Your Living Mind

The Mystery of Consciousness and Why It Matters To You

Edition One

Roger Christan Schriner

Living Arts Publications

YOUR LIVING MIND:
The Mystery of Consciousness and Why It Matters to You
Copyright © 2014 by Roger Christan Schriner

Living Arts Publications, Fremont, California
Printed in the United States by CreateSpace.com
Cover art based on a photo by Milan Jurek

Library of Congress Control Number: 2014912440
ISBN 978-0-9845840-1-7

Books by the same author:
(Earlier works used the author's middle name – *Christan* or *Chris.*)

Do Think Twice: Provocative Reflections on Age-Old Questions, by Chris Schriner. Creative approaches to topics such as the mystery of consciousness, mind and brain, moral relativism, free will, accepting mortality, theism vs. atheism, the limits of our knowledge, and the mismatch between human nature and the modern world. The book also offers strategies for personal and spiritual growth. Limited edition; contact the author for purchasing information.

Feel Better Now: 30 Ways to Handle Frustration in 3 Minutes or Less, by Christan Schriner, with an Introduction by Ken Keyes. Describes 30 specific techniques for quickly easing distress and explains how to use these tactics in dealing with everyday pressures and frustrations. Available from Jalmar Press (personhoodpress.com).

Bridging the God Gap: Finding Common Ground Among Believers, Atheists and Agnostics, by Roger Christan Schriner. Shows how to have honest and respectful conversations about religion. Order directly from the author or from Amazon.com.

An Adventure of the Mind
An Exploration of the Senses

Being conscious creatures makes us radically different from teacups, snowflakes, and lawnmowers, but we struggle to say just what it is that makes consciousness special. Today there is good news and bad news about this seemingly impenetrable mystery.

First the good news – philosophers and cognitive scientists have managed to articulate some of the key features that make consciousness extraordinary. The bad news is that these conceptual breakthroughs have led to further conundrums. It has been maddeningly difficult to reconcile some of our insights into consciousness with the way science thinks about the physical universe. This has reinvigorated the old mind-body dispute. How could consciousness occur within the brain, or relate to the brain at all? And what's really appalling is that it's hard to make sense of consciousness in any terms whatsoever – physical or spiritual, religious or secular.

Your Living Mind explains issues being hotly debated by experts who have studied consciousness in depth. If you liked *Consciousness Explained* by Daniel Dennett or *Soul Dust* by Nicholas Humphrey, or you enjoy readable books and articles about neuroscience, you'll enjoy *Your Living Mind*. It's a multifaceted meditation on "being a brain," and an invigorating workout for both your intellect and your imagination.

The author, who is a retired psychotherapist and Unitarian Universalist minister, has included a dozen exercises and techniques for personal experimentation and reflection. For those who try out these techniques, *Your Living Mind* will become both an intellectual adventure and an exploration of the senses.

Are you ready to become better acquainted with *your* living mind?

Dedicated to a Rather Odd Philosophical Couple:

René Descartes

and

Daniel Dennett

Seeking a Path Between the Extremes

Of These Conceptual Adventurers

A Book for Two Audiences

This version of *Your Living Mind* is partially intended for scholars, such as philosophers and cognitive scientists, but it was also written for a broad range of readers outside of academic circles. In addressing these two audiences, some compromises are necessary. I need to provide scholars with solid documentation and technical detail, but I do not want to burden others with wearisome complexity. Therefore a great deal of scholarly material has been placed in the footnotes. I have also marked some difficult sections as optional, in a way that will be explained in the Introduction.

Chapter Two and Chapters Four through Eight deal with subjects that are familiar to academicians, so they may want to lightly skim this material. Chapters Fourteen and Fifteen consider selfhood, artificial consciousness, and free will. Scholars will read, skim, or skip these according to their interests. I present my own account of consciousness in Chapters Three, Nine through Fourteen, and Seventeen.

Although it is difficult to write for two readerships, this unusual approach has unusual benefits. Lay readers can choose when to dive more deeply into topics that especially interest them, perusing footnotes and technical sections and reflecting on esoteric "thought experiments." Professionals may find that discussing consciousness in everyday language sheds light on longstanding controversies. Sometimes academic jargon obscures rather than clarifies.

While writing this book I have been excited at the continual unfolding of ideas in philosophy of mind. I was still reading recent publications while polishing the final draft. I have designated this release as *Edition One* because I fully expect that other editions will follow. But I have been fascinated by this topic for over twenty years, and at some point one must say, "Here is what I believe – subject to revision due to new data, new ideas, and further reflections." I am not ready to declare, "Here I stand!" but I can say, "Here I pause."

Acknowledgments. I owe a great debt of gratitude to those who have read all or part of the manuscript, at various stages of its development. These include Jack Alexander, Dean Beckwith, David Chalmers, Alvin J. Clark, Will Cloughley, David DeLange, Rocco Gennaro, Philip Goff,

Monica Hege, Mitch Landy, John Porter, Dominic Preston, Brit Pyland, Anthony Rifkin, William Robinson, Douglas Rodgers, David Rosenthal, Jo Ann Schriner, William Schwarz, and Christi VanEyken. In addition, Kenneth Williford offered valuable advice about terminology. Of course, I take full responsibility for all contents of the final publication.

I appreciate the conscientious work of my primary office assistant, Chun-Chi Chiu, as well as the assistance of Sabrina Huang and Sonia Sajja. Ms. Chiu also helped with several illustrations. I am grateful to Orange Coast Unitarian Universalist Church, the Unitarian Universalist Fellowship of Laguna Beach, and Mission Peak Unitarian Universalist Congregation for their generous policies of annual study leave, and for four periods of sabbatical leave between 1985 and 2007. These sabbaticals enabled me to investigate neuroscience and philosophy of mind without the interruption of other commitments. Finally, and most emphatically, I am grateful for the love and support of my wife Jo Ann, the dear daily companion of my life and my heart.

Regardless of whether you are a newcomer to consciousness studies or an experienced professional, I would value your comments about *Your Living Mind.* To contact me, search the Web for my blog or web site. I am currently writing about philosophy of mind at:

The Mystery of Consciousness, and Why It Matters
http://mysteryofconsciousness.wordpress.com

Roger Christan Schriner, August, 2014

CONTENTS

INTRODUCTION
Sprinting Through a Mental Hall of Mirrors

The most beautiful thing we can experience is the mysterious.
It is the source of all true art and all science. – Albert Einstein

Even in the hurried pace of everyday life we sometimes find ourselves stunned by fundamental mysteries, and three of these enigmas are especially arresting. The first mind-boggler is that anything exists at all. The second wonder is the appearance of living creatures. And the third jaw-dropper is that some living creatures have conscious experiences.

The second mystery, of course, is closely related to the third. When people speak of the wonder of life, what they often mean is the wonder of being conscious. Daisies and dandelions are amazing even if they lack a single shred of sentience, but adding consciousness to living matter is the slickest trick of all.

Consciousness is such a familiar miracle that we usually ignore it, but this remarkable phenomenon is at the core of our sense of self. We are intimately entangled with the flow of our own experiences, in every waking moment and even in our dreams. It seems to be the very essence of our existence. Christof Koch puts it bluntly. "Without consciousness there is nothing."[1]

Consciousness is also at the heart of our sense of value. We value sentient beings in a way that is radically different from the way we value anything else. Many of us would agree that it is wrong to casually destroy a conscious creature. By contrast, when I drink a glass of water I assume that nothing tragic occurs when it plunges into an acid bath in my stomach. I do not imagine the water silently screaming, *"Ohhh nooooo!"* – *SPLASH!* The difference in value between me and a tumbler of H_2O involves the fact that I am conscious and it is not.

The mind-brain problem

Your Living Mind is especially concerned with vivid and sensuous experiences – pleasures, pains, tickles, tingles, the *crack!* of thunder, the

---

[1]Koch 2012, p. 23.

luscious allure of chocolate mousse, and the hallucination of seeing two bright green gorillas grilling hot dogs in your kitchen. (Did you have a faint mental image of greenish apes just then?) We would not enjoy these perceptions if we were rocks, frisbees, or Deep Blue, the chess-playing computer. In this book we will consider a question that curious minds of all ages have contemplated. "What *is* this strange stuff inside of my mind?" (And some theorists reject the idea that conscious experiences are entities of any kind, or deny that "this stuff" is inside of us.)

Theologians have typically situated consciousness within the soul, but many scientists and philosophers believe it is somehow contained within the brain. When people report certain thoughts, emotions, impulses, and perceptions, brain scanners show characteristic kinds of neural activity. For better or for worse, we are learning to look into people's heads and know at least some things about what they are thinking and feeling.

The close connections between the brain and conscious experiences are especially obvious when illness, aging, or trauma damages nerve tissue. Dementia can make an old grump become docile or a pacifist turn homicidal. Any major brain malfunction alters the way we think, feel, plan, and/or behave. Clearly brain and mind are tightly intertwined.

Of course, recognizing that the brain is intimately involved with human experience does not prove that experiences are nothing but brain activity. The brain may be an instrument of the mind, a tool that the mind (or soul) uses to express itself. But even if that's true, it is important to discover whether certain key aspects of conscious awareness could literally *be* brain processes.

When I was young, I thought of consciousness as a sort of magical substance or energy that somehow appeared during the course of evolution. As animals developed from one-celled creatures into more complex organisms, at some point a miraculous light dawned in the darkness. But now I see that rather than being a ghostlike energy connected to the body, this light of awareness may be a new combination of the very same atoms that make up stones and water and stars.

As we will see, there are deep and disturbing questions about whether this could be so. How could a sensuous experience – the tingle of a caress, the scent of lilacs, the sight of day-glo orange – occur within a brain? Some contend that we can never answer this question satisfactorily. The basis of their skepticism varies[2] but they all agree that it is extremely difficult to show that experiences are brain events, in a way that makes any sense. They are not just worrying that consciousness is too complicated for us to grasp at this time. They believe that understanding how experiences occur within the brain is virtually impossible *in principle,* either because experiences do not occur within the brain or because we can never understand how this is so.

This book will wrestle with the remarkable issues associated with this conundrum, trying to show that human conscious experiences could be states of the brain.

Let me emphasize, we cannot yet prove that human consciousness is a brain state, but we are trying to discover whether this is possible in principle.[3] And if you are already convinced that the mind is wedged between our ears, don't be too sure that this is obvious. The puzzles involved are far more profound than I realized when I first immersed myself in this topic in the early 1990s. I feel as if I've been wrestling with a zen koan for two decades, and I have become excruciatingly aware of how hard it is to understand our own minds by looking within.

---

[2]*Dualists,* such as Sir John Eccles (1987), have argued that consciousness exists in a non-material realm rather than in the brain. *Mysterians,* such as Colin McGinn (1991), despair of ever understanding how conscious experience is related to brain activity. *Eliminativists* such as Daniel Dennett (1991) deny that inner, "introspectable" perceptions exist. And some *representationalists* deny that experiences are neural states. Instead, they consist of representations about external objects and bodily conditions; see Dretske (1995) and Tye (1995, 2000).

[3]William Robinson explains that understanding sensory experiences "is necessarily philosophical, and speculative, because the relevant science is still developing." Those who think these experiences are neural activities "must therefore speak not of results, but of *possible* results – statements about the brain, that is, that are clearly compatible with what is known in the brain sciences, but are not yet established" (Robinson 1996b, p. 66).

It's like trying to sprint lickety-split through an enormous hall of mirrors. Helmets and shin guards are strongly advised.

One reason this task is so difficult is that we are so close to our own awareness. It's as tricky as trying to look *at* my eye *with* my eye. By focusing on the stream of consciousness we access a source of information that is misleading in some ways, routinely dependable in other ways, and subject to no agreed-upon criteria for separating truth from error. Navigating a mental hall of mirrors may be the only way to proceed, but we had better drop bread crumbs along the way.

In negotiating this maze we will consider many different issues, any one of which could fill up a chapter or even a whole volume. Since I don't want this book to be so big that normal people cannot lift it, I will sometimes state my convictions without offering much argument. But when I say something especially controversial I will present reasons for making this claim.

I realize that after reading *Your Living Mind* you may end up deciding that the mind can't be in the brain after all. Regardless of your conclusions, I hope this book will remind you to appreciate the ongoing carnival of sensuous phenomena. Right now, as I see these words on my computer screen, the crisp black letters seem present in a remarkable way, vivid and obvious. I glance outside and a colorful panorama of luxuriant foliage seems spread out before me, manifest and undeniable. We owe it to ourselves to savor this astonishing gift, the living human mind.

One more point: Sometimes in exploring consciousness it seems as if a window has opened up unexpectedly and I have understood myself in a new way. I hope in reading *Your Living Mind*, new windows will open for you.

NO, you do not need to read all 400 footnotes

Those who read this book will differ widely in their interests. Some will be intrigued by the inventive conceptual moves of brilliant philosophers, the endless intellectual swordplay about subtle theoretical puzzles. Others will lose patience with minutia and skim ahead looking for the bottom line. To accommodate such differences, I have put many technical points into about 45 pages worth of footnotes. I have also segregated highly academic material into sections called *More Details.* If you wish, you can jump to the end of these sections by looking for this marker:

🐞 🐞 🐞 🐞 🐞 🐞 🐞

Although I have tried to write this book as precisely as possible, I have minimized scholarly jargon. For a handy guide to technical terms, book-mark the "Definitions" section immediately after the final chapter.

My personal fascination with the mind-body problem

I have always been interested in the big questions of life (philosophy, theology, ethics), and in why people think, feel, and act as they do (psychology, sociology, political science). Not surprisingly, introspection has been a hobby of mine. One of my favorite T-shirts shows a meditating Buddha above the caption, *"Inquire Within."* At age 20 I was wondering whether to take up a musical instrument. I decided instead to focus my energies on a project in which I could be at the "keyboard" all day long, the project of noticing my thoughts, feelings, beliefs, desires, memories, daydreams, and anticipations. Whenever we're awake, our own conscious experiences are always close at hand.

In college I majored in religion, philosophy, and psychology, and then earned a doctorate in religion and an M.S. in family therapy. I had planned to enter the ministry, but found myself drifting away from traditional religion. I became a Unitarian Universalist minister after learning that

Unitarian Universalism welcomes people of all positive faiths and philosophies. I served congregations in Costa Mesa, Laguna Beach, and Fremont, California, and my speculations about mind and brain found their way into sermons and classes in these settings.

Many Unitarian Universalists are interested in science, and no one has seemed shocked when I say that the mind might be part of the brain. In fact quite a few UUs are secular humanists (atheists or agnostics) who assume that all reality is physical. Others accept traditional theologies, and they have critiqued my ideas in helpful ways.

Although I have not been an academic philosopher, in my ministry I have been a hands-on consultant about real-life philosophical dilemmas, crises, and confusions. Since I am a "practicing philosopher" rather than a philosophy teacher, I have both an unusual vantage point and significant limitations. I know a lot about philosophy of mind, but less about philosophy of language, theory of knowledge, ontology, and so on. Even so, an outsider can sometimes bring fresh perspectives to issues that have been discussed half to death.

In addition to ministry, I practiced psychotherapy for 25 years, and in the 1980s I wrote some books about psychological issues. I like to study complicated and confusing topics, looking for ways to discuss them in clear and practical terms. But I shifted toward philosophy in 1992 after reading *Consciousness Explained* by Daniel Dennett. Dennett is an insightful thinker and a fine writer, but I found his book shocking. Like many others, I felt it should have been called *Consciousness Explained Away*. I immediately presented two lectures critiquing his theory.[4] I was particularly irked that he devalued introspection. Ever since I attended Gestalt Therapy[5] groups in the 1970s, I have felt that focusing on exactly what I am experiencing at this moment, including my thoughts, emotions, and bodily sensations, is a gateway to self-understanding.

In grappling with *Consciousness Explained,* I started seeing ways to solve the problems Dennett discussed. I followed through by joining the American Philosophical Association and immersing myself in philosophy

---

[4]Schriner 1992a and 1992b.

[5]Gestalt Therapy is an approach developed by psychiatrist Fritz Perls. It is loosely related to gestalt *psychology.*

of mind. I subscribed to journals, read many articles and books, and regularly attended conferences and colloquia. Over time more and more puzzle pieces fit into place. I also gained confidence in my work as an independent scholar, partly because my criticisms of Dennett have been similar to those of many academicians. Even so, I must sheepishly admit that some of Dennett's ideas now seem much more plausible than they did initially.

At this point I think I understand how, in principle, sensory experiences could occur within a brain, but powerful intellects have wrestled with this conundrum for centuries. If someone pokes gaping holes in my theory I will be disappointed but far from astonished. And if I actually have made progress toward solving this riddle, I will have done so only by learning from those who have gone before me, including Daniel Dennett.

An outsider's view of academic philosophy

No doubt there are still cocktail-party conversations about Descartes, Nietzsche, and Sartre, but I wonder how many Bordeaux-sipping intellectuals discuss Dretske, Nagel, and Kripke. The relationship between academic philosophy and the general public is nearly non-existent. Professors mostly speak to each other, in a technical language full of confusing terms with multiple definitions – "qualia," "intentionality," "representationalism," "epiphenomenalism," and so on. A few, such as Dennett, have written for a wider audience, but most of them remain within their own ivory towers. I have spent years as the proverbial fly on the wall, listening to professorial interchanges within these lofty retreats. *Your Living Mind* opens a window into the intriguing story of this hidden conversation.

I am more and more impressed with the need for philosophical analysis. Philosophy is extremely difficult and extremely important, because it deals with issues that the human mind is ill-equipped to address. Humans are easily befuddled by words that have multiple meanings and by concepts that are hard to articulate. We struggle to understand arguments that involve more than three or four steps. We often let our emotions think for us, while logic lags behind as a rationalizing afterthought. And we like to imagine that our personal intuitions about the Big

Questions are correct, assuming that those who disagree with us are either malicious or confused.

Philosophers are trained to surmount these limitations. They're especially good at analyzing murky topics that are hard to even formulate coherently. At a recent philosophy colloquium someone mentioned the need for dealing with problems about which there is little hard data, but a whole lot of speculation based on what little data there is. *"That's us!"* exclaimed the department chair, and hearty laughter ensued.

But there are problems with this profession, as many have observed. Freeman Dyson contends that compared to "the giants of the past, they are a sorry bunch of dwarfs. They are thinking deep thoughts and giving scholarly lectures to academic audiences, but hardly anybody in the world outside is listening. They are historically insignificant."[6] On the contrary, I think the finest philosophy today reflects disciplined inquiry by powerful intellects, but it's true that few non-philosophers ever hear about it.[7]

William Seager comments on the complexity of academic debates. "It is said that at the beginning of a course, the Russian physicist A. A. Blasov misspoke himself in saying that the purpose of the course was the 'deepening and development of difficulties underlying contemporary theory.' What is a misstatement for a physicist is a job description for a philosopher."[8] Or, as George Berkeley quipped in the eighteenth century, "Philosophers raise a dust and then complain that they cannot see."[9]

Articles in technical publications often use terms that are poorly defined, and are defined in different ways by different thinkers. As one

---

[6]Dyson 2012. And an editorial in *The Philosopher's Magazine* discusses charges "that philosophy is dead, that it has no content, it hasn't progressed in 2,000 years, it's unjustifiable, it no longer matters, and on and on" (Garvey 2013, p. 4).

[7]Seager reports that he "can't think of any real philosophical problem that has been satisfactorily dissolved; attempted dissolutions seem to rely upon their own set of controversial philosophical theses . . . that proceed to manufacture their own set of more or less intractable and genuine philosophical problems – this is called progress" (1999, p. 25).

[8]Seager 1996, p. 730.

[9]Cited by David Cole, 2011.

APA speaker stated bluntly, "terminology in contemporary philosophy of mind is a mess."[10] That may be surprising, since these are well-educated professionals with superb verbal skills and an obsessive interest in exact phrasing. But they may not always realize the way their use of terminology helps shape communication about consciousness.[11] And since these terms are often ambiguous, a lot of energy is expended precisely analyzing fuzzy ideas. Of course, it's easy to criticize people who are trying to do very hard things. The game looks simple, from the sidelines. "If the last century has taught us anything," writes Georges Rey, "it is that the provision of an adequate theory . . . of the mind . . . is stunningly more difficult than has been supposed."[12]

Scholars are humans, and ego clashes inevitably occur. Nicholas Humphrey reports that it is typical "for academics to be dismissive of each other's ideas. The psychologist Walter Mischel has wryly noted: 'Psychologists treat other people's theories like toothbrushes – no self-respecting person wants to use anyone else's.' Philosophers tend to be charier still."[13]

Theoreticians often see their own speculations as eminently reasonable, while being appalled at the quirky proposals of their colleagues. And despite following in the footsteps of skeptical Socrates, they sometimes underestimate their own fallibility. Scientist Christof Koch reports encountering "numerous philosophers who are utterly convinced of the

---

[10]Berger 2013.

[11]Scholars often define words in new and idiosyncratic ways, seemingly oblivious to the confusion this creates. Even basic terms such as "concept" have various definitions. "Questions such as 'What are concepts?' and 'What is it to possess a concept?'" are "notoriously difficult to answer" (Gennaro 2007, p. 1). Michael Tye laments "the failures of attempts to state necessary and sufficient conditions for terms of interest to philosophers . . ." (Tye 2009, p. 210). Although philosophers talk about "reducing" conscious experiences to physical states, "there are at least half a dozen different definitions of reduction . . ." (Searle and Freeman 1998, p. 731). This sort of thing sometimes even confuses professionals. "Crane . . . shows how much classical criticism of sense-data theories was flawed because of its misunderstanding both of the intentions of the sense-data theorists, and of the different ways the term 'sense datum' was used" (Maund, p. 277).

[12]Rey 2007, p. 123.

[13]Quoted by Humphrey 2011, p. ix.

truth of their ideas. Such confidence in one's own ideas – without being fazed by the myriad competing ideas of others, who can't all be right – is rare among natural scientists."[14] When their brilliant brainpower "is put to the service of harebrained intuitions, it yields logically dazzling but implausible results."[15] So wrote Thomas Nagel, and Georges Rey asks what it is "about our thinking about the mind that leads otherwise immensely intelligent people to say many of the extremely bizarre and foolish things that have been claimed about the mind? The psychology of philosophy is of a piece with the philosophy of psychology."[16]

Some have denied that animals or even human children are conscious.[17] Others have asserted that visual afterimages simply do not exist, either in the outside world or in our own minds. Some maintain that if a person who is absolutely identical to you or me somehow appeared out of nowhere, that being would not be conscious because it lacks an appropriate evolutionary history. Perhaps some of these ideas are correct, but they certainly seem strange on the face of it.

Nevertheless, philosophical innovation requires an intellectual courage that's akin to madness. To take a fresh look at age-old questions, philosophers must be willing to suspend preconceptions and set aside common sense, and sometimes they have a bit of fun following an idea to its "logical" conclusion. Rumor has it that C.E.M. Joad, a British philosopher, was once waiting at the Reading Station when a London train made an unscheduled stop. He leapt aboard, only to be told by a porter, "I'm afraid you'll have to get off, sir. This train doesn't stop here." Unabashed, Joad replied, "Don't worry then. If the train doesn't stop here, I'm not on it!"

---

[14]Koch 2012, p. 3.

[15]Nagel 1995, p. 8.

[16]Rey 1995, p. 131.

[17]Holt writes, "I have always marvelled at how the human species, in an effort to distinguish itself, would deny other species outright what they so clearly possess in some measure – tool use, reasoning ability, language understanding, moral significance, and yes, even perceptual consciousness" (Holt 2003, p. 27). Gennaro agrees, saying, "I am more sure of animal and infant consciousness than any philosophical theory of consciousness" (Gennaro 2012b); see also Gennaro 2012a, Chapter 8.

All things considered, I respect and appreciate the keen minds and the commitment to clarity of those who pursue this demanding discipline. "Philosophy," of course, means love of wisdom, and it is absolutely evident that most philosophers of mind have a genuine passion for gaining deeper insights. This isn't just their job; it is their vocation. Even older scholars seem excited about topics that first captured their imagination decades ago. And today many philosophers, especially the younger ones, seem less ego-driven, more comfortable and secure. Some have a keen sense of humor and don't mind laughing at themselves. I think of a delightful panel discussion of Joseph Levine's book, *Purple Haze: The Puzzle of Consciousness,* at which panelist David Chalmers illustrated his points with Jimi Hendrix graphics. (Each chapter title of *Purple Haze* is a lyric from the great guitarist, such as "Actin' Funny, but I Don't Know Why.")

Preview

Throughout this book we will focus on the question, "is it possible that conscious experiences occur within the brain?" Obviously we won't address everything that is labeled "consciousness." We won't discuss heightening our consciousness of class, race, gender, or other socio-political concerns, or elevating consciousness through meditation. Eventually, however, we will talk about enhancing the quality of consciousness.

After laying some groundwork in the first chapter, I discuss intriguing discoveries about the brain in Chapter Two. In Chapter Three I consider the way our minds interweave conscious and unconscious processes. Chapters Four and Five explain why the mind-body problem is so challenging, and the next three chapters discuss valiant attempts to deal with this issue. I present my own proposal in Chapters Nine through Fourteen, and I relate this theory to our understanding of selfhood and personal freedom in Fifteen and Sixteen. Chapter Seventeen suggests additional implications, and concludes.

As you read, watch for insights that you find especially meaningful, and think of ways to reflect upon these concepts in real-life situations. Any book's benefits will be multiplied if we actively apply its principles. Drawing upon my background as a therapist, I have suggested several exercises and techniques that can make the ideas of this book more useful and accessible. I have placed these in shaded boxes marked with this symbol: ✎

I would find it unsatisfying to think about consciousness without engaging in personal exploration, but not everyone feels this way. I therefore emphasize that all exercises and techniques are optional. Try out some of them, all of them, or absolutely none of them, as you prefer. Realistically, however, it is difficult to deepen one's understanding of this topic without experiential engagement, and no doubt many readers are already familiar with disciplines similar to the ones I will suggest. For those who practice at least some of the book's exercises, *Your Living Mind* will become both an intellectual adventure and an exploration of the senses.

I'll close this Introduction with a candid comment by Michael Tye:

Philosophy is a hard subject – too hard, I sometimes think, for human beings. This seems especially true when it comes to the topic of consciousness. . . . In thinking about consciousness, I have often had the sense that I am like the man in a room described by Wittgenstein. The man is expending great effort to find a way out, but it does not occur to him to pull on the door instead of pushing. The door, which is unlocked, opens inward, and he can simply walk outside.[18]

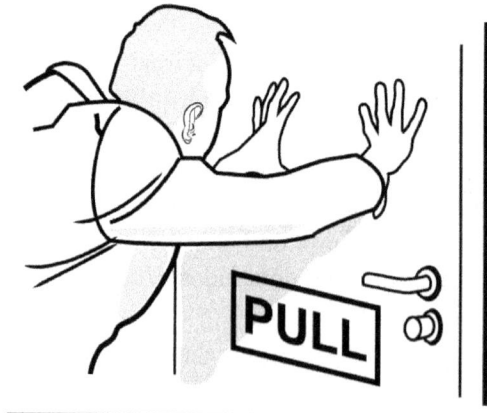

---

[18]Tye 2009, p. xiv.

My own journey has taken me through a whole series of conceptual and experiential doorways. Most of them were easily opened once I firmly grasped the handle, but they have a nasty tendency to swing back shut. You and I will approach three important conceptual and experiential portals together. Some readers will go through them. Others will not.

So let's take a deep breath now, and open up the question, "Could our rich, vivid, complex, and precious *conscious experiences* exist wholly within a brain?"

Chapter One
Our Most Familiar Stranger

Your Living Mind is about the ongoing flow of personal experiences. What is this world of awareness that you and I enjoy, and that snowflakes and bowling balls seemingly lack? Although consciousness is closer to us than our own breathing, trying to grasp its nature is like trying to pick up smoke. It is so familiar, and yet so very strange.

Conscious experiences include thoughts, perceptions, and bodily sensations. "Thoughts" is a big circus-tent of a term that covers many different mental processes, including those that could be expressed as: *"I believe ____ is true," "I wonder if ____ is true,"* and *"I want ____."* Thoughts, sensations, and perceptions help constitute our:

- dreams
- impulses
- memories
- moods and emotions
- imagined episodes, fantasies, and anticipations
- altered states, such as mystical experiences and hallucinations

Some of these categories overlap and some can also occur unconsciously. And although many writers distinguish the terms *consciousness, awareness, experience,* and *sentience,* I'll usually treat them as synonyms to avoid monotonous repetition.

> It's important to remember that conscious experiences occur *right now.* You cannot experience a state of mind that you had yesterday or that you're going to have five minutes from now. But people are often confused about whether they are reporting a fresh experience that just happened, remembering what they felt a few minutes ago, or talking about what they typically experience. *Reading this book should help you learn to focus on what you're experiencing at this very instant.*[19]

---

[19]In very short time frames we sometimes get mixed up about which part of an experience comes first. In the experimentally-induced tactile illusion called the cutaneous rabbit, a sensation seems to "hop" up the arm in a way that does not match the timing of the stimulus (Dennett 1991, pp. 142-43). Ned Block (2012) writes that there may be a "moving window" of time in which it makes no sense to ask which part of an experience occurs first.

So you're barefoot, strolling in the surf, on the beach at Waikiki. You savor the salt spray, the lulling sun, the water splashing your ankles, the sounds of laughing children. And if you're philosophically inclined you may be thinking, *"It's good to be conscious."*

And now imagine another pleasant scene – dining out with good friends, showered with an array of sensuous inputs – sounds, sights, scents, and tastes.

To round out the picture, remember what it's like to have a nasty toothache. Now you're in touch with the cost of consciousness for creatures like us. These experiences matter. They are the stuff of life. We'll return to these three episodes later, but if you didn't personally relate to these scenarios you can think of your own examples – one highly sensual experience, one social interaction, and one intense pain.

But what IS consciousness?

Many authors suggest that precisely defining consciousness is impossible,[20] so instead of offering a definition, I will roughly indicate what I mean by *human* consciousness. (At times I will mention other forms of consciousness, such as that of animals, machines, and space aliens.) To clarify, I'm not focusing on why we are conscious in the sense of being awake instead of asleep. I'm dealing with the items that float along in our "stream of consciousness," such as thoughts, bodily sensations, and perceptions. These experiences are the subject of *Your Living Mind.* So without claiming to present a comprehensive list, here are five typical characteristics of human conscious experiences.

1. Conscious experiences are available to the mental systems that control our behavior. Our experiences therefore serve as a sort of "global workspace"[21] which can be accessed by many mental mechanisms. Hu-

---

[20]"Unfortunately, it seems to be impossible to define phenomenal consciousness (Chalmers, 1996). The best we can do is to point to instances of it" (Levy 2014, p. 129).

[21]Bernard Baars (1988) popularized the idea that consciousness is a global workspace. Daniel Dennett compares consciousness to "political influence – a good slang term is *clout"* (2005, p. 137). But even though "fame in the brain" is a useful idea, it may not get at what we mean by conscious experiences. Note

mans continually cope with challenges such as walking down the street without flipping heels-over-head on a banana peel. If we are to survive these challenges, our sensory experiences must be accessed by the mental agencies that think, make decisions, and instigate actions. If you are wrapped in a warm embrace, for example, this experience is available to these control-agencies. As a result you might have *thoughts* about this embrace, make *choices* (shall I keep hugging, or disengage?), and use the experience to guide further *actions*.

Consciousness is especially useful when we need to concentrate, as in typing a long password to access a web site. At these times our action-guidance systems need laser-focused awareness. Anything that degrades consciousness makes these tasks more difficult.

2. You are the only one who has your experiences. I can't tune in to what's in your mind the way you can. So for one of your mental events to be conscious it must be conscious *to you*.

Philosophers often leave terms such as *I, the self,* and *the subject of experience* undefined. In this book, these terms will usually serve as shorthand ways of referring to the part of us that monitors, enjoys, and suffers our experiences. I think of the self as an extremely complex team of brain mechanisms working together, but the exact nature of this system or systems is not crucial for our purposes. Even if the idea of "self" changes quite radically, it is difficult to imagine utterly abandoning the notion that something within us suffers and savors our torments and delights.

One big difference between people and non-conscious things such as rocks is that something within people "gets" their experiences. Suppose we figured out that some specific pattern of brain activity is absolutely

---

that even though your experiences are famous in your brain, they aren't famous in mine. They are conscious to you, but not to me. Similarly, they are broadcast to many of your brain modules, but not to all. If there is truth in the brain-fame model, certain neural events must be famous *to certain brain systems*. Not just any sort of widespread influence will do. For example, Ned Block suggests thinking "of perceptual mechanisms as suppliers of representations to consuming mechanisms that include mechanisms of reporting, reasoning, evaluating, deciding, and remembering" (2007, p. 491).

identical to the sensations that agitate you when someone tickles your feet. Even if we managed to move that neural activity pattern into the middle of a boulder and keep it functioning, the rock would not feel any urge to giggle. Unless we transplanted the entire experiencing self, nothing in the rock would be equipped to *experience* the ticklish sensation. The sensation would just sit there, unknown and unappreciated. We cannot have an experience without an experiencer.

What does it mean to say that an experiencing subject or self *has* experiences? When I have an experience, I typically know about it, but there's more to consciousness than acquiring knowledge. For one thing, I am also *impacted* by what I experience. To have a pain or to notice a noise changes me. Experiencing the scent of garlic involves believing that I'm aware of a pungent odor, but in whiffing that evocative stink I am also being altered, penetrated, reconfigured by this scent. Perhaps I'll realize that it's making me hungry, whereas someone else might respond by fleeing from the kitchen.

3. Experiences are typically remembered, at least briefly. (Experts disagree about whether all details of our experiences are held in short-term memory.)

4. At least some aspects of an experience are typically reportable, in creatures that are able to make reports. These reports are often vague. I may say, "I saw that tree blowing in the wind," without being able to specify which leaves and branches appeared to be jiggling.

Reportability, of course, is made possible by the fact that conscious experiences are typically remembered, and are available to the mind's behavior-guidance systems. Isn't it remarkable that some team of obscure mental mechanisms enables us to *speak* about our own states of mind? If I think about what to eat for dinner or I feel a twinge in my toe, I may find myself reporting these mental events in comprehensible English. We have hardly a clue how that happens.

5. Some of our experiences, especially body sensations and sensory perceptions, seem "present." Philosophers find it difficult to explain how brain activities could generate a sense of presence, so let's consider this slippery notion.

Manifest presence

Many conscious episodes seem real and tangible. I can mentally examine them, in a way that seems somewhat like examining a physical object. When I hear a symphonic finale, I can track what I experience as it begins, changes in quality and intensity, and ceases. The same is true of coffee tastes, gasoline smells, skin shivers, and blazing sunsets. In each case it seems as if we are encountering something with a definite form which we can partially describe. Such experiences are, in some sense, *present* to us as conscious creatures.

The sort of presence I'm talking about is hard to pin down in words. I will often speak of *manifest* presence, which is really just a way of pounding the table to emphasize the point. I'll also use the philosopher's term "phenomenal."

Even though I know some things about what is happening in my own unconscious mind, and in the conscious minds of others, these mental states are not manifestly present, whereas my own sensory experiences are *thus-there-now*. Similarly, I can think about Paris while I'm in Madrid, but when I'm actually experiencing Paris I seem to see, hear, smell, feel, and taste that city.

Present-seeming experiences are introspectable. Narrowly, introspection means paying attention to our own mental processes. ("Does my vision seem fuzzier today?") But we briefly and casually notice our own experiences all day long.[22] One might have a fleeting awareness, for example, of an unusual sound, thinking of it as an experience of *sound* rather than as something nearby that is making an odd noise.

Manifest experiences seem to be obviously real. It would be strange to say, "I am conscious of a searing pain in my left side, but I'm not sure if I am now in pain." They speak to us assertively. "I'm here, pay attention to me!" they insist, and we have little choice but to obey.

---

[22]Gennaro suggests that we "distinguish between two kinds of introspection: *momentary focused* and *deliberate*. Momentary focused introspection is merely having a momentary conscious awareness of one's own mental state" (Gennaro 2012a, p. 53).

✎ *Got it.* To deepen your understanding of the fact that you are automatically aware of conscious states, notice yourself "registering" each experience. Begin by closing your eyes and sitting for five or ten minutes, noticing every sound you hear. With each new sound, think, "got it," meaning, "I notice that I have just experienced this sound." Sense the way these sounds are impacting you, perturbing you, sometimes gently and sometimes more forcefully. Then do the same thing with bodily sensations: *"Got it, got it, got it."*

You can also try this with thoughts, and eventually with every conscious episode.

In short, typical conscious experiences are *available for use by the parts of the mind that control behavior, are your experiences rather than someone else's, are remembered at least briefly, are at least partially reportable, and (in many cases) seem manifestly present.* There may be other characteristics of consciousness as well, but this list will point us in the right direction.

Welcome to the labyrinth

Realistically speaking, it is dreadfully easy to get lost in our mental hall of mirrors. Part of the problem is that words are pitifully cumbersome tools for understanding and communicating about the mind. Wittgenstein called philosophy "a battle against the bewitchment of our intelligence by means of language."[23]

Consider the relationship between having an experience and communicating about it. Once we have had an experience, a series of other events ensue, such as:

- ❀ remembering the experience
- ❀ thinking about these recollections
- ❀ entertaining silent "mental sentences" which express those thoughts
- ❀ stating these sentences aloud or putting them on paper

---

[23]http://www.brainyquote.com/quotes/quotes/l/ludwigwitt101117.html#9buo Oi3g1FTM3dh4.99.

❀ discussing these statements within some linguistic community, such as English-speakers, neuroscientists, or philosophers

Feeling dizzy yet? That probably means you're paying close attention. And you are in splendid company. I suspect that many scholars have wished they had become chicken-sexers or chimney sweeps instead of philosophers of mind. Conceptual vertigo aside, it's crucial to remember that thoughts about our own experiences are not the same as the experiences themselves, and philosophical discussions are even further removed from the right-now immediacy of the living mind.

Conscious vs. unconscious

Let's contrast things that we do and do not experience. Right now, notice the sensations in your legs. You probably weren't aware of your legs a moment ago, unless they were uncomfortable or you had just moved them. And yet your brain was continually receiving neural signals from those lower limbs. If a rattlesnake had started slithering up your ankle, you would hopefully have noticed a change in sensation. (Did you feel a creepy little tingle, just reading that last sentence?) Complex sensory information is constantly flowing into your brain, but the brain has cerebral sentries posted, tasked with letting some things "into" consciousness and keeping others out. These gate-keeping mechanisms recruit a small fraction of your current perceptual inputs into sensory awareness.

Imagine, for example, that while you're watching television your eardrums are struck by sound waves from some sort of beeping device. At first you aren't conscious of the noise, because your attentional mechanisms are giving priority to the TV program. But after the beepings persist, these mechanisms open the gate and let them in. Then you wonder, *"Is that my phone, your phone, one of our computers, my watch, your watch, our alarm clock, the oven timer, the oven preheat, the washer, the dryer, the smoke detector, the carbon monoxide detector, Dale's car alarm, Jenny's video game, or Jack's truck backing up?"* After being unconscious of the noise and then experiencing it faintly, you zero in on the sound with cocked ear and furrowed forehead. Selective attention makes this possible.

The difference between consciously "present" and non-conscious mental events is partly a difference in the way we know things. If I'm paying attention to my legs I know they exist because I can feel them. But suppose someone gives me a drug that prevents me from feeling my legs for the next hour, and blindfolds me as well. Although I would still know my legs exist, "knowing my legs are there" without being conscious of them is different from knowing my legs through feeling them and seeing them.

Is everything in your mind either conscious or unconscious? Some say yes and some say no. I suspect that in borderline cases there is no fact of the matter about whether a mental event is conscious.[24] For example, I was once watching a TV show about hippopotamuses. My mind began to wander and suddenly I realized that the TV had been showing zebras instead of hippos for a minute or two. It seems likely that in some sense I did experience the shift from one animal to another, but at first I was not fully aware of this change. Even if there's a gray area of semi-awareness, however, some mental events are clearly conscious and others are definitely unconscious.

In case you'd like to practice focusing on your own stream of consciousness, here are a few ways to do that. (Chapter One contains several exercises, but don't treat these as burdensome obligations. It's up to you to decide which ones you'll try and which you'll skip.)

✎ *Just notice.* In a quiet place, set a timer for perhaps 10 minutes, close your eyes, and notice the flow of your own awareness. As in the previous *got it* exercise, start with sound-experiences. Every time you hear something new, even if it's very soft, just think *sound.*

---

[24]"Attention is not an all or nothing affair," writes Jesse Prinz. "I think it can come in degrees, and hence consciousness too, which depends on attention in grades" (Prinz 2007, p. 195). Metzinger reports that "research has shown that the distinction between 'conscious' and 'unconscious' is not simply all-or-nothing" (1995, p. 33), but Uriah Kriegel seems to disagree. "Consciousness strikes me as akin to a light with a dimmer switch: one can turn the light up or down, and one can also turn the light off entirely, but there is no vague area where the light is neither determinately on nor determinately off" (2012, p. 482). I tend to side with Metzinger here.

Then do the same thing with bodily sensations, thinking *body* in each case. Eventually you can do this with everything that moves through your mind: *smell, taste, thought, emotion, sight* (noticing visual patterns with your eyes closed), and so on. Of course at times you will start pursuing thoughts about some topic and fall away from this exercise. Just say the word "thoughts," silently, and return to your focus, until the timer rings. This standard meditation technique has numerous benefits in addition to acquainting us with our own mental processes. It will help you become more "conscious of consciousness," more aware of your own inner life.

> ✎ *I observe – I assume.* This technique from Gestalt Therapy highlights the difference between experiences and thoughts about experiences. For this experiment you'll observe other people without distraction. Sitting in a restaurant or watching TV are two excellent opportunities. Look at someone unobtrusively and notice something you observe about that individual. Then notice what you are assuming, inferring, or speculating about this person. "I observe that he is wearing a tie. I assume he is a rather formal fellow." "I observe that she is wearing a red blouse; she probably likes that shade of red." "I observe that he is laughing; I speculate that he has a nice sense of humor."

Continue alternating between things you observe and things you guess or assume. See if you can catch yourself confusing an assumption for an observation. For example, "I observe that she is sleepy" is false. You aren't inside of her head and you can't be sure sleepiness is what she is experiencing. "I observe her yawning, and I assume she is sleepy" would be correct. By practicing this technique you can begin to see how much of what we take as obvious facts are merely conjectures. It is remarkably easy to live within our concepts instead of our actual experiences.

Communication check

Now let's see if we're on the same page, so to speak. Look at this list of items and ask yourself: Which of these are sensory experiences? Which are conscious but non-sensory? Which are not conscious at all? You need not agree with my answers, but this exercise will at least clarify the way I use terms such as "sensory experience."

1. A cat is sitting on my lap. As Kitty purrs, I feel vibrations against my abdomen.
2. While looking at a Chinese vase, I notice how beautiful it is.
3. I remember the terrible backache I had yesterday.
4. While reading a book, I notice the dark lettering and the light color of the page.
5. A psychotherapist asks Amos how he feels about his brother. "I feel he is unfair to me," Amos replies.
6. He then adds, "I guess I tend to resent him."

Item 1 is clearly a sensory experience. I am feeling Kitty's vibrations, here and now.

In item 2, I am seeing a vase, but am I having a sensory experience of beauty? In one sense the answer is No. I am not perceiving something called beauty that is "in" the physical vase. As the old saying goes, "beauty is in the eye of the beholder." But I may be aware of my reaction to the way this object looks – "I find this vase beautiful." In that sense I am in touch with an *experience* of beauty, an inner state of finding something lovely. Whether this experience is more like a sensory state or more like a thought is debatable; I think it's a mixture of both.

Item 3 may also be an experience of a thought: "Yikes, what a brutal backache!" And it's also a sensory experience, if remembering the backache is associated with current physical sensations.

Item 4 is a sensory experience, noticing how things look to me here and now.

The fifth item is tricky. Notice that even though Amos says, *"I feel,"* he is talking about a thought rather than a feeling. Perhaps he was also having sensory and emotional experiences, but these are not mentioned. And actually this statement may not express a conscious experience at all. Sometimes we blurt out thoughts we did not know we had. Rather than noticing that he thought his brother was unfair and then putting that realization into words, this statement may have erupted straight out of his unconscious mind. Hearing himself say "he is unfair" might have been the first time he knew that he felt this way.

The last example ("I guess I tend to resent him") is conscious in the sense that he was aware of what he was thinking, but it doesn't sound like he was tapping into a current emotional experience. To say that he tends to resent someone may or may not express the way he feels *now*.

The complexity of experience: an experiment

Many have commented on the rich complexity of consciousness. My favorite example involves a movie – a Beatles cartoon-film, I think – in which big, brilliantly-colored, whimsically-shaped numbers were flashed on the screen, one per second, for 60 seconds, illustrating how much we can absorb in just a single minute. Here's another way to highlight this idea:

> ✎ *Instant complexity.* Sit in front of a television in a quiet room, and turn up the volume so that it's loud but not painfully so. Hold the TV remote with your finger ready to press the "mute" button. Close your eyes and focus intently on the sound for a moment. Then as you hit "mute" to eliminate the sound, open your eyes and focus your attention on your *bodily sensations.*

While you were listening to the loud TV, your body was probably not in the foreground of your awareness. But when the sound disappeared and you turned your attention inward, you probably noticed many sensations, and just by opening your eyes you immediately absorbed a great deal of visual data. Thus within three or four seconds you noticed all sorts of details about what you were feeling and seeing.[25]

---

[25]Some have argued that the seeming complexity of consciousness is an illusion. In speaking of consciousness as a workspace, Koch writes that this "workspace is very small, though, so only a single percept, thought, or memory can be represented at a time" (2012, p. 122). Although we sometimes do overestimate the amount of detail in our experiences, the above exercise shows that a very brief span of awareness can be quite rich.

In here or out there?

Suppose you're at a jazz concert, and you're aware of horn-like noises and a visual experience of someone working the slide of a bright, brassy trombone. Assuming that you are perceiving accurately and not hallucinating, here are two ways of thinking about this episode:

1. You are directly experiencing someone playing a trombone.
2. You are directly experiencing mental states (sounds and sights), and this leads you to *infer* that someone is playing a trombone. This inference happens with such lightning speed that you don't even notice it. You just think, "great solo!"

If version two is correct, we do not directly perceive the world. Instead, we are aware of an inner simulation of worldly objects, and we (mostly) treat this simulation as the real thing. Philosophers call this indirect realism. We know about real things in the real world, but we know them indirectly.

Mental phenomena such as hearing horn sounds or visually perceiving a trombone have sometimes been called *sense data*. The sense datum theory was developed about a hundred years ago, and many thought sense data were non-physical. They were influenced by the seventeenth century philosopher René Descartes, who believed that physical matter and the conscious mind were two separate domains. But those who think everything is made of matter reject the "dualistic" Cartesian account of consciousness. Because it is historically, and at times unfairly, associated with Cartesian dualism, indirect realism has acquired a rather bad odor these days.

Many scholars have abandoned the "internalist" idea that conscious perception is an inner simulation of worldly objects. Waving the banner of externalism, they contend that conscious experiences only tell us about things in the outside world. Michael Tye, for example, has famously proclaimed that sensory phenomena *"ain't in the head."*[26]

---

[26]Tye 1995, p. 151. Tye admits that "orthodoxy in the philosophy of mind has favored phenomenal internalism. The received view has been that phenomenal externalism is obviously false." ("Phenomenal" refers to the phenomena of conscious experiences.) Even so, he maintains that "phenomenal externalism

Tye concludes a recent book by calling scholars to the barricades:

For the thoroughly modern materialist, the thesis of phenomenal internalism . . . should be 'committed to the flames.' Only then will all vestiges of Cartesianism be eliminated from the materialist worldview.[27]

So often, disputes are based on two opposite hunches, both of which make sense. Are conscious phenomena in here or out there? Our perceptions inform us about the outside world, so we do seem to be aware of something outside of our minds. But internalists, including indirect realists, are also tuned into important truths. Dreams and hallucinations, for example, are definitely internal states rather than experiences of the outside world.

An indirect realist can reject mind-body dualism, and say that conscious experiences are brain states. In that case, a pain "in" your toe is actually located in your brain. If pain-signals stopped entering your brain, someone could smack one of those little piggies with a hammer and you wouldn't feel a thing. And if a surgeon stimulated the right spot in your brain, it might seem as if something ghastly was happening to your toe even though no one was touching it.

In one experiment during the 1950s, doctors installed electronic probes in the brain of someone with a severe mental illness. This ethically problematic procedure produced vivid results. "The patient giggles again, transformed from a stone-faced zombie into a little girl with a secret joke. 'What in the hell are you doing?' she asks. 'You must be hitting some goody place.'"[28] This experiment offers evidence that experiences are internal mental states. (In another experiment, rats were allowed to press a lever that shot a jolt of electricity into their pleasure centers. "Some

---

is a plausible and appealing position that goes naturally with the thesis that *phenomenal character is itself out there in the world"* (Tye 2009, pp. 193 and 198). In Chapter Seven we'll unpack the enigmatic claim that I've italicized.

[27]Tye 2009, p. 199.

[28]Hooper and Teresi 1987, p. 156.

would push the magic button thousands of times until they passed out from exhaustion or hunger.")[29]

Sensory perceptions are actually much less world-like than we may imagine. Perceptions are processed in all sorts of convoluted ways, and the resulting experiences may be quite different from the things we're perceiving. In fact, systematic visual illusions begin at the point where the surface of the eye meets the air! The air is full of atomic particles, but I visually experience air as if it were nothing. If I perceived air in the same way I perceive walls, I would be as blind as if my head were encased in concrete. It is an enormous distortion of reality to experience air as nothing and a wall as something, and consciousness involves many of these useful illusions. Furthermore perceptions offer *clues* about what an object is, rather than presenting us with full details about it. Even if we see it clearly, we are merely detecting a small percentage of the electro-magnetic radiation bouncing off of one side of it.

Indirect realism also fits the obvious fact that if something in the outside world changes, we only perceive the change if it registers in our minds. And when our perceptions change (or if we hallucinate), it seems as if the world has changed, even if it has not. Want to make it seem as if all of the objects in front of you have disappeared? Just close your eyes.

Convinced? Well, not so fast. In recent years *direct realism* has fought back, proclaiming that perceptions put us directly in touch with the world. Direct realists explain perceptual errors and hallucinations by saying that "we directly perceive external arrangements, but do not always perceive them as they actually are."[30] Direct realists don't have to show that we perceive perfectly or that we perceive everything. We can't hear some sounds that dogs can hear, and they can't see colors as we can. But we're perceiving the world, and so is Bowser. For "direct realist theories of perception . . . there is nothing standing between us and the objects we perceive."[31]

---

[29]Hooper and Teresi 1987, p. 147.

[30]Brown 2008, p. 53.

[31]Jackson 2012. Harold Brown states that in both philosophy and everyday life, "direct realism is the default position, and philosophical 'defenses' of this view largely consist of replies to arguments against direct realism" (Brown 2008, p.

To counterattack, internalists can whip out their ultimate trump card, the famous brain-in-a-vat scenario. A mad scientist of the future keeps a brain alive in a liquid solution, while stimulating it in a way that triggers seemingly normal sensory experiences. The brain therefore thinks it is inside of a body that's walking around and living a normal life – the ultimate virtual reality simulation – but it is only in touch with its own internal states.

Some externalists deal with envatment by flatly denying that this brain would experience anything at all, even if its neural states happened to be identical to, say, the states of your brain right this second. Does that make sense, or do you vote for internalism on this one?

But could it be both?

Can one and the same mental state be an experience of both the outside world and our own minds? Obviously it's possible to detect two or more things by focusing on the same item. Think about a TV newscast. By watching it, you are monitoring (1) its content (what it's telling you about world affairs), (2) the screen images that help convey this content, and (3) the dotty little pixels that constitute these images, at least with low-resolution TVs. (On the other hand, unless you are God or Superman,

---

45). But Colter makes it sound as if direct realism is on the ropes. "Michael Tye purports to defend . . . direct realism about perception against criticisms ordinarily taken as conclusive" (Colter 2009). Siegel observes that internalism "is motivated by the idea that there need be no phenomenal differences between the states of seeing two qualitatively identical table settings, or between these and a hallucination of just such a table setting. Whether or not internalism is true, there are clearly pairs of perceptions that seem the same from the subject's point of view." Internalism "provides an account of what these pairs of experiences have in common" (Siegel 2010, pp. 169-70).

you are not detecting the atoms that make up these pixels – not detecting them *as atoms*.)

So a single stream of stimuli can tell us about several different things. Could it be that a multiple-detection process of some sort is occurring in consciousness?[32] And yet even if a single experience puts us in touch with something inside of our minds *and* something in the outside world, we run into trouble if we use this approach to answer the basic question, *what are conscious experiences made of?* Contrast these two claims:

❀ Seeing a giraffe gives me information about both what's happening inside of my head and what's happening in the outside world. I can tell that I am perceiving this animal in a certain way (seeing it clearly or fuzzily, for example), and I can also tell that there's a giraffe in front of me.
❀ The stuff that I detect when I have an experience of seeing a giraffe is both the giraffe itself and a visual experience of that beast.

The second claim, which says what this experience *is*, just sounds silly. Tall spotted creatures and mental events in human heads are very different kinds of things. How could one thing actually *be* both of these? Compare: "I now see a red shape on my TV screen. This shape is both a screen image of a fire truck and the fire truck itself." No. I'm seeing a screen image that I imaginatively experience as a fire truck.

✎ *Multi-layered awareness.* Here's a way to practice thinking of your mind as a multi-layer detection device. Turn on music and close your eyes. Start by listening in your usual way. Then focus for a few minutes on each of the following interpretations: (1) Think of the sounds you hear as states of the instruments themselves – the vibration of piano strings or drum-heads, or what a horn's doing as the air flows through it. (2) After a while, think of the music as sound waves striking your ear. (3) Then think of it as experienced sound, the auditory perceptions that make you tap your feet.

---

[32]Robert Van Gulick advocates a "pragmatic pluralism" in which "for some purposes a more internalist mode of characterizing mental kinds and contents may be best, while for other purposes some more externalist scheme would serve better . . ." (2011, p. 145).

Did it seem as if you were in touch with the outside world (interpretations 1 and 2) or your own mind (interpretation 3), or both?

You can do the same thing with other sensory modes, such as taste. Are you directly experiencing a hot pepper or indirectly detecting it through taste phenomena? With scent, are you directly or indirectly detecting the particles within an onion that make it smell so strong? With touch, are you directly detecting the surface of this book or indirectly experiencing it through tactile sensations? Again, try to alternate between external and internal interpretations. This may help you empathize with both sides of this debate.

The inner eye illusion

When people think about visual experiences as inner, mental states, a TV set analogy may come to mind. We look at something and the mind conjures up an internal display, as if a little person inside of us is watching a movie.[33] Do you see the fallacy? If we explain how we perceive visual phenomena by saying that a mysterious mini-me re-perceives these phenomena, how do we explain this inner observer's perceptions? There has to be another re-perceiver inside of the first one, and so on, an endless series of tiny people inside of other tiny people.[34] Furthermore the idea of inner re-perception often goes hand in hand with the belief that we know our own experiences in a way that is direct and virtually infallible. I hope to thoroughly convince you that this is not so.

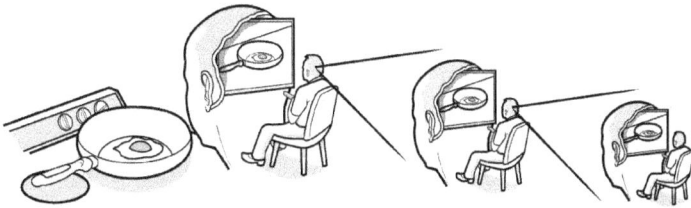

---

[33]"We talk loosely about the mind's eye," notes Pollock, "but no one thinks there is literally a sense organ in the mind surveying what is occurring there" (1989, p. 5). Even so, Daniel Dennett (1991) argues persuasively that we are insidiously influenced by a naive inner-sense account of our own experiences.

[34]Block (1981, p. 3) and Güzeldere (1995a, p. 353) discuss this problem. See also Sydney Shoemaker 1994a, pp. 254-55 and Michael Tye 1991, p. 20. However some philosophers have affirmed versions of the inner perception model. Armstrong, for example, suggested "that consciousness . . . is nothing but *perception or awareness of the state of our own mind"* (1980, p. 198).

The inner eye metaphor is useful in some respects, but it is hard to know which aspects of this idea are helpful and which are misleading. I will try to identify ways in which "looking within" does put us in touch with our own minds, while rejecting the ways in which introspection leads us astray.

Now that we've covered some basics, I'll refine my earlier statement about the focus of this book: *It seems as if some states of mind are "conscious" and others are not. Could these conscious experiences, in principle, be states of the brain?*

And the brain is our very next topic.

Summing up

Consciousness is a hydra-headed word with meanings that spiral out in several directions. This book deals with what is often called *the stream of consciousness.* What we possess, and what computers and corpses presumably lack, is an ongoing stream of experiences – thoughts, feelings, and perceptions that each of us detects as we notice our own mental processes. Some typical characteristics of conscious experiences include being available to the mind's control-systems, being conscious to the self, being remembered at least briefly, being reportable (in creatures that can make reports), and (at least with perceptions and sensations) seeming to be "present."

Some philosophers say we do not directly perceive the world. Instead, we are aware of a partially correct mockup, a simulation that resides within our minds, and we treat this simulation as if it were real. Others deny that we access anything in our own heads. Perception only informs us about the outside world. Both interpretations have merit, neither is entirely satisfying, and it is difficult to combine the virtues of each into a satisfying synthesis.

Chapter Two
A Three-Pound Universe

To know whether the mind could exist within the brain, we need to understand the brain itself. Although this chapter may seem like a digression, many readers will find it the most fascinating material in *Your Living Mind*[35] – and it's an essential foundation for the rest of the book. I should warn you that I will sometimes speak as if it has already been proven that the mind is, or could be, contained in the brain, even though that is exactly the point that this book tries to prove. I could repeatedly say things like "*if* visual experiences are brain states, then . . ." but that would become tedious after about two pages. So even though I will sometimes speak as if the mind is definitely in the brain, I realize that this has not yet been established.

What your brain can never understand . . .

. . . is itself. There is no way any of us can fully grasp the astonishing capabilities that are packed into a few inches of cranial space. Do not be deceived by this organ's small size – remember how much data can be written on a computer chip. I invite you to treat this chapter as a meditation on the brain's prowess. Then later in the book, if you find yourself thinking, "a brain couldn't do *that*," think again.

The human brain contains about 100 billion nerve cells (neurons). The word "cell" may seem to imply simple shapes, like little boxes, but neurons look more like bushes or trees, with luxuriant branches and tendrils projecting from the cell body. One winter's day while driving through the countryside I realized that every one of the bare trees lining the highway looked roughly similar to an individual neuron. So next time you're in a forest or a botanical park, imagine that you're looking at your own inner "garden."

---

[35]If you'd like to dig deeper, *The Three-Pound Universe* by Judith Hooper and Dick Teresi, *The Evolution of Consciousness* by Robert Ornstein, and *Neurophilosophy* by Patricia Churchland are engaging and informative even if somewhat dated. Andy Clark's *Being There: Putting Brain, Body, and World Together Again* is a helpful treatment by a philosopher. William Robinson's *Your Brain and You* explains brain functioning well, in simple and concise terms. *The Human Brain Book* by Rita Carter also contains a lot of pertinent information, clearly stated.

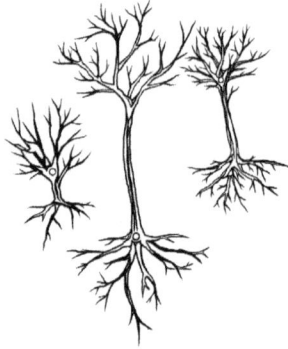

Popularized descriptions of the brain tend to be simplistic. When authors refer to brain structures such as channels, pumps, and receptors, they are talking in almost cartoon-like fashion. According to George Johnson, these terms are more like metaphors than like literal descriptions of molecular processes. He says that "faithfully simulating a single neuron would take an entire supercomputer."[36] So just *one* of your nerve cells is as complicated as a computer, and you have roughly 100 billion of them!

Furthermore, the basic building block of brain power is not the individual nerve cell. It's the synapse, *the connection between the cells,* and your brain contains at least one hundred **trillion** of these linkups.[37] Suppose you started counting the links between neurons in your brain, one connection every second, twenty-four hours a day. At the end of a year you would have counted around thirty million. But to count all of the interconnections would take you over three million years.

And that's just the beginning. We've been talking about how many connections there are in your brain at this instant, but these connections are changing all the time. How many possible sets of interconnections *could* your brain have? Philosopher Owen Flanagan has suggested that the number of possible link-ups in the average brain is *ten to the one*

---

[36]Johnson 1991, p. 99.

[37]Koch estimates that the human nervous system contains "perhaps 1,000 trillion synapses linking about 86 billion neurons." That's one *quadrillion* synapses. If this is correct, counting them at one per second would take about 30 million years.

hundred trillionth power.[38] By comparison, Paul Churchland estimates that the number of elementary particles in the entire universe is about 10^{87}.[39]

Can you see why each person is unique? Can you see why we might have amazing abilities? As one neurologist said, *"100 trillion different connections – hell, you can do anything with that. That's more than enough to contain a soul."*[40]

The brain is a very big place in a very small space.

The point that matters here is that *each of us lives in a giant brain.* I have come to believe that I am inside of this huge little thing.

If we pay attention to our own mental processes we'll occasionally catch a glimpse of the brain's prowess. For instance, it processes information with incredible speed. Once a friend of mine began uttering a word that started with the sound "gro . . ." Before she even finished that syllable I thought she was saying "gross," but when she completed the word a millisecond later it was "growth." How remarkable that my brain could auto-complete her word (erroneously) in such a short time.

Patterns within patterns within patterns . . .

The brain processes information through *patterns of neural activity.* An electrical impulse flows through a nerve cell, causing chemicals to jump across the gap from one nerve cell to the next. The arrival of this chemical message increases the chance that another electrical impulse will ripple through *that* neuron, so that another signal hops across another synaptic gap, and so on. A single activated neuron can signal thousands of other cells, which may then signal thousands more, forming a particular pattern. This ongoing dance of synaptic firings is like a constantly-changing kaleidoscope, and each turn of the kaleidoscope creates a unique experience. One brain pattern might be a visual experience

---

[38]Flanagan 1992, p. 37.

[39]Cited by Flanagan 1992, p. 37. Flanagan states that is is impossible to fully write out ten to the hundred trillionth because this number "would fill all imaginable space and then some."

[40]Hooper and Teresi 1987, p. 31, emphasis added.

of a bright red slice of watermelon. Another pattern might be the ice cold sweetness of that first delightful bite. Still another kaleidoscope configuration might be a memory of a picnic last summer, enjoying an especially tasty melon slice.

"Neural activity pattern" sounds rather abstract, and when I lecture on this topic I sometimes illustrate this idea physically. "Please rise if your last name begins with A through L. Now make contact with at least one other person. This is like the way nerve cells connect through synapses, and let's say that this combination of links is the experience of hearing a bell. Now everyone whose name starts with M through Z can connect up. Let's say this is the way the brain creates the experience of seeing *red*. By linking up cells, as you linked up your bodies, the brain creates your experiences."

Someday we may be able to detect precisely which neural activities constitute, say, a visual experience of a single cherry blossom, but this will certainly not be easy. Compare the task of identifying precisely which electromagnetic waves in the signal from a TV satellite constitute an image of the seams of a football being passed during the Superbowl. We assume that this part of the video signal is a physical event, and our inability to precisely specify it does not make us puzzled. But the difficulty of knowing just which brain activities constitute a particular experience may make us wonder whether this experience *could* be in the brain. Complexity confuses us, *so beware of the complexity trap.*

I recall a lecture in which the speaker announced that he was going to display his model of the neural correlates of consciousness, or NCC. The NCC is whatever cluster of neural activities correlates with conscious experiences, and finding such a correlation would be a big step toward showing that experiences are constituted by neural processes. He then showed us a diagram that looked roughly like this:

He was joking, of course, because we have no idea how to sketch the NCC. But because neural processes are so intricate, we are forced to oversimplify them by drawing tidy diagrams. From time to time we need to remind ourselves that the brain is much more complex than we can comprehend, and that **we are in** this convoluted mish-mash.

Your own little Truman Show

"Reality . . . what a concept!" This title of a CD by the late Robin Williams suggests that what we think of as reality is our own conceptualization. In a sense, the brain assembles the only reality we are able to know. Every message we receive through our ears, eyes, nose, tongue, and skin is elaborately processed before we become aware of it. There is no way to experience life as raw data. Our brains feed us French toast rather than kernels of wheat topped with unshelled eggs. In that sense the direct realist's claim that nothing stands between us and the objects we perceive is rather misleading.

Perceptions are processed in ways that help us cope. For example, visual information is cleaned up and enhanced after it arrives in the brain. Suppose we are looking at an object that is equally bright all over its surface, according to exact measurements of brightness levels. To us its brightness will not seem uniform; it will seem brighter at the edges and corners than in the middle.[41] By artificially brightening edges and corners the brain exaggerates boundaries, so that it's easier to tell one thing from another. How convenient to see a universe of specific objects instead of a swirl of bewildering stimuli. Changes are also exaggerated, making it easier to notice the movements of an animal. And when we watch a moving object, we experience it as being slightly ahead of its actual location. This helps a baseball player hit a fastball that's ripping along at nearly 100 mph – and helps pitchers fool batters by throwing them a curve.[42]

There are blood vessels in the eye, right in front of the retina, and it would be confusing to peek out at the world through a grillwork of capil-

---

[41]Ornstein 1986b, p. 38.

[42]". . . when targets are moving, they are seen ahead of their actual retinal location because they are seen at their predicted next location" (Cavanagh 2013, p. 15).

laries. So how does the brain solve this problem? Very simply. Anything that stays perfectly still in relation to the eyeball is invisible. Whenever the eyeball moves, the blood vessels move with it, so the blood vessels aren't seen except under unusual conditions.

As you look at an object, a river of information flows up the 1.2 million fibers of your optic nerve into your brain. Once it arrives there, an early stage of processing establishes edges. One neural system graphs the horizontal lines and another attends to straight-up-and-down vertical lines. Others monitor an object's shape, color, location, or name.[43] Sometimes people who have had a small stroke will lose one of these subsystems, but the others will remain intact. For instance, they may be able to name an object they are looking at and accurately describe it – but they have no idea where the object is located in relation to other objects! Their visual experience has changed in a way that is virtually impossible for normal people to imagine. They've lost their inner map of object location.

In a film called *The Truman Show*, the main character starts to suspect that what he thinks is real is just a made-up story. Eventually he discovers that the world he had known since birth was actually an enormous stage set. *And we are all the stars of our own Truman Show.* The brain manufactures our world and fabricates the way we feel about it. Presumably a lot of this brain-made story is reasonably accurate, but some of it is pure fantasy.

I like to picture my brain as a huge Tinkertoy sculpture, with billions of interconnected spools and dowels. Activate the connections of these units in one way and you feel like dancing. Switch around their activation patterns and you sink into existential angst. It seems as if "reality" has changed, but it's all just patterns in our heads. If you change the pattern, you change yourself.

---

[43]Raggett discusses areas of the visual cortex: "V2 imposes more order relative to boundaries and the separation of objects from backgrounds; V3 is related to visual depth; V4, or a subsidiary area V8, is thought to be related to colour, and V4 may also be related to texture; V5 is related to motion" (Raggett 2014, p. 216).

Brilliant simpletons and loopy links

So we're learning about the brain's complexity and the way it creates what we take as reality. We're also learning about the way it is organized. I won't say much about that, except to emphasize that the brain is less unified than we once thought. It's actually a system of systems. Each of us has a left brain system and a right brain system, and lots of other systems as well.[44] Our cranial universe is more like a multiverse.

Commenting on the brain's organization, Robert Ornstein states: "A brain is actually built like a ramshackle house, built first at one time for a small family, then added onto over several generations of growth. The original structure remains basically intact, but some of its functions are moved somewhere else in the house, as when a new and modern kitchen is built, and the old one remains, but is now a pantry. . . . The lower part of the human brain is strikingly similar in appearance to the entire brain of reptiles, but the functions are no longer the same. . . . We'd often like to think that we live exclusively in that modern rationally designed part of the house, but this is an illusion."[45]

Ornstein says the brain is organized into *squadrons of simpletons,* legions of cellular machines toiling away inside our heads. The individual units are unintelligent – Ornstein shows them wearing dunce caps – but working together they can add up to an Einstein.

Has this ever happened to you? You were about to leave a room, carrying a few objects. Then you stopped, realizing you had meant to bring another item, but you weren't sure what it was. Some of your brain mechanisms had forgotten about it, but another team of simpletons tapped you on the shoulder, nudging you to recall the missing item.

Many cerebral squadrons are arranged like maps, especially the parts of the brain that deal with sensory information and physical

---

[44] A great deal of nonsense has been written about how the "right brain" and "left brain" function. For example, we have ". . . no hard evidence that the size of the left or right hemisphere affects one's personality, despite pop neurology assertions" (Duncan 2009, p. 66).

[45] Ornstein 1986a (cassette tape).

sensation. There are over 30 maps of the visual field in monkeys and we believe the same is true in humans.[46] Somehow all of these maps of the visual world – maps that chart edges, shapes, colors, locations and so on – are fused together so that we see one picture. The brain takes visual reality apart and puts it back together again.

So where in the brain does it all come together? Is there some neural agency that unifies our experiences? We have already discovered multi-sensory neurons, which increase their activity level if they are receiving information from two senses at the same time. This might happen, for example, if a person is seeing an object and hearing a sound that both come from the same location in space. But many experts doubt that there is a single brain system where the separate ingredients of consciousness are integrated.

Philosopher Daniel Dennett says it never comes together. And yet in some sense we must have unified experiences as a basis for unified actions. Evidently an elaborate coordination process enables all of the separate maps and agencies to work together well. The brain is well designed for such coordination, because different brain regions are connected to each other by highly repetitive feedback loops.[47] So even if there are 30 maps of my visual world, each one of those maps may be functionally interlaced with the others.

The feedback loops that link different assemblies of nerve cells help integrate the various mappings of visual space into a single pattern. They even help resolve conflicts when two different systems seem to be seeing two different things. Here's an example:

---

[46]According to David Heeger "[t]here are about 30 secondary visual areas after V1. Most lie in the occipital lobe. But some are in the parietal and temporal lobes as well" (Heeger 2006). To see these areas in the macaque monkey, go to: http://www.cns.nyu.edu/~david/courses/perception/lecturenotes/what-where /what-where.html.

[47]"Churchland explains that 'it is a general rule of cortical organization that forward-projecting neurons are matched by an equal or greater number of back-projecting neurons . . .'" (Gennaro 2012a, p. 282).

When most people look at this diagram they see a white triangle with the apex pointing upward. But there is no white triangle! This shape is implied rather than depicted, so what's going on? According to Semir Zeki, the part of the visual cortex called V1 does not "see" the triangle. V2, however does register it. V2 has "larger receptor fields and more analytic functions," and it assembles the triangle out of bits and pieces of other shapes in the diagram. So V1 and V2 are in conflict, but V2 sends a message to V1 to resolve this contradiction.[48] Thus even though two parts of the brain are telling two different stories, there is an orderly procedure for marginalizing one account and canonizing the other.

One way the brain creates our sense of reality is by making memories, but memories are not stored in the way that we stack videos in a cabinet. Memories are stored as *the ability to generate experiences which create partial simulations of previous experiences.* Think of a child's set of plastic bricks. The buildings that the child can make with those bricks are not all warehoused in a little box. The bricks are in the box, and the child knows various ways of arranging them. Just so, our brains can rearrange neural activations into the remembered faces of friends. When something reminds us of an event in the distant past, partial re-creations of old sights, sounds, smells, tastes, and tactile sensations come flooding in. As George Johnson writes, "memory is a construct, not a videotape." He then warns us that when different people experience the same event, their "brains will pick different features to put into their memory structures, and they will build them in different ways. . . . A single eyewitness report – whether in a scientific experiment or a criminal trial – should always be open to skepticism."[49]

---

[48]Zeki 1992, p. 76.

[49]Johnson 1991, p. 165. Similarly, John Searle writes, "A very traditional view of memory is of a kind of storehouse of mental representations. You want to

Do colors exist?

Colors are one of the most widely discussed features of consciousness, but it's hard to know where they are actually located. Think of a bright yellow lemon, for example. When scientists examine the brain, they find grayish neurons, and when they examine the fruit itself, they just find a lot of molecules in motion – no color at all.

I wonder where the yellow went.

It seems natural to think of colors as being "on" physical objects, as if every speck of matter sports a paint job, but is that really so? Here are six ways of thinking about this problem:

1. Colors are surface properties of physical objects. They are not inner experiences.
2. Colors are inner experiences. Strictly speaking, it is a mistake to say that objects are colored.
3. "Color" is a word for two different things – features of the surfaces of objects and experiences within the mind.
4. Colors are one thing, located in two places – the surfaces we see and our experiences of those surfaces.
5. Colors are whatever cause us to have color experiences.[50]
6. Colors don't exist.

---

remember Herbert Hoover, so you go back and get the Herbert Hoover dossier out of your storehouse of memory. That is clearly a misconception of memory, which we now understand to play a much more creative, active part. You don't reach into an existing store: you create a present memory-experience . . ." (Searle and Freeman 1998, p. 726).

[50]In other words, colors are whatever cause us to be in states that we refer to *as* colors. You could have what you take to be an experience of one particular shade of orange on many different occasions, and each time it might be caused by something different. Similarly, each time you are amused, this feeling might be caused by something different, such as hearing a joke, being tickled, or being hypnotized to feel amused. One could then define the feeling of being amused as the long list of things that can cause it. I think this approach loses touch with our intuitive sense of what "feeling amused" – or "experiencing a color" – means.

I am comfortable with Options Two or Three as long as we remember that surface colors and experienced colors are quite different. But it's hard to override our common-sense view that "yellow" is both out there and in here, unproblematically one and the same.[51]

Brain science sheds some light on this issue. Most of us learned in school that colors are perceived with the help of "cones" in the retina. There are three kinds, which respond to short light waves, medium waves, and long waves. Color experiences are based on complex mathematical relationships among the reactions of the three sets of cones, so even if you are terrible at math your brain calculates quite precisely in creating color vision.

We could think of these cones as three different slots in a vending machine. One takes nickels, another dimes, and another quarters. The machine adds them up and gives you the total, and different inputs could give you the same bottom line. You could insert ten dimes or two quarters and ten nickels, and both add up to a dollar. In the same way, two or more very different wavelength patterns may appear to be exactly the same color. It just happens that the mathematical relationships among the

---

[51]"The difficulty in finding a plausible objective property that the visual system is responding to in the case of color has led many philosophers . . . to subjectivism about color" (Dretske 1995, p. 89). In color projectivism, "worldly objects have no color in and of themselves, but our conscious experiences project their qualitative character onto them . . ." (Kriegel 2009, p. 65). According to Jeffrey Gray, "it is almost universally agreed that colours, as such, are not properties of the objects that we perceive as being coloured" (Gray *et al.* 2002, p. 29). However Tye maintains that projectivism is a "descendant of the Descartes/Galileo view. Their position is that colors are really intrinsic properties of subjective sensory fields (akin to sense data) that perceivers mistakenly project upon things outside the mind" (2000, p. 146). Seager seems to agree with Tye. "Experiences are *not* themselves red, or audible, tasty or smelly. . . . (no little red Canadian flags . . . appear in my brain, or anywhere else in the natural world, when I imagine the flag)" (Seager 1999, p. 139). (Notice – if the natural world is all there is, the imagined flag does not exist anywhere!) And thousands of years ago the Greek philosopher Democritus denied "that perceptible qualities other than shape and size (and, perhaps, weight) really exist in the atoms themselves: . . . 'by convention sweet and by convention bitter, by convention hot, by convention cold, by convention color; but in reality atoms and void' . . ." (Berryman 2010).

responses of the three cones come out the same, in the brain's color calculations. This is called a metameric color match.

If I say that two colors look the same, I might be claiming that I see two *surfaces* that share certain features, or that I am having two color *experiences* that are the same. With metamers, the first statement is false, and the second statement is true. Those who state that two objects are the same color often assume they are talking about something these objects have in common, something about what is "on" their surfaces. But this color match results from the way the brain processes wavelength information.

If you look through a microscope at the surface of objects, you will not find any feature that is obviously the object's color. C. L. Hardin's excellent book, *Color for Philosophers,* lists fifteen different features of physical objects that influence the color appearance of those objects. He also lists nine ways that color is created in the eye and the brain, including migraine headaches, pressure on the eyeball – and even the *bombardment of the visual system by cosmic rays.*[52] All of these considerations make trouble for "externalist" theories that place colors and other sensory experiences out in the external world.

When brains go bad

We can learn a lot about the brain by noticing what happens when it is damaged by aging, accident, or illness. For example, sometimes an injury or a stroke alters neural structures that help constitute our core sense of reality, including concepts of front and back, left and right,

---

[52]Hardin also reports that color experiences can be caused by "blackbody emission, reflection, refraction, scattering, and polarization . . ." (2008, p. 143). He adds that "a color realist's appeal to 'normal' or 'standard' conditions to determine the 'true' or 'actual' colors of objects is mere hand-waving unless there is some clear reason for preferring one set of illumination or background conditions to another. So far, nobody who has held a realist position has been prepared to propose and defend such a set of conditions" (p. 145). And Harold Brown points out the fact that a visual perception becomes conscious only "after massive disassembly. . . . The very complexity of the process leaves the claim of numerical identity [between object-surfaces and color-experiences] beyond the reach of plausibility" (Brown 2008, p. 52).

clockwise and counterclockwise. Then it's as if one of the stage sets for our personal Truman Show has suddenly collapsed.

In rare cases after a stroke a "patient's visual experiences are a mirror image of normal experiences, so that he can only read books held up to a mirror, write[s] the mirror image of his signature, runs around the baseball diamond from home plate to third, to second, to first, and home again and attempts to drive on the left-hand side of the road."[53] That's a fairly basic reality shift!

Or consider hemineglect (half-neglect), in which people ignore half of their world as if it isn't there (usually the left half). When asked to copy a drawing of a flower they only draw the right side. They still realize that every object has two sides, but the brain modules which structure their experience of the world in terms of left and right have been damaged.

Neurologist Oliver Sacks tells of a stroke patient who would only eat the right half of a plateful of food. She could, of course, have turned the plate around after eating half of her meal. Then the neglected left half would have become the effortlessly-noticed right half. But since it was so hard to focus on "leftness," she had to physically move, turning around in a circle *to the right*. Looking at the plate again she would see the remaining food – or at least the right side of what was "left" over. She would do this several times, consuming one half after another until only crumbs remained.

This patient was highly intelligent and could even joke about the conceptual predicament of hemineglect. "It may look funny, but under the circumstances what else can I do?" When she tries to rotate the plate rather than rotating herself, "it is oddly difficult, it does not come naturally, whereas whizzing round in her chair does, because her looking, her attention, her spontaneous movements and impulses, are all now exclusively and instinctively to the right." "'It's absurd,' she says. 'I feel

---

[53]Churchland 1986, p. 234.

like Zeno's arrows – I never get there.'"[54] So even though she knew she was succumbing to an illusion, her compelling inner sense of *the way things are* overwhelmed her intellectual insight.

Object blindness. If a person sees all parts of an item, does that constitute "seeing the item?" Right now, for example, you see black letters on a white background. Doesn't that make it obvious that it's a page of text? No it doesn't, and this is a striking example of the way hidden mental machinery assembles our world. Some people can see objects in detail and draw them accurately, but their minds cannot put the pieces together so as to experience their wholeness. If you ask them to identify something, they will look at its parts and guess, often incorrectly. One might, for example, say that a dish is a frisbee.

A closely related disability is *face blindness,* a breakdown in the brain complex that recognizes faces. If this system isn't working, the details of another person's countenance won't add up to a face. I attended a lecture by a face-blind fellow named Bill Choisser.[55] As a child he was teased by other youngsters because he had trouble telling them apart. He had no way of knowing how most of us see each other.

Bill learned to recognize people by their hair and clothing. Then he joined the Navy and was surrounded by people in uniforms with short hair. It must have seemed as if everyone had turned into penguins. He had a nervous breakdown in five days. Eventually Bill developed more effective techniques for recognizing people in spite of his condition.[56]

Normal disabilities

Those of us who are "normal" also find ourselves experiencing the world in ways that we know are irrational. For example, some of us have become convinced that colors are located in our minds and not on physi-

---

[54]Sacks 1970, pp. 77-78. The Greek philosopher Zeno asked how an arrow could ever arrive at its target, since before landing it has to go halfway, before going halfway it has to go 1/4 the distance, before that 1/8, and so on *ad infinitum.* Thus the stroke patient consumed half of her food, 1/4 more, and so on.

[55]Choisser 2000.

[56]See http://www.choisser.com/faceblind.

cal objects, but it still seems as if those hues are out in front of us.[57] And most of us also suffer from perceptual disabilities, some of which we are only beginning to discover. The following examples drive home the point that perception does not just duplicate the outside world, as if we were photocopy machines.

Inattentional blindness. It may seem as if we would surely be aware of anything we're looking at directly. But if people are paying attention to one thing they may not see something else, *even if they are gazing straight at it.* In one study subjects were asked to stare at a fixed point, but they had to report whenever an **X** appeared a few inches *away* from the point they were gazing at. So they were looking at one point but staying alert for randomly appearing Xs nearby. Partway through this task, without warning, some letter or shape would appear at the fixation point, right where they were looking.

Here's the surprise. Many did not see what unexpectedly appeared, even though they were looking right at it! However some kinds of items were usually noticed. "The two most reliable of this small group of attention-capturing stimuli are one's own name and the iconic representation of a happy face."[58] But if even one vowel in the name is incorrect, we are unlikely to detect it, "suggesting that it is the *meaning* of the stimulus that captures attention and not some lower-level stimulus attribute."[59] This elegantly demonstrates the way some perceptual activities within the brain become conscious while others do not. After information about what we are staring at travels up the optic nerve into our brains, cerebral sentries note the *meaning and significance* of this perceptual data, and decide whether to let it become conscious.

Here's a frightening example of inattentional blindness. Pilots in training use a simulator to practice flying while they're safely on

---

[57]"As a philosopher, I must continually remind myself that colour is *not* pasted on to the surfaces of objects, since no amount of theoretical commitment allows me to *experience* it otherwise" (Ellis and Newton 1998, p. 421).

[58]Mack 2002, p. 108. A circle at the attention point was seen only 15% of the time, but 88% of the time people noticed a happy face. See Mack and Rock 1998, pp. 139 ff.

[59]Mack 2002, p. 109.

the ground, watching a screen that duplicates what they would see out the windshield of an aircraft. At one point NASA was testing a display that projects navigational information *onto* the windshield, as if the information were floating out in front of the airplane. Sometimes pilots were "using a display, commenting on how nice it was, while landing their aircraft right on top of another aircraft taxiing onto their runway in plain view." Their attention was on the new display, so they overlooked a huge moving obstacle right in front of them.[60]

Change blindness. It may seem as if we see what's in front of us in full detail, so that we have an essentially complete picture of the visible world. We now know this is false, thanks to the discovery of change blindness, the failure to see changes in a visual scene. In one demonstration[61] the audience watched as a picture was flashed repeatedly on a big video screen. We were warned that part of the picture would change from one flash to the next, and then back again. I did not notice the change at first, but when I did the difference was dramatic. A cathedral jumped back and forth from one part of the picture to another. The chimney of a house leapt to the opposite end of the roof. At first, only a few people would notice these shifts, and then others would laugh and gasp as they saw what was happening.

If visual experience just copied what's in front of us, people would notice these changes immediately, but they don't. This "comes as a surprise to most subjects. It has also come as a surprise to many seasoned vision researchers."[62]

This one's just amazing. Daniel Simons and Daniel Levin "set up a kind of slapstick scenario in which an experimenter would pretend to

---

[60]D. Levin 2002, p. 127.

[61]O'Regan 2000.

[62]Davies *et al.* 2002, p. 75. Here's another example: "Subjects are shown a video, the title of which is 'The Color Changing Card Trick.' They attend closely, expecting to see a color change involving the cards. One of the cards does change color. The subjects are then told that . . . there were four other color changes – one involving the color of the tablecloth upon which the cards were resting, one involving the color of the backdrop, and two involving the shirts of the experimenters. This is shocking news to nearly all subjects. When the video is played again, the color changes are obvious" (Tye 2009, p. 170).

be lost on the Cornell Campus, and would approach an unsuspecting passer-by to ask for directions. Once the passer-by started to reply, two people carrying a large door would (rudely!) walk right between the enquirer and the passer-by. During the walk through, however, the original enquirer is replaced by a different person. Only 50% of the direction-givers noticed the change. Yet the two experimenters were of different heights, wore different clothes, had very different voices, and so on."[63]

Daniel Dennett tells a story about change blindness that sounds like science fiction, but it's fact. There's a machine that can track the movements of a person's eye so as to predict where he or she is about to look. If you were hooked up to this eye-tracker while watching a computer screen, the machine could predict where you were going to look on the computer screen in the next millisecond. Some researchers hatched the idea of presenting a computer screen full of text, set up so that after the machine predicted where a person's eyes were going to focus next, *the words they were about to see would change before they saw them.* The person whose eyes are being tracked doesn't notice that the text is changing, because the change occurs during the split second between the instant that the eye starts to move and the time that it winds up gazing at another part of the screen. But those who are watching the experiment will see words changing all over the screen as the subject glances around. Dennett writes:

> When I first encountered an eye-tracker experiment, and saw how oblivious subjects were (apparently) to the changes flickering on the screen, I asked if I could be a subject. . . . While I waited for the experimenters to turn on the apparatus, I read the text on the screen. I waited, and waited, eager for the trials to begin. I got impatient. "Why don't you turn it on?" I asked. "It *is* on," they replied.[64]

Digression: After watching a change blindness video at a consciousness conference, I started noticing *un*-consciousness everywhere I turned. In listening to presenters, for example, I was struck by the way highly competent individuals seemed unable to handle simple tasks. One would

[63]Clark 2002, p. 185.

[64]Dennett 1991, p. 361.

think that prominent authors who have spoken in public many times would be aware of how close they should stand to a microphone in order to be heard. Not so. Furthermore several famous speakers showed us slides that were absolutely illegible in a large auditorium. Nor did most of them bother to clarify technical terms. In one session four experts discussed quantum mechanical effects within microtubules. Not one of them defined "microtubules," even though they knew that this conference included many who were unfamiliar with their particular field of study. Evidently a microtubule is a little doohickey inside of our cells, but I would have liked something beyond the notion that it's a teeny-tiny biological whatchamacallit.

Our intellectual sophistication is partly the result of specific training for specific situations. Like mice who have been moved to an unfamiliar maze, once we are outside of our usual social and vocational context we may suddenly overlook what "ought" to be obvious.

Summing up

There is absolutely no way any of us can fully grasp the abilities that are packed into a few inches of space between our ears. Whenever you think, "the brain couldn't accomplish *that*," think about the problem again from the giant-brain perspective. The brain is a *very* big place in a very small space.

The brain writes our stories. It makes up our world and our life, and tells us how to feel about it. Each of us is therefore the lead character of our personal Truman Show. Every message we receive through our ears, eyes, nose, tongue, and skin is elaborately revised before we consciously experience it. It's especially obvious that the brain is creating an internal mockup of the world when illness or trauma damages the cerebral stage-set. An injury or a stroke may alter one's core sense of reality in ways that seem bizarre even to the patient. This, plus normal disabilities such as inattentional blindness and change blindness, provide evidence for the possibility that conscious experiences are brain states.

Chapter Three
Mindweaving

The hidden sources of simple choices

I'm in an ice cream shop, wondering whether to order chocolate or strawberry. I look back and forth at these two flavors, feeling indecisive. "Dunno what I want." Then I feel drawn toward the chocolate. Do you see the gap in my decision-making process?

There is something missing between not knowing what to order and knowing I want chocolate. While I was puzzling about this decision an impulse popped into my head, seemingly out of nowhere. And if we closely examine our thought processes, we will see that we often jump from one step to another, with gaps in between.

I will be emphasizing an idea that I call mindweaving,[65] and we can begin to understand this phenomenon by noticing what is *not* in consciousness – the blanks, the gaps, the missing links. Experiences are woven from an intricate interplay of conscious and non-conscious processes. Many different considerations could have influenced my decision about ice cream, and in each case I might or might not have been aware of my motivation. Suppose the deciding factor was the dark, velvety color of the chocolate. Would I realize that this consideration tipped the scales? Perhaps, but perhaps not. Or it could be that:

❀ A conscious or unconscious childhood memory of eating chocolate swayed my decision.

❀ I consciously or unconsciously hoped that caffeine in the chocolate would wake me up.

❀ I consciously or unconsciously recalled disliking this store's strawberry flavor.

Sometimes, of course, I know exactly why I make some selection. I might even tell the server "I had strawberries at lunch; I want a chocolatey flavor, just for variety," and this might be the real explanation. But if we examine decision-making sequences closely it will often seem as if we are hopping from one step to another rather than smoothly flowing with no gaps.

---

[65]The first part of this chapter draws upon Schriner 2009.

If we loosely compare our minds to a stage in a theater, conscious experiences are on-stage and unconscious mental processes are off-stage. (I will sometimes use "scare quotes" to remind us not to take this metaphor too literally.) In the ice cream example, I was aware in a conscious, "on-stage" kind of way that I couldn't decide what to order. This feeling of indecision alerted various "off-stage" brain agencies and they went through some secret mental maneuvers. As a result of their labors, I become aware of an impulse to say, "Two scoops of extra-dark chocolate, please."

But why is this important? So I'm ambivalent about what to order, a bunch of nameless brain agencies perform neurological gymnastics, and I go for the chocolate. Big deal. Yes, it is a big deal, because there are lots of these gaps. Hidden brain mechanisms impact what we experience in consciousness every single second.

Researcher Michael Gazzaniga writes about the way thoughts seem to show up out of nowhere. "It has been a major assumption of many investigators in psychological research that the elements of our thought processes proceed serially in our 'consciousness' for construction into cognitions. I think this notion of linear, unified conscious experience is dead wrong. . . . [W]e frequently ask ourselves where particular ideas came from when they appear in our consciousness. For example, when we write, we suddenly think of the exact way to phrase an idea. Where does such an insight come from? We don't seem to know."[66]

Gazzaniga is expressing an increasingly common opinion. Philosopher Owen Flanagan reports that authorities generally agree "that most mental processing is unconscious."[67] Sloman and Chrisley call this the iceberg conjecture. "Consciousness as we know it is *necessarily* the tip of an iceberg of information processing that is mostly . . . inaccessible to consciousness."[68] Interestingly, many artists and poets have said that their

---

[66]Gazzaniga 1985, p. 4. William Robinson makes a similar point. "The sentences in our inner speech are like gifts from our brains. As with ordinary gifts, we do not go out and get them by our own efforts. Instead, our thoughts *come to* us" (Robinson 2010, p. 71).

[67]Flanagan 1992, p. 173.

[68]Sloman and Chrisley 2003, p. 139.

inspirations materialize out of the blue. "As Mozart once said of his musi-cal ideas: 'Whence and how do they come? I do not know and *I have nothing to do with it*'"[69]

The loom of experience

Mindweaving involves more than just the fact that unconscious brain systems work like busy little bees putting together thoughts and impulses which they then dump out into consciousness. Once we become aware of those thoughts and impulses, some of our non-conscious brain agencies give them special attention, as if they were brightly illuminated. These hidden agencies then react to what's been happening out in the exper-iential spotlight, perhaps by manufacturing new thoughts and urges. Some of these then march onto the "stage" of consciousness and seize the lime-light. This again impacts what's going on out in the wings, and again, part of what is off-stage comes on-stage.

Here's an example: As I'm driving, barely audible sound waves cause nerve cells to fire in my auditory cortex. My brain treats this sound as significant and focuses on it through selective attention, and I think, *I'm hearing a siren.* Unconscious neural systems then take the consciously-experienced siren sound into account, as they shape my thoughts, actions, and emotions. I notice a feeling of apprehension and I find myself glanc-ing in the rear view mirror. If I then spot a red vehicle with flashing lights, various neural agencies will respond to this updated information, unleashing a cascade of new experiences such as an impulse to move to the shoulder and stop my car.

I call this the woven-mind or mindweaving model because every experience involves an entanglement of conscious and non-conscious events. Our lives are stitched together from darkness and light. There is an endless game of "tag" going on between experiences we notice and the anonymous mental modules that react to these experiences, a resonating, ricocheting, echoing interaction between what is hidden and what is intro-spectively obvious, interwoven with such speed that we cannot possibly keep track of it all.

---

[69]Dennett 1984, p. 13 (emphasis added by Dennett).

Beyond the Freudian unconscious

It was once commonly believed that all thought occurs within con-sciousness, in the clear light of day.[70] This assumption supported the now-amusing notion that humans are rational animals. Then Freud shocked the world by emphasizing powerful unconscious dynamics that had largely escaped our notice. Because people were accustomed to thinking that cognitions such as beliefs and desires are readily introspectable, Freud's concept of unconscious mental processes "met widely with stark denial and incomprehension."[71]

Today we can go farther than Freud. Freud's conscious-unconscious dichotomy distinguishes mental states which we can access introspec-tively from states we are not aware of at all. But in addition, processes that are *obviously conscious* are closely entwined with hidden brain events. "One of the most fundamental results in cognitive science" writes George Lakoff, "is that most of our thought is unconscious – not unconscious in the Freudian sense of being repressed, but unconscious simply in that we are not aware of it."[72]

Suppose I'm in a Mexican restaurant and I ask someone to pass the salsa. This is clearly a conscious action; I knew I was doing it. Ad-mittedly, unconscious dynamics may have been involved. Maybe I asked for salsa because I unconsciously wanted to irritate a dinner companion who already thinks I'm hogging the hot sauce. But even if nothing from the Freudian unconscious was involved, non-conscious agencies were still at work. I wanted to perk up a boring entree, and hidden mechanisms of behavior-selection chose a remedy. Other modules then picked the proper words and activated my speech-generating muscles. But I have no idea how my mind remembers that hot sauce adds zip to bland food or how it phrases my request in coherent English.

Most of the time we ignore the gaps between one thought and the next, one impulse and the next. We connect the dots, treating each mo-

---

[70]Tye notes that at one time "many philosophers subscribed to the view that the mind is wholly transparent to introspection" (1991, p. 14).

[71]Hofstadter 1981a, p. 12.

[72]Lakoff 1996, p. 4.

ment of experience as if it were a direct link in an unbroken chain. But this useful simplification can lead us astray. Psychotherapists often find that their clients blame others for emotional upsets, assuming that their emotional responses occur as a direct result of events that please or displease them. If a friend says something critical and I immediately see red, I may think the remark directly caused my anger, like one domino knocking over another. But there were "invisible dominoes" between the remark and my anger, mental processes that analyzed the remark's meaning and triggered a reaction. Perhaps the criticism involved something I already felt guilty about. Since I didn't want to be reminded of something I was ashamed of, I became angry.

Instead of: *REMARK* ⭢ *ANGER*
the sequence was: *REMARK* ⭢ *GUILT* ⭢ *ANGER*

Or perhaps my critic reminds me of someone I dislike. If the critical comment is the first domino, the next (unconscious) domino might be, "This sounds like my grandfather scolding me again!" So I blow up. Therapists have to painstakingly teach their clients that the statement, "You made me mad," is always false. An action I consider irritating is evaluated by many mental agencies in the split second before my flash of anger. *Someone else might have been amused instead of irritated,* again because of hidden brain processes that analyzed what happened and selected a reaction. And yet we easily slide into giving other people full credit or blame for the way we respond.

Our ignorance of background mental processes also reinforces the illusion that our reactions are objectively correct and logically necessary. Would any of us regard our political, religious, or moral judgments as being logical and objective if we could see a cutaway view of the way we actually construct them? The thought makes me shudder.

Although the brain's hidden operations can trick us into doing irrational things, they also do lots of useful work for us. For example, one day while preparing a lecture I noticed that I had two main topics to present, and they didn't fit together. Then I noticed a common thread that linked the two themes. But soon I realized this was too much to cover in half an hour. Before long a solution drifted into my mind as if it had floated down by parachute. "I'll cover one topic in detail and briefly mention the other."

Each of these thoughts, both realizing the problems and realizing the solutions, arrived as gifts. It was like getting money in the mail without any return address. On the surface, the process of planning the lecture seemed conscious. It was only by looking closely that I noticed the gaps, the seconds or milliseconds when creative mental agencies were cooking up suggestions. Suitably enough, many of the new ideas I've had while writing this book first greeted me upon awakening.

Actually it's very good that most mental processes occur off-stage. It would be dangerously distracting to know about the 77 steps that assorted mental modules went through just to produce this sentence. We need the high points in the story, the abridged version, so most mental activity happens discreetly out of sight.

But what if *all* of the action happens unconsciously? What if all of our believing, our desiring, our reasoning, our planning, our choosing happens off-stage, and then the results of these non-conscious activities are displayed within consciousness? What if human awareness is not an active, creative agency, but just a freeloading hitchhiker who comes along for the ride? These worries are unnecessary. Although we have underestimated the role of non-conscious processes, we needn't go to the opposite extreme. When people suffer injuries or illnesses that interfere with conscious mental processes, they are often severely handicapped as a result. Consciousness is crucial for optimum functioning.

> ✎ *Mindwatching.* If you want to become familiar with the way your mind interweaves on-stage and off-stage operations, observe your stream of consciousness while you are resting or engaged in a low-cognition activity such as weeding or jogging. Notice the ideas, memories, mental associations, anticipations, and impulses that pop up like mushrooms.

When a conversation goes badly, do you mentally replay it, to make it turn out better? Instead, review the conversation looking for clues about hidden thoughts and impulses that made you say things you later regretted. We can also look for gaps in our awareness when we surprise ourselves by doing something unusually positive. So learning to watch our own mind-weavings has many practical benefits.

Now let's consider a puzzling possibility. Could it be that some states of mind are "off-stage," not overtly introspectable in the same way as sensations and perceptions – and yet conscious?

Consciousness beyond the spotlight

In Chapter One we discussed the seeming *presence* of some experiences. Perceptions and sensations, for example, seem to be definite, tangible entities that we can describe as they arise within our minds – a ticklish sensation, "seeing stars" after bumping one's head, or a menacing face that intensifies a nightmare. We are also aware of thoughts as they occur, but thoughts do not have the tangible character of sensuous phenomena. Of course thoughts can be accompanied by sensory phenomena. While telling a friend about a dream, a ghastly face from that nightmare might float back into one's mind, but thinking about a bad dream is more than just dredging up spooky imagery. Even more obviously, thinking about intellectually sophisticated issues (e.g., the mind-body problem or the political and economic consequences of World War I) does not seem to consist mainly of tangible phenomena that we can describe as we describe seeing stars or feeling a tickle. So if thoughts are not tangible and describable in the same way as sensuous experiences, are thoughts conscious or unconscious?

Here's a related puzzle. Many scholars say that when we have visual experiences we are only aware of "spatial properties, color, shape, motion, and illumination."[73] But some say that we are also visually aware

---

[73]Siegel 2010, p. 7. "Do you just visually experience arrays of colored shapes, variously illuminated, and sometimes moving? Or does visual experience involve more complex features, such as personal identity, causation, and kinds of objects, such as bicycles, keys, and cars?" (Siegel 2010, p. 3). Van Gulick (2014) elaborates. "Some have argued for a so called 'thin' view according to which phenomenal properties are limited to . . . basic sensory properties, such as colors, shapes, tones and feels. According to such theorists, there is no distinctive 'what-it-is-likeness' involved in believing that Paris is the capital of France. . . . Some imagery, e.g. of the Eiffel Tower, may accompany our having such a thought, but that is incidental to it and the cognitive state itself

of things like *causation* and *object-identity*. We are conscious of one thing causing another, and conscious of what things are.

When you see a pass-rushing linebacker flatten a quarterback, does your visual experience include the fact that his beefy mass is *causing* the QB to go down, or is that a conclusion you immediately and automatically draw based on the visual experience? And regarding object-identity, do you see *that* you're looking at football players, or do you experience colored shapes and instantly *infer* that these are Seattle Seahawks and New England Patriots?

Causation is tricky because some visual phenomena strongly suggest causation, as when one auto strikes another at high speed. But now let's play Fantasy Football for Philosophers. Suppose our minds had been evolved differently, so that when the linebacker collided with the quarterback we automatically assumed that the QB had drawn the LB toward him through a sort of magnetism, pulling this hapless adversary on top of him by falling backward. We could hold this radically different interpretation of what-caused-what, *without changing anything about the manifest experience of color, shape, or motion.*

The question of whether features such as causation and identity are literally part of visual phenomena is a lively controversy, and I could argue the case either way.[74] But even if we say that causal relations and

___

has no phenomenal feel." Others advocate "a 'thick' view according to which . . . beliefs and thoughts . . . have a distinctive nonsensory phenomenology."

[74]When we are aware of some experience, it is often hard to tell whether we're in touch with the experience itself or a post-experiential judgment. "Discovering

the identities of objects are part of our conscious experiences, these features are not experientially *present*. We can inwardly "point" to football-player-like shape-and-color combinations, but we cannot focus on some particular detail of a visual experience and say, "*There* is the cause of the quarterback's collapse, and *that* is where his identity is located." (We may see his name on his uniform, but that's just a series of letters. It's not his identity.) Causation and identity may be conscious in some sense, but they are not *explicitly present* in the way that color, shape, and motion are present.

Now let's consider whether thoughts are truly conscious. Most philosophers say that they are, but I used to disagree with this consensus because of the mindweaving considerations mentioned earlier. Since only fragmentary aspects of our thoughts are introspectable as manifestly present phenomena, I maintained that thoughts and similar cognitions are mostly unconscious.

Here's an example: You're driving and someone cuts you off. This triggers a state of mind that could be expressed as, "*I want to honk at that #$%@?&!*" But what aspects of this thought are explicitly introspectable? You might be aware of sub-vocal speech that states this idea in a complete and grammatical sentence, but in the heat of anger one's inner-speech productions tend to be terse. Perhaps you sub-vocalized the word, "*Idiot!*" and fantasized punching the horn button – or punching the driver in the headlights. Such partial sentences and fleeting fantasies offer hints about what we are thinking, but thoughts are much more than these impressionistic flitters.

Even if I express myself in a full sentence (either aloud or silently), such as, "I hope that fool gets a ticket!" that is not a thought either. It's just a series of sounds, or sound-like mental phenomena. Suppose I notice sub-vocal speech that would be written in English as *morning*, and a Mandarin speaker notices sub-vocal speech that would be written in pinyin as *zǎo shàng*. We are thinking similar thoughts, because we both have in mind the interval between sunrise and noon. But what we're

---

which properties figure in experience is difficult," Siegel warns us, pointing out that "in many cases introspectively reflecting on an experience does little to help one decide whether a property is presented in visual phenomenology, or farther downstream" (2010, pp. 52-53).

"hearing" in our heads is entirely different. One is hearing sub-vocal English noises, as you will right now if you silently think, "morning." The other is hearing Chinese sub-vocalized noises. The way sub-vocalized words sound in our heads is not the same as a *thought*.[75]

We often know our thoughts as effortlessly as we know sensory experiences, but we mostly know the content of these thoughts, the ideas they are conveying. We don't know much about the "thingy" aspects of thought. Thoughts are not "displayed" in the same way as sensations and perceptions. A pain may seem small and roundish or large and longish, but a thought about justice does not seem justice-shaped. It may not seem to have any shape at all. Nevertheless, I now recognize that some thoughts are truly conscious experiences. This change of heart is grounded in an overall impression that I am aware of thoughts themselves rather than merely being conscious of various states of mind that are related to thoughts, such as scraps of sub-vocal speech, tidbits of emotionality, and miscellaneous bodily sensations. What tipped the scales for me was the question of whether we consciously know what words mean.

Suppose your friend George says, "I want to quit my job!" At that moment you are aware of (1) the sound of his voice and (2) your interpretation of what those noises mean. It seems that you are genuinely conscious of both (1) and (2), *but in very different ways.* You did not notice your interpretation of what George meant in the way you noticed his spoken words. Experiences of sounds seem like tangible entities that we notice as they begin, persist, and end, but experiences of knowing sound-meanings are not deployed in this thing-like way. Furthermore, we might change our interpretation of someone's statement without changing our recollection of how the statement sounded.

Amazing! Phenomenal! And these two words aren't synonyms!

Academicians talk about the issues I've been discussing by saying that sensory experiences are *phenomenal,* but they do not mean remarkable or astonishing. They are referring to the phenomena that seem to be "right

---

[75] As David Pitt notes, some do see thoughts as sub-vocal sentences. "[S]ome philosophers have been tempted into *defining* thought as inner speech.) . . . But sentences in one's head are no more thoughts than are sentences on paper" (Pitt 2004, p. 24).

there" in the stream of consciousness. To the extent that thoughts do not show up in this way, thoughts are non-phenomenal. Although scholars chat comfortably about phenomenality and non-phenomenality, many people find these labels mystifying. I have tried to find words that communicate more clearly, but I'm not yet satisfied with my terminology. I have sometimes said that sensory phenomena (such as word sounds) are *explicitly* conscious and that some non-sensory states (such as language comprehension) are *implicitly* conscious. I still like this dichotomy but readers found it confusing, so I will also use other pairings:

> Manifest - unmanifest
> On-stage - off-stage
> Phenomenal - non-phenomenal[76]
> Sensory - non-sensory

I will often use that last pairing, even though some manifest phenomena are not typical sensory states.[77] The sensory vs. non-sensory contrast is an oversimplification but close enough for our purposes.

In any case, there are important differences between the way we know our own thoughts and the way we know sensuous experiences. Those who write about the mystery of consciousness sometimes gloss over these differences, and this can lead to confusion. "Getting" the meaning of words is not introspectable in the same way as sensory perceptions, such as the arresting fragrance of a nearby skunk, but it

---

[76]In this book "phenomena" refers to aspects of experience which seem overtly present, such as the qualities of sensory experiences, but philosophers use this term in several different ways. For example, Van Gulick (2014) suggests that "phenomenal consciousness" involves far more than these qualities. Later we will consider Ned Block's distinction between phenomenal consciousness and *access* consciousness.

[77]For an example of an experience that is phenomenal but not truly sensory, think about trying to remember a word that's on the tip of your tongue. Many report a *feeling* connected with this experience, almost like a physical sensation. Some say, for instance, that it feels as if the word is trying to push itself "into the light." But in general, the difference between phenomenal and non-phenomenal experiences is roughly the same at the distinction between sensory and non-sensory experiences.

does fit most of the other criteria of conscious experiences mentioned above. If this point is still fuzzy or you'd like to explore it further, read on:

More Details: Let's consider whether understanding "I want to quit my job!" fits the characteristics of conscious experiences listed in Chapter One. It isn't overtly present in a thing-like way, so it doesn't fit that criterion. But what about the other four hallmarks of consciousness? I should emphasize that the characteristics I have listed are not meant to be absolute criteria that unfailingly distinguish what is conscious from what is not. But it would be odd if some state of mind fits most of these characteristics and yet is utterly *un*conscious.

1. Experiences are "broadcast" to the mental machinery that controls our actions. When we listen to someone talk, for example, our interpretation of what is being said is available to action-guiding mental agencies. In fact these agencies are usually less interested in how words sound than in what they signify.

2. Experiences are conscious to the person who is experiencing them, and again, knowing word-meanings fits this criterion. When people speak we consciously register both the sounds they are making and what we think they're saying.

3. We typically remember our experiences (at least partly and briefly), and when we remember a sentence we typically recall what it meant. Actually we're more likely to remember the "gist" of a statement than to recall either the words or the way the words sounded. I once saw a speaker ask his audience, "Who can repeat the exact words I used two sentences ago?" After an embarrassed silence only a couple of us put up our hands, but I'd guess that most of us were following his ideas fairly well. Our interpretation of what words mean (such as your interpretation of what you're reading now) becomes part of our memory record. That's one more reason that it makes no sense to say that our apprehension of word-meanings occurs unconsciously.

4. By the same token, experiences are typically reportable, and we can typically report what we believe someone was trying to communicate. We can make these reports because we remember what we think was being communicated, not because we remember the sounds of the words that

were used. In principle we could be making an inference about the meaning of words, after remembering how they sounded, but that seems cumbersome and unnatural.

Importantly, when we hear a statement, our sense of this statement's meaning is conscious *in contrast to states that are truly unconscious.* For instance, we have little conscious access to the mental mechanisms that interpret strings of letters as words. Most activities of these mechanisms are not conscious at all. Admittedly, the act of understanding words is not conscious in the same way as perceptions and bodily sensations, but it does fit several criteria of consciousness. And this is just one example of a more general principle. *Many states of mind that do not seem overtly "present" in our awareness nevertheless deserve to be considered conscious,* or at least they deserve some label that makes it clear that they are not unconscious.

❦ ❦ ❦ ❦ ❦ ❦ ❦

I realize that some will object to using the word *consciousness* in talking about language comprehension and other "off-stage" mental states that I will discuss later. I respect this terminological preference, but these states are not entirely unconscious either. They should not be consigned to a sort of philosophical limbo and ignored in discussions of the conscious mind.

I've used understanding words as an especially clear-cut example of implicit, non-phenomenal consciousness, but now I will broaden my claim considerably, maintaining that many of our thoughts are conscious even though they are not "present." Since the word thoughts is rather vague, I'll offer:

More Details: Here are examples of the kinds of thoughts that tend to be "implicitly" conscious:

❀ *Judging what is happening now.* If my Northern California house starts rocking and rolling, I will consciously think we're having an earthquake – even if my mind does not produce an overtly introspectable thought expressing this idea.

❀ *Knowing whether one is feeling positive or negative.* Suppose Jane is trying to decide whether to buy a Honda Civic. As she finds out more about the vehicle, her inclination shifts from "buy" to "don't buy" and back again to "buy." While she is vacillating, she may know about each of these flip-flops even though they are not phenomenally conscious. These shifts may be *accompanied* by sensory phenomena, e.g., butterflies in her stomach. These funny feelings give her clues about her own inclinations, but Jane may also be conscious of her positive or negative leanings without using such clues.

❀ *Knowing why one is feeling an emotion.* Suppose that at a particular moment a person is explicitly aware of an intense feeling of gloom. I believe that this individual might be implicitly conscious of what this feeling is about, e.g., whether this dismal mood is due to "my car needs a new motor" or "yesterday they sentenced me to hang." And one may be conscious of this information regardless of whether one is introspectively aware of automobile images, or the scowl of an angry judge.

These examples all fit under a very broad umbrella. We are often conscious of *having a thought about some fact* – believing, imagining, doubting, hoping, fearing, or entertaining the possibility that a particular fact is true – even if we are not aware of such thoughts as manifest sensory phenomena.

Look back at these examples. When you have similar experiences, are you aware of only the overtly introspectable aspects of the experience? Or do you seem to be conscious of more than that?

❦ ❦ ❦ ❦ ❦ ❦

Our minds intermingle three kinds of processes, woven together with exquisite intricacy to produce our awareness of sensations, perceptions, thoughts, and emotions:

Phenomenal ("on-stage") aspects of experiences
Non-phenomenal ("off-stage") aspects of experiences
Unconscious mental states

The distinction between manifest and unmanifest conscious experiences will be useful as the book progresses. Importantly, most of the deepest questions about how experiences could be brain events involve manifest phenomena such as colors, tastes, and pains.

Summing up

The mind is the loom of experience. Human sentience is a cunning tapestry of conscious and non-conscious activities. This fabric is woven so cleverly that many of our mental processes seem fully visible unless we look quite closely. Yet in reality, every introspectable detail of awareness is densely entangled with anonymous "off-stage" mechanisms.

The mindweaving concept has revolutionized the way I think about myself. Instead of clearly separating the conscious mind and the unconscious mind, I now realize that the intermingling of sensory experiences, non-sensory experiences, and unconscious mental states is as close and continuous as the blending of dye, cotton, and wood pulp in a sheet of fine stationery.

Even though hidden mechanisms shape our experiences every second, we seldom notice the gaps from one instant of awareness to the next. We treat each moment of experience as a direct link in an unbroken chain. If we pay attention to these gaps we will sense the interplay of conscious and non-conscious processes, weaving the mind from darkness and light.

Many states of mind that do not seem "present" as sensory phenomena nevertheless deserve to be considered conscious. One example would be your current conscious experience of understanding the words in this sentence.

Chapter Four
Is Consciousness Physically Impossible?

Is there any connection we could imagine to exist between certain movements of certain atoms in my brain on the one hand and, on the other hand, those facts that are basic, indefinable, and undeniable for me: "I feel pain, pleasure, I taste something sweet . . ."
– E. Du Bois-Reymond, 1872[78]

Nobody has the slightest idea how anything material could be conscious. Nobody even knows what it would be like to have the slightest idea about how anything material could be conscious. So much for the philosophy of consciousness. – Jerry Fodor, 1992[79]

What is it like to be a bat? Nagel's conundrum revisited

In 1974 Thomas Nagel challenged behaviorism with an essay called "What Is It Like to Be a Bat?" According to behaviorists, if we want to learn about bats, we study the way bats behave. But what about knowing how it is to be the bat itself? Isn't that rather important if we want to understand what bats *are*?

Nagel chose bats because they use an exotic navigation system called echolocation. They send out high-frequency shrieks and monitor the way these sounds are echoed back. Since we do not typically navigate in this way, we don't know what it's like to have this sensory ability. Echolocation highlights the difficulty of knowing another creature's perspective, and the implications of this example go far beyond furry flying beasties. Nagel suggested that for every conscious organism there is *something that it is like to be that organism,*[80] and it is this what-it's-like aspect of experience that is left out by behaviorism. For instance, if you knew everything that could possibly be known about me except what it's like to be me, would your knowledge of me be complete? Importantly, many

---

[78]Quoted by Pauen 2011, p. 92.

[79]http://web.media.mit.edu/~minsky/eb4.html.

[80]Nagel wrote that "an organism has conscious mental states if and only if there is something that it is like to be that organism – something it is like for the organism" (1974, p. 436).

theories of mind are logically compatible with there being absolutely nothing it's "like" to be a bat, or a person.

Nagel claimed that "to form a *conception* of what it is like to be a bat . . . one must take up the bat's point of view."[81] But if we can only understand an organism's experience from its special vantage point, how can science ever understand consciousness? Science strives for objectivity, and Nagel declares that "any shift to greater objectivity – that is, less attachment to a specific viewpoint – does not take us nearer to the real nature of the phenomenon: it takes us farther away from it."[82]

Nagel's essay was only 15 pages long, but it had more impact than most hefty tomes. In time "a consensus . . . emerged that Thomas Nagel's expression, 'what it is like to be' succeeds in capturing well what is at stake" in discussions about consciousness.[83] But even though it was a stunning intuitive breakthrough, some people doubt that it has any clear meaning. Rosenthal complains that the term "'what it's like' is not reliable common currency" and quotes William Lycan as saying that this phrase is "positively pernicious and harmful."[84] We seem to have needed such a term, but perhaps we will eventually find better ways to express what Nagel was getting at.

Nagel and many others wonder if we will ever understand consciousness in terms of brain events. Are they worried that the brain is so complicated that we can't find consciousness within its tangled circuitry? Are conscious and unconscious processes so tightly intertwined that we will never know which is which? Those are very real difficulties, but theoreticians seldom lie awake fretting about them. In fact, philosopher David Chalmers says that these are among the "easy problems" of consciousness, not to make light of them but to contrast them with what he calls . . .

---

[81]Nagel 1974, p. 442.

[82]Nagel 1974, p. 445.

[83]Varela and Shear 1999, p. 3.

[84]Rosenthal 2011, p. 434. For example, some say that what-it's-like includes only sensory experiences. Others say that non-sensory mental states such as highly abstract thoughts can be "like something."

The Hard Problem

In 1995 Chalmers described a puzzle that is "hard" in the sense that once we understand the issue we have no idea how to address it. Suppose in the distant future neuroscience has discovered precisely which brain structures and processes are correlated with specific conscious experiences. The scientists can even display their prowess with a mind-reading demonstration. Experimental subject X79 reports that she is recalling a teenage love affair. The researcher then reveals that the brain scanning machine had already printed out a report, just before X79 spoke: "subject is remembering a high school sweetheart." Isn't it clear that we now understand the neural basis of consciousness? Aren't the neural structures and activities that the scanner detected simply identical to the experience X79 reported?

Not necessarily. Two things may be tightly correlated without being the same. Maybe the brain event that the scanner detected caused her to speak about her old flame, *and also caused her experience of remembering him.* In that case the scanner has detected what caused her experience rather than the experience itself. "Even if every behavioral and cognitive function related to consciousness were explained," writes Chalmers, "there would still remain a further mystery: Why is the performance of these functions accompanied by conscious experience? It is this additional question that makes the hard problem hard."[85]

In trying to solve the Hard Problem we seem to be perpetually stuck at square one. Nagel has stated bluntly that "we have at present no conception of what an explanation of the physical nature of a mental phenomenon would be. Without consciousness the mind-body problem

---

[85]Cited by Kriegel 2009, p. 271. Chalmers also states that scientific observations tell us about "structure and function; that's all. Such observations give us no reason to postulate any new class of properties, except insofar as they explain structure and function; so there can be no analogue of a 'hard problem' here." But with consciousness "alone, we can have access to something other than structure and function" (1997, p. 6). At a recent colloquium Chalmers reiterated these comments in discussing the conceivability of creatures that are physically identical to us and yet not conscious (Chalmers, 2013). We'll discuss these creatures shortly.

would be much less interesting. With consciousness it seems hopeless."[86] And William Seager concludes his book, *Theories of Consciousness,* with this dispirited admission: "It is indecent to have a ragged and unpatchable hole in our picture of the world. Cold comfort to end with the tautology that an unpatchable hole is . . . unpatchable."[87]

Pleasures, pains, and colors in the brain?

In addition to these philosophical considerations, conscious experiences don't *seem* like neural activities. "Neural transmissions just seem like the wrong kind of materials with which to bring consciousness into the world," declares Colin McGinn. "What has matter in motion got to do with the way a rose smells? What is it that converts brain 'gook' into visual experience?"[88]

Part of the problem is that when we compare our own descriptions of sensory experiences with scientific descriptions of brain states, we find all sorts of mismatches. For example, suppose we ask whether anything in the brain matches our descriptions of visual experiences.

● Does the brain's way of configuring the *spatial relationships* in a visual scene correspond to our experience of the scene? Look at what's in front of you right now. Does your brain contain a little tableau that precisely maps out what you're seeing?
   ● Vision also seems to mimic complex *motions* of objects and *relationships* among these movements, as when you see a flying flock of birds. Could neural processes exactly match such movements?[89]
   ● Visual experience appears to disclose *unified objects,* but neuroscience suggests that fragments of visual perceptions are scattered through the visual cortex and beyond.

---

[86]Nagel 1974, pp. 436.

[87]Seager 1999, p. 252. Ellipses are in the original text.

[88]McGinn 1991, pp. 1, 100.

[89]Georges Rey asks if the parts of a mental image are "contiguous in the ways the parts of the mental image seem to be? . . . Or [is] introspection just dead wrong about all this?" Rey reports that in some cases a philosopher "simply bites the bullet" by asserting that mental images in our brains "enjoy precisely the same three full dimensions in ordinary space . . ." (1981, p. 121).

❀ We also seem to be in touch with the *qualities* of experience, such as experienced blueness, bell sounds, and sugar tastes. Many theorists find it hard to understand how these qualities could be neural events.

❀ Sensory experiences seem manifestly *present*. In normal sight, for example, an array of visual phenomena seem vivaciously obvious. How could any sort of brain activity constitute manifest phenomena?

This is not an exhaustive list, but it points up some striking inconsistencies between our descriptions of experience and science's descriptions of the brain. It is as if science and consciousness encounter entirely different "surfaces." If you were developing a theory of consciousness, how would you deal with these mismatches? Which ones seem hardest to resolve?

Misleading metaphors and other befuddlements

Some seeming contradictions between experiences and brain events boil down to a mismatch between metaphorical language and literal language. For example, Alistair Hannay worries that "pains can be sharp, thoughts amusing, and desires burning, but brain states none of these things . . ."[90] Similarly, some find it puzzling that sensuous experience seems to be "rich" and "full."

All we need to do here is rephrase poetry as prose. When I say a pain is sharp, I mean that it feels as if something sharp were jabbing me. I don't mean I can use it to slice cucumbers. When a thought seems amusing, our amusement may seem fused with the thought, as if it has been decorated with levity. When we say that human experience is "rich," do we mean "has a big bank account?" Do those who say experience is "full" estimate that it's at about 94% of capacity? Of course not. We are merely describing our own experiences in poetic language.

The apparent mismatch between experiences and brain events is reinforced by resistance to new ways of thinking and speaking. The words we use to describe consciousness evolved long ago, and using these terms in the same breath with scientific jargon seems as incongruous as mixing King James English with instructions from a computer manual. Some commentators are still aghast at the idea that we could talk

---

[90]Hannay 1990, p. 50.

about experience in neurological terms. Maxine Sheets-Johnstone, for example, scoffs at the notion that "the brain of any reader reading this article feels now like having a chocolate bar. Such outlandish claims obviously make brains rather than people the subject of experience, a practice not in the least uncommon in neuroscience, but on the contrary and lamentably, an engrained practice."[91] This "lamentable" practice reflects conceptual and linguistic flexibility, the willingness to express old ideas in new terms. Speaking personally, I feel no distress whatsoever when I think that my brain (or some part of it) would like a Hershey bar.

(As noted earlier, sections marked *More Details* are optional.)

More Details: Some have questioned the idea that the brain contains color experiences, claiming, e.g., that for the experience of blueness to be in the brain, nerve tissue would have to appear blue to an outside observer. Right now you're seeing black type on a white page. If visual awareness is in the brain, why can't we look inside your head and find this phenomenon? If we could open your skull without harming you, all we'd see would be a sort of glisteny gray.

William Lycan calls this *the stereoscopic fallacy.* It's as if one eye looks at the physical brain and the other eye focuses on our own experiences, and we are alarmed that the two do not match.[92] But even if we could point to a pattern on a brain scan and know that it is precisely identical to an experience of hearing Sarah Vaughan hitting high C, obviously we are not detecting the high-C experience in the same way, *from the same vantage point,* as the person who is accessing this experience from within. It is completely unsurprising that they seem different from these different perspectives. The only question is whether what we find from the experiential perspective could turn out to be the same thing that scientists detect.

❦ ❦ ❦ ❦ ❦ ❦ ❦

---

[91] Sheets-Johnstone 2011, p. 154.

[92] Lycan 1987, pp. 76-77. David Papineau cites "the standard rhetorical ploy used to put the argumentative onus on materialism: 'How can technicolour phenomenology arise from soggy grey matter?' asks Colin McGinn." "Still, fallacious as it is, the move is terribly seductive. I would say that it is ubiquitous in everyday discussions of consciousness, and by no means uncommon in philosophical contexts" (Papineau 2005a, p. 145).

Now let's turn to several other problems with understanding how "what it's like" states could occur within the brain, starting with one of the most contentious controversies of all:

The qualia wars

> *Qualia* is an intriguing concept, and this term has no simple everyday equivalent. Please do not skip ahead without reading this material!

Qualia rhymes with Som*alia* and the singular is quale, pronounced *qua*-lay or *qua*-lee. Qualia are the qualities of sensory experience. Think about your own vivid sensory perceptions – the snap of firecrackers on July 4th, the scent of oranges, the flavor of peppermint ice cream. Each of these perceptions is experienced as a quale, a special quality that is difficult or impossible to describe. How would you explain the smell of rotten eggs, for instance, to someone who has never been able to smell anything? "Well, umm . . . it's just . . . *like that.* It has a certain quality that I can't put into words."

Qualia include:

❀ Color experiences – pale pinks, bilious greens, the electric blue of a peacock's feathers
❀ Auditory phenomena – frog chirps, fingernails on a chalkboard, the rumble of thunder
❀ Smells – garlic, cigar smoke, sizzling fajitas
❀ Tastes – popcorn, overripe bananas, kung pao chicken
❀ Tactile qualia – paper cuts, rib-tickles, foot rubs with warm lotion
❀ Internal sensations – spine-tinglings, *mal de mer,* the overwhelming rush of an orgasm

Should we add thoughts to that list? Traditionally, many theorists have divided mental states into two categories, qualia and thoughts. Qualia supposedly have no thought-like features, and thoughts have no qualitative, *what-it's-like* features.[93] Thoughts do not show up in con-

---

[93]David Pitt writes, "It is a traditional assumption among realists about mental representations that representational states come in two basic varieties . . . those, such as thoughts, which are composed of concepts and have no

sciousness in any tangible *right-there* manner, although they may be accompanied by all sorts of qualia. But some philosophers now say that thoughts themselves are qualia.[94]

More Details: Unfortunately, discussions about qualia are confusing and contentious. "Some theorists find them so obvious as to not require justification, while others reject them as if they belong to the powers of darkness."[95] Part of the problem is the crazy-quilt complexity of scholarly terminology. "It is hard to find a description of qualia with which two (let alone all) philosophers would agree . . ."[96] Beyond these complications, the basic problem is that it is hard to explain how sensory qualia such as pains, tastes, and color experiences could exist within a brain.

We describe some aspects of experience quantitatively. I am now visually experiencing two drinking glasses on my desk and three books. The bigger glass seems about 25% larger than the smaller one, and one

---

phenomenal ('what-it's-like') features . . . and those, such as sensations, which have phenomenal features but no conceptual constituents" (Pitt 2013).

[94]"Several philosophers have recently argued that purely cognitive states – propositional attitudes with no sensuous qualities whatsoever – can be phenomenally conscious . . ." (Kriegel 2009, p. 311). Cf. Gennaro 2012a, p. 27: "It does indeed seem right to hold that there is something it is like to think that rabbits have tails, believe that ten plus ten equals twenty, or have a desire for some Indian food."

Although psychology emphasizes the importance of individual differences, we don't know much about individual variations in qualitative experiences. Clearly many philosophers believe that their thoughts lack "what it's like" features, and they may well be correct. But others may actually *experience* thoughts in ways that more closely resemble sensory phenomena.

[95]Maund 2008, p. 269.

[96]Dretske 1995, p. 73. "It will become plain at once," reports Edmond Wright, "that supporters of qualia do not agree about the nature of them" (2008, p. 23). Tye notes that some define qualia as "intrinsic, consciously accessible, non-intentional features of sense-data and other non-physical phenomenal objects" (1994, p. 161). But Flanagan argues against those who define qualia as "atomic, nonrelational, ineffable, incomparable, and incorrigibly accessible from the first-person point of view" (1992, p. 61). He thinks qualia can be redefined in physical terms, and I agree.

book looks twice as far away as the other two. But we wouldn't say red is twice as low as pink or that blue is a little faster than green. We can compare colors in terms of lightness and darkness, but the quality of the color itself is just its own quality, period. Similarly, the sound of a flute has a special quality, and we aren't sure how to speak of it quantitatively. A musical tone vibrates at a certain number of cycles per second, so we can talk about a sound wave in quantitative terms, but that's not a sound-*experience*.

❦ ❦ ❦ ❦ ❦ ❦ ❦

Science, of course, deals with quantities, not qualities. Qualia seem to be another sort of beast entirely. But it would make perfect sense for humans to *categorize* mental states in qualitative terms when they are actually quantitative. In order to survive, we had to evolve the ability to very quickly tell one thing from another. In the jungle, we needed to distinguish ripe bananas from the green leaves that surrounded them, and from the viper gliding nearby. Thus the visual information profiles of yellow, green, and black must be represented differently in our minds.

Colors, sounds, tastes, scents, and body sensations must also contrast with each other. We would become discombobulated, for example, if tactile sensations suddenly seemed like part of the visual field. Sensory inputs must be clearly "labeled." If neural activities constitute sensory phenomena, they could be clustered into families and subfamilies that we automatically *think of* in qualitative terms. Science, of course, would analyze these same brain states by making quantitative measurements of neural functioning. So the seemingly qualitative nature of sensations and perceptions could be accommodated by physicalism.

Setting aside perceptual oddballs such as bats, what is it like to be the person sitting next to you? Presumably there is *something* it is like to be that individual, but are your qualia the same? I imagine most of us as children wondered about whether some people's color experiences might be unusual or even reversed. And philosophers worry about the possibility of *inverted spectra,* meaning that your color spectrum might be reversed, relative to mine. Perhaps when you look at a ripe banana the color you see is the same color I call "blue," and when you look at the sky on a smog-free day you experience what I call "yellow." It seems intuitively as if this sort of thing is possible.

Colored numbers, tasteable shapes

We can also reflect upon qualia by considering synesthesia, a remarkable syndrome in which a perception that typically occurs through one sensory system (such as hearing) can also be represented in another (such as sight). For instance, some people both hear and "see" sounds. They experience the same auditory inputs with two different types of qualia. "Some synesthetes hear what they see, others see what they hear. One of them felt tastes with his hands. The taste of mint, for instance, felt to his hands as smooth, cool columns of glass. Every taste had its systematically associated feel, and he found this quite useful as an aid to creative cooking."[97] "Synthaesthetes often report 'odd' or weird colours they cannot see in the real world but see only in association with numbers."[98]

Let's play with the concept of synesthesia by using a *thought experiment*. Thought experiments are imaginary and often bizarre scenarios that are intended to shed light on philosophical problems. Dennett calls them "intuition pumps," because they stimulate new insights into subtle issues. Sometimes these scenarios invoke the concept of God as a metaphorical way of erasing practical difficulties which are irrelevant to the basic idea behind the experiment.

Suppose an all-powerful being altered our bodies so that we started detecting pain as tastes. Instead of feeling a stabbing sensation, a person who stepped on a tack might notice a terribly bitter taste in the bottom of her foot. This taste would represent the damage done by the tack. If something like this is possible, then perhaps when we notice the distinction between tactile and taste sensations, we are noticing

---

[97]Davies *et al.* 2002, p. 75.

[98]V. S. Ramachandran and E. M. Hubbard 2001, p. 5. "For example, the number 3 may lead to a perception of copper green, the word 'kiss' may flood the mouth with the flavour of tomato soup, and the key of C# minor may elicit a slowly expanding purple spiral" (Brogaard and Marlow 2013, p. 28).

something which goes beyond detecting the features of bodily states – *something about the mental states that represent these body-states.* This would support the internalist claim that we experience states of our own minds rather than just states of the world.

Digression: I have learned to respect the value of thought experiments such as this one.[99] They can lead to error or confusion if used carelessly, especially if we pile one experiment on top of another on top of another. But play with this book's thought experiments and see if you gain new insights.

As a psychotherapist I have often said that people live in their concepts instead of in their bodies and their feelings, but that isn't quite accurate. We live on the *surfaces* of our concepts, seldom bothering to look at them closely or probe their components. We move them around like chess pieces, or re-arrange their connections with each other as if they were simple mechanical parts that we could plug in wherever we please. But philosophical concepts are far more complex and jerry-rigged than they might seem. If we are used to them, we may think we know them well, but familiarity is not understanding. Studying consciousness can help us dig into concepts more deeply, and this can help us probe puzzles about other topics such as ethics, religion, and politics.

The problem of duality

In this section and the next we'll consider two issues that have been discussed by Joseph Levine. First, there's the problem of duality. Many believe that consciousness involves both *what* we are experiencing and the *act of experiencing it.* And our language reflects this duality, treating "experience" as both a noun and a verb. It is:

- ❀ the object of our awareness – the experience I'm having is *pain*
- ❀ our being aware of it – *I experience* pain

---

[99]"It certainly seems as though many important zeitgeist shifts in twentieth-century philosophy owe primarily to thought experiments and the specific beliefs they elicit" (Holtzman 2013, p. 36).

So "experience" is a two-sided term that sometimes emphasizes what is being experienced and sometimes emphasizes the act of experiencing it. (However speaking of an "act" of experiencing is a bit misleading. It makes consciousness of our experiences sound more voluntary and deliberate than is usually the case.) We can also speak of the *process* of experiencing, and this usage is both verb-like and noun-like: "Experiencing four hours of Wagnerian opera caused classic symptoms of PTSD."

If there were nothing "in" consciousness, we would experience nothing. No visual qualia – no visual experience. But if there is no one who is having the experience, no experiencing self, there would be no experience either – no awareness of vision or anything else. Unfortunately, it is hard to understand how these two aspects of consciousness are related. Levine notes that it seems as if "the very same state is both cognitive apprehension and object of cognitive apprehension"[100] and wonders how this could be literally true. How could *the very same state, at the very same instant,* be both what is being experienced *and* the act of experiencing it? Some people have dealt with this by saying experiences are "self-presenting" or "self-intimating," but others find these ideas mystifying.

―――――――――――――

[100]Levine 2001, p. 176.

Here's a way to get hold of this elusive notion:

✎ *Exploring duality.* First, focus on the act of experiencing, using the exercise from Chapter One in which you notice the way sensory experiences "register" within you. Close your eyes and sit for several minutes noticing every sound. With each new noise, think *"got it,"* meaning, "I notice that I have just experienced this sound." You can do the same thing with bodily sensations and other manifest experiences: "Got it, got it, got it." Then to focus on *what* you are experiencing, turn your attention to the perceptions and sensations themselves. Again, close your eyes and notice all sounds. With each new noise, think: *"there"* or *"thus,"* as a way of affirming that you are detecting something real and specific. Sense the way each sound seems to be arrayed, concentrating on its "shape" and quality. How is the next sound arrayed differently? Then you can do the same thing with bodily sensations, etc.

These exercises highlight the subtle distinction between the sense that **you** are experiencing something and the sense that you are experiencing **something**. These are the two sides of duality.

The problem of duality arises because whenever we have one thing that detects another, mistakes can occur. Suppose you are looking at a ripe strawberry and your brain's visual systems are processing its red color in the usual way. But suppose your experiencing self is grotesquely malfunctioning, so that it's in the state which would normally occur if you were perceiving the color green. In that case, what is this experience "like" for you? What experience are you "really" having, red or green (or something else)? We'll come back to this question in later chapters. Now we'll consider one more problem addressed by Joseph Levine.

Levine's unbridgeable gap

In a famous 1983 article, "Materialism and Qualia: The Explanatory Gap," Levine asked a tough question about sensory awareness. "To put the point starkly: what is it about the firing of a neuron, or the nature of a synaptic connection from one neuron to another, or any complicated assembly of such connections and firings, that could explain the reddishness of my experience of the diskette case?"[101] He also added a particularly tricky twist: How could we ever explain why a brain event is one particular quale rather than another? For instance, how could we ever know why a certain pattern of neural activity would turn out to be an experience of redness instead of an experience of blueness? Levine concluded that even though experiences are physical, we cannot explain how this could be so.

Over thirty years after Levine's paper, many theorists believe that the explanatory gap is no closer to being bridged. Ned Block recently commented that "no one has a glimmer of a clue of an idea of how to think about it."[102] **Trying to solve this riddle is like trying to show how you could add up a column of numbers and get letters of the alphabet as your answer.** To many theorists, sensory experiences and brain events seem to belong in two different universes.

Some philosophers "hope to close the explanatory gap not in a single step but by building multiple theoretical links from both directions . . ."[103] Others, such as Thomas Nagel, David Chalmers, and Galen Strawson, "think that we need a conceptual breakthrough in our understanding of matter before we can solve the mind-body problem . . ."[104] I agree that we need a new way of thinking about the relationship between qualia and neural activities, but I'm betting that the big conceptual breakthrough will be in our understanding of qualia, not our understanding of physical matter. More on that later.

---

[101]Levine 2001, p. 94.

[102]Block 2011a, pp. 422-23. And Oliver Kauffmann states that "nothing that we now know, indeed nothing that we have been able to hypothesize or even fantasize, gives us an understanding of why the neural basis of the experience of green that I now have when I look at my screen saver is the neural basis of *that* experience as opposed to *another* experience or no experience at all" (Kauffmann 2011, p. 48).

[103]Van Gulick 2011, p. 143.

[104]Robinson 2008, p. 243.

Summing up

Although many now believe consciousness is a brain process, the obstacles to seeing how this could be so seem all but insurmountable. Many have wondered why, if consciousness is in the brain, our experiences don't seem like neural activities, and several considerations suggest that they are not. Thomas Nagel maintains that consciousness is a state that is "like something" for the creature that IS conscious. If we want to understand a bat, we need to understand what it is like to have the bat's perspective, but how can we have *objective* knowledge about a *subjective* viewpoint? Chalmers has argued that even if we understood every structure and function related to consciousness, we would still not see why the presence of these structures and the performance of these functions is accompanied by conscious experience. It is also puzzling to ask how the same state of mind could be both having an experience *and* the experience we are having. And how could we possibly explain why some brain event is one particular quale instead of another?

Next, two celebrated thought experiments that shed more light on the nature of qualia.

Chapter Five
Mary and David Meet the Zombies

Mary gasps in the garden

Some of the most important works in philosophy of mind are short articles such as Thomas Nagel's "bat" paper, David Chalmers' essay on the Hard Problem, and Joseph Levine's analysis of the explanatory gap. In 1982 *Philosophical Quarterly* published an essay by Frank Jackson with the catchy title of "Epiphenomenal Qualia," following up with "What Mary Didn't Know." Thirty years later "more than a thousand published papers, innumerable conferences, and even several books" have responded to these articles.[105] Jackson's two little essays seem to have hit a very big nerve.

Students of consciousness have found that as they think about how sensuous experiences could be neural processes, the two keep coming apart, as if they could not possibly be the same. Jackson's article highlighted this problem with an intriguing thought experiment. Jackson eventually decided that his argument was flawed, but many believe he was right the first time and should never have recanted.

Jackson asked us to imagine a time in the future when our knowledge of the physical aspects of color perception is complete. We know all there is to know about this topic. In that distant era, there is a neuroscientist named Mary who has absorbed all of this information. She has soaked up everything about color that books, teachers, and computers can possibly tell her about this topic – but Mary has never seen a color! She grew up in a black-and-white room, was prevented from ever seeing her own skin, and so on. Then one day she is released from her achromatic domicile, free to see colors for the very first time.

I'll embroider Jackson's account by stipulating that the first colorful thing she sees is a garden full of dazzling red roses. And here's the crucial question: When she experiences colors for the first time, *does she acquire new **knowledge?*** If she does, Jackson claimed, this shows that "[T]here are truths . . . that escape the physicalist story."[106] In other words, Mary's

---

[105]Garvey 2012, p. 68.

[106]Jackson 1986, p. 293.

discovery shows that some facts about color experiences are not physical facts. This also implies that qualia in general are not physical.

If this doesn't make sense yet, imagine that before she was set free in the garden Mary happened to see a shade of gray that she had never seen before. Since she knew everything about the physical aspects of color experiences, she could have said, "Ah, I recognize that shade as charcoal #27, just lighter than 28 and just darker than 26, both of which I have seen before. And I know just exactly what brain patterns constitute this visual experience." Seeing charcoal #27 would have been a new *experience*, but it doesn't seem clear that it would have given her an amazing new *fact*.[107] But seeing red, green, blue and so on would seem to involve learning something new about the universe.

"Physicalism" (sometimes called materialism) claims that everything that exists is made of physical matter, and so any facts about things that exist are facts about physical things. But Jackson's knowledge argument implies that knowledge of physical facts is not complete knowledge, because after her release Mary learns new facts *over and above the complete physical knowledge she already possessed*. If all things are physical, including human experiences of colors, Mary would have learned nothing new when she walked into that garden. Since she did, the argument suggests, some things are not made of matter. "Therefore, physicalism is false."[108] That may sound to you like dualism, the doctrine that mind and matter are two different sorts of stuff. If so, you are exactly right. Jackson was indeed a dualist,[109] and Mary gave him a persuasive way to justify his anti-physicalist leanings.

---

[107]Actually, seeing a new shade of gray might have been problematic in the same way as seeing colors for the first time. In fact, if Mary had reflected on the qualia she had been experiencing for years, she might have decided that every time she accessed any quale, she was accessing a fact that her textbooks didn't teach her about. The point of the thought experiment is that seeing colors for the first time seems to *obviously* involve learning new facts.

[108]Jackson 2004, p. xvii.

[109]"I had been a dualist for years. I was taught by Michael Bradley, and he had some good arguments for dualism" (Frank Jackson, cited by Garvey 2012, p. 69).

The knowledge argument

Many people think it's obvious that when Mary is set free she learns something she has never known before, i.e., what color experiences really are. In fact one might expect her to gasp with astonishment at this revelation.[110] We certainly see this reaction in the real-world case of "Kevin Staight, who was born with a rare eye defect that resulted in his seeing the world in black and white. As a teenager, Kevin was fitted with revolutionary contact lenses that enabled him to see in color." After he put in the lenses, he reports, "I went for a walk and slowly saw the world in color for the first time. Up until then I didn't have any idea what color was because I couldn't see it. I couldn't stop crying because the world looked so different from what I was used to. The reds just kept on jumping out at me and I had to ask my grandparents which colors were which because I didn't have a clue." He concludes: "It has opened up a whole new world for me. I never realized just how beautiful things like trees and flowers are."[111]

But of course, one can be amazed at a new experience without learning a troublesome new fact. Suppose I have never been to the Grand Canyon, but I watch movies about the canyon and read books about it, becoming so familiar with its appearance that I could draw a detailed sketch of it from memory. Nevertheless I'm likely to be awestruck when I actually stand at the rim, even though in doing so I have not learned any new fact that is philosophically puzzling.

On the other hand, one could learn something radically new without being gobstruck. If Mary had been given a powerful anti-amazement medication prior to being released, she might have discovered "red" without her jaw dropping. So her emotional reaction is beside the point. Regardless of whether Mary goes agog in the garden, *does she learn anything new*, and if so does this discovery demonstrate that qualia are

---

[110]Some deny that she'd be amazed. Dennett, for example, tries to show how this super-scientist might have a ho-hum reaction to the first dazzling blast of color, being "not in the slightest surprised" (1991, p. 400). I find his proposal just incredible.

[111]Tye 2009, p. 125.

not physical?[112] Remember, if physicalism is true she would have nothing new to learn about color perception. She already knew absolutely everything about the physical aspects of color perception.[113]

Because few modern scholars are dying to embrace dualism, hundreds of papers have tried to explain why Mary does not learn anything new when she first sees colors.[114] I won't delve into the hyper-technical details, but lurking behind most of these analyses are questions regarding what we can know about conscious experiences. Suppose we reject the idea that we know the quale "red" because a little eye in the brain is peering at it. Since there is no inner eye, it's hard to know what we do accurately know about this quale and what we erroneously think that we know.

Why Frank jilted Mary

In the mid-1990s, Frank Jackson abandoned his claim that Mary's color discovery refutes physicalism and establishes dualism. He had come to accept a theory of consciousness called representationalism, which we'll consider in Chapter Seven.[115] However Michael Tye, one of the

---

[112]Mary would have known about the concept of qualia, so she would have expected that color experiences would involve color qualia. "That rose looks splendid, but really weird," she might have murmured. "I must be experiencing new qualia. It's different from other qualia I have known, but it does remind me of the qualitative aspects of sounds, tastes, smells, and body sensations."

[113]If color qualia are brain events, Mary could have detected them without experiencing them herself. She could have monitored someone else's brain activity and said, "this complex of neural activities is Mark's experience of the color purple." But she's not doing that sort of thing when she herself sees purple. Detecting color qualia from her subjective vantage point is different from detecting them on a brain scanner, and this difference allegedly involves perplexing facts about consciousness.

[114]One widely-accepted physicalist explanation "is to claim that Mary acquires new concepts when she leaves her room: phenomenal concepts" (Tye 2009, p. 125). She doesn't discover some new entity when she spots those roses. Instead, she gets in touch experientially with a brain event that she already knew about from her scientific studies. This experience gives her new *concepts* with which she can think things like, "Ah, there's that reddish quale again!" Tye eventually rejected this strategy, but others still endorse it.

[115]Jackson says that he cannot see how he could have changed his views about

most prominent representationalists, now thinks Mary *does* acquire new knowledge when she starts seeing colors. "Surely if anyone ever made a significant discovery, Mary does here."[116] How remarkable that these two eminent professors have traded places! Jackson has convinced Tye that Mary learns puzzling new facts, and representationalists such as Tye have convinced Jackson that she does not. And now Jackson, like Tye, is a physicalist rather than a dualist.

"On the face of it," Jackson still maintains, "physicalism . . . cannot be right." Nevertheless, "I now think that what is, on the face of it, true is, on reflection, false."[117] For one thing, Jackson now rejects epiphenomenalism (the idea that qualia do not cause any physical consequences). He calls epiphenomenalism "a triumph of philosophical ingenuity over common sense. This is what someone who's done a good philosophy degree can somehow make seem all right, but if you look at it in a more common-sensical way it's actually pretty implausible. So the epiphenomenal stuff was just very hard to believe."[118] (I'll say more about epiphenomenalism in just a bit.)

Jackson concludes a paper called "Looking Back on the Knowledge Argument" on a nostalgic note. "In many ways, I wish I could still accept it."[119] And at the end of another essay he tosses out this tantalizing comment. "The considerations at the end of ['Epiphenomenal Qualia'] can be no reason to hold that Mary learns something new . . . but rather that there may *(may)* be a lot about fundamental nature that we and she can never know."[120] I asked Frank about this remark after a recent colloquium and he emphasized the importance of intellectual humility and the limitations of human knowledge.[121] I appreciate the fact that even after decades of reflection he is not trying to tie it all up with a neat little ribbon.

Mary "without going via representationalism" (Jackson 2004b, p. 439).

[116]Tye 2009, p. 55.

[117]Jackson 2004a, p. xvi.

[118]Quoted by Garvey 2012, p. 72.

[119]Jackson 2004a, p. xix.

[120]Jackson 2004d, p. 420.

[121]Personal communication at Stanford University, May 17, 2013.

Look out! Here come the zombies!

Now let's turn to another famous thought experiment, Australian philosopher David Chalmers' notion of "philosophical zombies." Those who have been reading every footnote may be feeling like philosophical zombies, but that's not what David has in mind.

Chalmers proposed the zombie idea to highlight the Hard Problem of consciousness, the problem of understanding how conscious experiences result from (or are identical to) brain activities. A philosophical zombie is a hypothetical creature whose brain has precisely the same physical structures as ours and functions in the same ways that our brains do, but without consciousness. Actually the creature *would* be conscious in the ways that psychology understands the structures, abilities, and functions of consciousness. "He will be awake, able to report the contents of his internal states, able to focus attention in various places, and so on." Furthermore a psychologist studying you and your zombie twin would discern no difference in behavior. But even though it would be conscious in a certain sense, it would lack conscious *experiences*.[122] It would be utterly devoid of qualia, and it would never be in any state that is "like something." Thus, as Philip Goff notes, when it screams it is not in pain. "Its smiles are not accompanied by a feeling of pleasure. Its negotiation of its environment does not involve a visual/auditory experience of that environment."[123]

Remember the distinction between explicit, manifest, phenomenal aspects of consciousness and implicit, unmanifest, non-phenomenal aspects. Zombies would have the latter and lack the former. For example, they would have thoughts, if these thoughts did not include any conscious perceptions or sensations. So a zombie that is screaming might think, "I'm in pain!" But it would have no pain qualia, no phenomenally evident sensations of pain. This is an example of the important difference

---

[122]Chalmers 1996, p. 95. Chalmers was suggesting that there is an ontological gap between conscious experiences and brain states, not just the sort of epistemic gap that Joseph Levine has discussed. In other words, qualia and brain states don't just seem different; they really *are* quite different kinds of fundamental "stuff." In this way Chalmers was following in the footsteps of Saul Kripke, whereas Levine was trying to avoid Kripke's ontological conclusions.

[123]Goff 2013.

between aspects of consciousness that do and do not seem "present." The philosophically puzzling states are the ones that seem *thus-there-now*, and zombies don't have them.

Several people who read early drafts of *Your Living Mind* dismissed zombies as irrelevant. The whole idea is moot, one of them remarked, since it would be impossible for us to know that such a creature *is* a zombie. But Chalmers' scenario is an example of both the value and the subtlety of thought experiments. If there actually could be such creatures, then conscious experiences are not brain events. Therefore physicalism is false.[124] Since there has been a strong trend toward saying that all real things are, in some sense, physical, that would be a revolutionary finding.

Michael Tye clarifies Chalmers' idea with an omnipotent-being scenario. "One way to picture what is being claimed here is to imagine God laying out all the microphysical phenomena throughout the universe. Having done so, and having settled all the microphysical properties of those phenomena along with the basic microphysical laws, God did not then have to ask Himself 'Shall I make lightning flashes or caterpillars or mountains . . . ?' No further work was needed on His part."[125] Why? Because a lightning flash simply *is* a group of microphysical entities operating according to certain laws. By making all these particles and deciding how they would interact, the Creator would have ensured that lightning flashes, caterpillars, etc. would exist. But what if consciousness is not physical? In that case zombies are possible. "Even if God had no

---

[124]The zombie story asserts that *if there could be* a creature that is physically identical to you, but not conscious, then consciousness is not a state of your brain. We could dispute this claim by arguing that even though a creature physically identical to you could exist without being conscious, nevertheless consciousness is a state of *your* brain. But that won't work. Let's call your current brain state *CBS*. If your brain's being in state CBS is *sufficient* for your being conscious, then if some other brain is in CBS, it would also have to be conscious. So you could not have a physically identical zombie twin. (No doubt that's a relief.) On the other hand, if a brain's being in state CBS is not sufficient for its being conscious, then consciousness is not a brain state. We would need a brain state *plus* something else to have consciousness – or we would just need the "something else." There are lots of complications we could consider, but the basic idea is that if zombies are truly possible, qualia are not brain states.

[125]Tye 2009, pp. 25-26.

further work to do in determining whether there would be a tree in place *p* or a river in place *q* or a neuron-firing in place *r*, say, having settled all the microphysical facts, God did have more work to do to guarantee that we were not zombies."[126]

Conceivably, then, there could be an exact physical duplicate of you, right down to the last whirling electron, that does not enjoy a single millisecond of conscious experience. Chalmers emphasizes that he is not trying to prove that a zombie duplicate of you or me could really exist in this universe – only that this sort of thing is conceivable.

But what does "conceivable" mean? Now the fog drifts in. There are several types of conceivability, including a contentious notion called "ideal conceivability."[127] Philosophical professionals have not yet sorted out these intricacies and "it remains a matter of considerable debate whether conceivability arguments are capable of doing the work they are asked to do."[128]

More Details: People used to think it was inconceivable that living organisms could "merely" be physical matter. Surely there must be some extra vital essence that enables a worm, a weasel, or a Wall Street speculator to function as a life-form. This doctrine was called vitalism, and back in the nineteenth century a vitalist could have conceived of a frog that could *not* conceive, even though it was physically identical to a frog that could. Today this sounds silly to most scientists. If Freddy Frog can beget little tadpoles, and Frodo Frog is physically identical to Freddy, then Frodo gets to sire tadpoles too. As Daniel Dennett writes: "Vitalism – the insistence that there is some big, mysterious extra ingredient in all

---

[126]Tye 2009, pp. 25-26. Tye is not actually suggesting that a deity created consciousness. He's just noting that this is one way of understanding Chalmers' scenario. (I believe Tye's analogy was first used by Saul Kripke.)

[127]"People use terms like 'logically possible,' 'metaphysically possible,' 'conceivable,' 'conceptually possible,' and 'epistemically possible' in different ways" (Levine 2001, p. 39). Scholars also discuss *"prima facie* versus *ideal, positive* versus *negative,* and *primary* versus *secondary* conceivability" (Pereboom 2011, p. 50). For additional comments on the conceivability of zombies see Kirk, 2012.

[128]Botterell 2001, p. 21.

living things – turns out to have been not a deep insight but a failure of imagination."[129]

The English philosopher John Locke considered "an explanation of the physical state changes of water" to be "just as unimaginable as an explanation of mental properties."[130] And "Descartes argued . . . that a purely physical being could not possibly use language intelligently. C.D. Broad argued similarly that the chemical facts of this world must be metaphysically distinct from the physical facts." In each case, "their mistake arose from simple ignorance of relevant facts. Descartes was unfamiliar with the modern notion of computation. Broad did not know about the quantum theory of chemical bonding. Once the ignorance was remedied, later thinkers had no difficulty in seeing how the physical facts determined both language use and chemical bonding."[131]

🐛 🐛 🐛 🐛 🐛 🐛 🐛

David Chalmers does think zombies are conceivable in some sense that shows consciousness is more than just a brain event.[132] But before venturing further into the shadowy zone of zombieland, let's consider an odd syndrome that makes some people partially resemble real-life philosophical zombies. In certain ways they function as if they could see, without having visual experiences.

Blindsight

Some individuals have suffered brain injuries that make them partially blind. Portions of the visual field are still intact, but a lot of it is missing. They might, for example, be able to see a light flashed off to the left but not over to the right. And yet some of them can say with remarkable

---

[129]Dennett 2005, p. 178.

[130]Pauen 2011, p. 86.

[131]Papineau 2007.

[132]Because of his reflections on the Hard Problem, Chalmers has suggested that experience may be a fundamental property of the universe, "alongside mass, charge, and space-time" (1995, p. 210). At this point he is still considering alternatives for understanding the nature of qualia.

accuracy what is present in the blind part of their visual field, *if you ask them a yes-or-no question.*

At first those with blindsight may refuse to answer a question like, "did a light flash?" because they have no idea what the answer is. Then they are amazed at how well they're doing. "How can I know that a light flashed when I didn't *see* anything?" Eventually they realize they are accessing information without being aware of it. Some can even tell whether a color patch is red or green, if forced to choose between just these two alternatives.[133]

Since these people can access visual information without being conscious of what they are detecting, why don't we all function this way? Why not just process information about light rays that fall upon our eyes, without having any awareness of light or color? What's the *point* of being visually conscious? Was vision merely evolved so we could enjoy Dancing with the Stars?

Actually we can discover clues about consciousness by reflecting upon what people with blindsight do not do. In general they do not spontaneously affirm that some perception is manifest to them, detectable in a way that is all but impossible to deny, and that carries with it a compelling sense of presence: "*this* is real to me, *right now.*" Sensory experiences tend to seize us by the lapels and demand our attention, but those with blindsight are not grasped by data in the blind part of their visual field.

Blindsight also reminds us that normal consciousness involves a subjective aspect. What's dramatically missing in this syndrome is the fact that a human subject, a *person,* "gets" perceptual data. So even

---

[133]Hardin 2008, p. 152. Holt notes that these individuals "can detect and locate targets and discriminate shape, pattern, orientation, motion, and colour. They can also pick up and even catch objects with a skill comparable to normal perceivers – all without visual consciousness. When left to their own devices, patients behave as if blind, but when forced to choose between a pair of provided options (e.g., 'red/green') or cued to the appropriate action (e.g., 'Catch!'), they perform with astonishing reliability, up to 100 per cent in some cases" (Holt 2003, p. 21). Blindsight is discussed in Weiskrantz 1988. Something similar occurs in other sense modalities, so we can also speak of, e.g., blind touch.

though they can guess about the blind part of their visual field, a hugely important aspect of normal functioning is left out – the detection of experiences by an experiencer.[134]

Returning to David Chalmers' notion of philosophical zombies, let's consider a scenario in which:

David and Mary meet their zombie twins[135]

Pondering the possibility of zombies is an excellent way to explore the intuition that experiences are not neural events, so let's delve into this idea further by imagining that David Chalmers and achromatic Mary learn that there are physical duplicates of themselves, David-Z and Mary-Z. Intrigued by the prospect of meeting their own "twins," they decide it would be fun to go on a double date and discuss philosophy and science. The two Marys have just been granted permission to leave their black-and-white residence, so the two Davids drive over to pick them up, chatting lickety-split about philosophy of mind and Australian politics.

The Marys are set free in a rose garden. Both display astonishment at finally seeing vivid shades of red. They embrace, grateful for having shared this dazzling moment, wiping their tears on their black shirt-sleeves. When the Davids arrive they all discuss this episode and its implications for consciousness studies.

Suddenly this erudite quartet is startled by a thunderous roar. A bearded stranger dressed in flowing robes appears in a whoosh of white smoke, and shocks them all by proclaiming that Mary-Z is a zombie. Even though she has just finished choking up with emotion while describing her first-ever color experience, she has had no such experience, and in fact she never experiences anything at all. Throughout her entire life she has been talking about conscious episodes that do not occur. Like

---

[134]Recall the five hallmarks of conscious experiences from Chapter One. Blindsight visual data is not spontaneously available to the brain's mechanisms of behavior-control, not accessed by an experiencing self, not spontaneously remembered, not spontaneously reported, and of course, not introspectively present as entity-like manifestations.

[135]Thanks to David Chalmers for being a good sport about my including him in this story.

humans, she *detects* perceptual inputs, but unlike humans she is never *conscious* of them.

Remember that the brain of a philosophical zombie has the same abilities, functions, and physical structures as ours, even though it lacks consciousness. In fact it usually *is* conscious in the sense of being awake rather than asleep, and its brain possesses complex self-monitoring abilities that parallel those of human brains. If Mary and Mary-Z are both looking at a rosebud, Mary-Z will do just as well as Mary in detecting internal states such as perceptions (or perception-like states), attitudes, and desires pertaining to this flower.

David Chalmers, in real life, has expressed confidence that he is not a zombie. "The justification for my belief that I am conscious lies not just in my cognitive mechanisms but also in *my direct evidence*: the zombie lacks that evidence . . ."[136] This sounds fishy to Daniel Dennett. "Chalmers fervently believes he himself is not a zombie. The zombie fervently believes he himself is not a zombie. Chalmers *believes* he gets his justification from his 'direct evidence' of his consciousness. So does the zombie of course."[137]

Now back to our story, as the plot thickens. The mysterious fellow in the fancy bathrobe now reveals David-Z's zombiehood, but the accused automaton angrily rejects this charge. "That is patently absurd. I can tell that I am conscious by simply noticing my own stream of thoughts, feelings, and perceptions. I have *direct evidence* of consciousness, and a zombie would lack such evidence."

Soon, however, Dr. Chalmers decides that this frightening visitor is telling the truth – David's double is indeed unconscious. The be-robed stranger seems eminently credible. He calls himself Yahweh, repeatedly turns water into well-oaked Chardonnay, and seems to be omniscient. Since David-Z's brain works just like David's, he also becomes convinced. "Good heavens – evidently I *don't* have conscious experiences. Well that's a letdown!"

---

[136]David Chalmers, quoted by Dennett 2005, p. 48. Emphasis added by Dennett.
[137]Dennett 2005, p. 48.

We must hope Yahweh is truly omniscient and doesn't get the twins mixed up, telling *David* he's a zombie. David-Z would then feel sorry for Chalmers. "Hmmm. David says he has direct evidence that he is conscious, but Yahweh knows that he isn't. It must be terrible for a zombie like David to realize that he is bereft of sentience. Of course, he isn't actually *experiencing* anything terrible. Nevertheless I have a very strong urge to console him."

The notion of philosophical zombies is a helpful "intuition pump," pointing the way to a deeper understanding of consciousness. And yet when we consider zombiehood in this double dating episode, the whole idea seems less and less plausible. What then, is wrong with this thought experiment? I will offer three conjectures, and perhaps you can think of more.

1. Although zombies would speak about qualia in the same ways that we do, it seems as if their lack of consciousness would eventually become obvious. For example Mary-Z, freshly released into the garden, would find herself weeping with joy about a startling new perception. If she then reflected on this episode she might become alarmed. "It's true that I now visually detect certain optical wavelength data that I have never accessed in this way before, but this should be no more astounding than noticing some shade of gray for the first time. Why am I burbling with emotionality over a perceptual event that is far from earth-shaking? And why do I think I have gained a strange new insight into the nature of color perception? This makes no sense at all. I'd better call my psychiatrist."

David-Z might similarly wonder about his personal relationship to the mysteries of qualia. "Why do I keep blathering on about the inner light of consciousness, when I notice nothing like this in myself? And despite my proven intellectual prowess, why don't I get the point of worries about bat-consciousness, the Hard Problem, phenomenal presence, inverted spectra, and the explanatory gap? I discuss these issues quite cogently, but I'm not sure why they matter."

2. As we drill down into the details of this scenario, the parallels between people and zombies grow closer and closer. Zombies can comment on their own perceptual or quasi-perceptual states in the same ways that we can. In understanding word meanings, they would detect both the sounds of words and the meanings of those word sounds, just as we do. They would realize that the sounds seem "present" but their interpretations

of word meanings do not. Thus the distinction between "on-stage" and "off-stage" mental events would make perfect sense to them, and they might very well describe on-stage events just as we do. Visual experiences seem spread out in space. Sounds and smells seem different from each other, and the difference seems to be one of quality rather than quantity. And all sensations and perceptions have features that seem impossible to put into words. "It's just . . . *like that.*"

If a zombie has states of mind that are suitable for being described in these ways, perhaps having these mental states *actually is what we call consciousness.*

3. If David-Z says exactly the same things about conscious experiences as David Chalmers does, this may contradict the assumption that he is physically identical to Chalmers. Why? Well suppose David-Z talks about his qualia in exactly the ways that David C. does. Then he must have brain mechanisms that lead him to do so without being prompted by the actual experience of qualia. But the zombie scenario stipulates that their brains function identically. If so, then David Chalmers' brain must also contain mechanisms that would prompt him to talk about qualia even if he did not have them! There is no reason to think that humans would have evolved such mechanisms.

We could also imagine a possible world which is identical to ours except that all of the human-like creatures on that planet are zombies. Would their philosophers think about consciousness as ours do, arguing about the Hard Problem, what it's like, Mary, and the explanatory gap? Why would they, given their lack of consciousness? And if they did not, they would not be behaviorally identical to humans.

The zombie brain must be physically identical to a normal brain, and zombies and humans must behave in the same way. These are both core requirements of this thought experiment. But here's a dilemma. If the zombie brain is identical to our brain, it would not spontaneously believe that it has qualia. And if we use some sort of Rube Goldberg work-around that makes zombies speak of qualia even though they don't have them, we are adding something to the zombie brain that we lack. Therefore this scenario is *not* coherently conceivable, and the zombie objection to physicalism fails.

Although I am confident in stating this conclusion, I realize that this is a complex topic. Dr. Chalmers may well marshal rebuttals which I have not remotely anticipated. And even if this intuition pump turns out to be leaky, it is an effective way to highlight our doubts that qualia could be physical. Later I will suggest a way of addressing the problem of consciousness that deals with the puzzles posed by both Jackson and Chalmers.

Are we all just whistling zombies?

The concept of philosophical zombies is often proposed in conjunction with the idea that consciousness is epiphenomenal.[138] Epiphenomenalism was discussed in the nineteenth century by T. H. Huxley, who compared conscious mental processes to the steam whistle of a locomotive. The whistle *accompanies* the locomotive's operation, but it does not help the train move forward. It is an epiphenomenon, a side effect. Today some scholars contend that all conscious experiences are epiphenomenal. They do not cause any of our actions. They're only along for the ride. They may *be caused by* physical states such as neural activities in the brain, but they have no physical consequences. It's a one-way street:[139]

Brain event ⟶ experiences ⟶ dead end; no physical effects

So even if you and I are in some way acquainted with our own qualia, this acquaintance does not impact our behavior. It's an intriguing notion, so if you're game here are –

---

[138]Even though the zombie idea is often thought to support epiphenomenalism, Chalmers believes that it is also compatible with two other exotic options, panprotopsychism and interactionism (Chalmers 1999, p. 493). And Philip Goff shows that one could have zombies without epiphenomenalism if a certain form of pan-psychism is true. See http://ndpr.nd.edu/news/44734-the-conceptual-link-from-physical-to-mental.

[139]"Traditionally, epiphenomenalism amounts to the claim that mental events are caused by physical events in the brain although mental events themselves do not cause anything" (Pauen *et al.* 2006, p. 7; cf. Horowitz 1999, p. 421). However some say that non-physical conscious experiences do have effects on *other* non-physical conscious experiences. At that point things become very, very complicated. Frank Jackson comments on various sorts of epiphenomenalism in Jackson 1982, p. 133.

More Details: Joseph Levine suggests that the "main alternative to materialism is epiphenomenalism . . ."[140] So do qualia affect the physical universe or not? If your bare foot stomps on broken glass, do the pain qualia you experience contribute to the physical action of lifting your foot? If your nose itches, does the itchy *feeling* make it more likely that you'll rub your proboscis? If you bite into a hot pepper, does your *experienced sensation* make you reach for a water glass? If qualia do help shape your actions, epiphenomenalism is false.

If qualia have no physical consequences, it's hard to figure out how we'd know about them.[141] Former epiphenomenalist Frank Jackson has concluded that if there were "anything nonphysical about our psychology, . . . no indicative traces of it would survive in memory, in reports, in articles called 'Epiphenomenal Qualia. . . . This creates an insurmountable epistemic problem for the views of my former self."[142]

Another difficulty: If qualia are not physical and have no physical effects, this leaves us with a severely impoverished understanding of ourselves. It would mean that humans, to the extent that they are bodily, *function as zombies.* (Epiphenomenalism, remember, claims that consciousness is not a brain state.) On this view we are zombies in almost every respect. Our immaterial experiences merely accompany the activity of our zombie brains, rolling along beside the brain like a side-car attached to a motorcycle.

---

[140]Levine, 2001, p. 22.

[141]". . . if genuine knowledge requires causal interaction, as some philosophers have maintained . . . there can be no knowledge of epiphenomenal entities or phenomena" (Kriegel 2009, p. 141). ". . . epiphenomenalism would even seem to be *self-defeating* because it seems that if it were true, it could not be known to be so . . ." (Pauen *et al.* 2006, p. 10).

[142]Jackson 2004a, p. xvi.

The picture isn't quite as bleak if we assume that we have a complete, epiphenomenal, non-physical mind rather than just a series of epiphenomenal qualia. In that case we have an entire psyche, complete with thoughts, perceptions, and sensations, riding along in that side-car. But the brain would also contain a complete set of *non*-conscious thoughts, perceptions, and sensations, and these would be doing all the work. The non-physical conscious mind might think it was holding the handlebars and pressing the pedals, but that would be a delusion. Conscious mental processes would have zero influence on what we do physically – how we act and what we say. Human society would consist of nothing but zombies plus extraneous minds.[143]

So are we all just whistling zombies? Zombies plus epiphenomenal tagalongs?

🐝 🐝 🐝 🐝 🐝 🐝 🐝

Importantly, if conscious experiences have no effect on our actions, then *every single syllable* that has ever been written about the mystery of consciousness has been produced by non-conscious brain mechanisms. None of it has actually been influenced by the existence of consciousness itself. That seems ironic, to say the least.

If thinking about all of this makes your head hurt, you may be getting close to the source of our confusion, the hidden core of the problem of consciousness.

Summing up

The case of Mary and the possibility of philosophical zombies are useful and intriguing thought experiments that highlight the difficulty of

---

[143]Another concern: If living things are strongly shaped by evolution, and all survival-related actions are caused by non-conscious states, why would an entire conscious mind have evolved? Our conscious mental states would be irrelevant to our practical concerns, just as the steam whistle produced by a locomotive is irrelevant to the train's forward progress. We would therefore need some non-evolutionary explanation for the development of conscious minds.

Epiphenomenalists have suggested various responses to those who critique their view of consciousness. See for example Robinson 2006 and Gadenne 2006. Lycan calls Robinson "probably America's most committed and ingenious defender of epiphenomenalism" (Lycan 2009).

explaining consciousness in scientific terms. Mary has all the knowledge about color that science can ever provide, but it seems as if she acquires new information when she first experiences colors – new knowledge that she could not have deduced before. If so, then there are knowable facts that are not physical facts, and some real entities are not physical (or are not entirely so). A philosophical zombie is a hypothetical creature whose brain has the same physical structures as ours and operates in the same ways that our brains do. The zombie also acts just as we do, but it has no experiences. I have argued that zombies are not coherently conceivable, but if they are, this would undermine the claim that consciousness is a brain event.

In the next three chapters we will explore proposals for solving the problem of consciousness. After that I will outline my own theory and discuss its practical implications.

Chapter Six
Changing Fashions in Consciousness Studies

What is mind? *Never matter.* What is matter? *Never mind!*

Dualism, pan-psychism, and the any-stuff problem

In this chapter we'll consider several ancient and modern attempts to comprehend consciousness, beginning with two of the most venerable theories, pan-psychism and dualism. Today most scholars reject these strategies,[144] but they are enthusiastically endorsed by traditional religions. They are also accepted by some contemporary philosophers for reasons that have little to do with theology.

Asian religions such as Hinduism have emphasized pan-psychism, the idea that everything is in some sense mental. In pan-psychism "even the lowliest of material things has a streak of sentience running through it, like veins in marble."[145] Since it's hard to see how experiences could literally *be* brain activities, perhaps we should conclude that all matter, including all gray matter, is already blessed with experiential attributes. In fact, John Perry once quipped that all philosophers of mind eventually become pan-psychists, or go into administration.[146]

The noted neuroscientist Christof Koch is a recent convert to the doctrine that "consciousness is a fundamental, an elementary, property of living matter."[147] "I used to be a proponent of the idea of consciousness emerging out of complex nervous networks. Just read my earlier *Quest*. But over the years, my thinking has changed. Subjectivity is too radically different from anything physical for it to be an emergent phenomenon. A kind of blue is fundamentally different from electrical activity in the cone photoreceptors of the eyes, even though I'm perfectly cognizant that the latter is necessary for the former."[148]

---

[144]Moody (2014) comments on these two options. "Panpsychism gets little love in contemporary philosophy. Indeed, it is generally dismissed as absurd" (p. 181). And "dualism finds nearly as little support as panpsychism . . ." (p. 185).

[145]McGinn 2012, http://www.newstatesman.com/ideas/2012/02/consciousness-mind-brain.

[146]John Perry, cited by Chalmers, 2013.

[147]Koch 2012, pp. 119, 132.

[148]Koch 2012, p. 119.

Many scholars dismiss pan-psychism, partly because it seems to wipe out the difference between consciousness and unconsciousness. If everything is in some sense conscious, then "unconscious" brain processes are also conscious! But the experiences that we typically consider conscious seem different from unconscious events, different in important ways that need to be explained. So rather than solving the problems of consciousness, pan-psychism reshuffles them.[149]

Pan-psychism also needs to explain the moral distinction between beings that are conscious and things that are not. If even dead matter is sentient, why do we think it's OK to "unplug" someone who lacks brain activity associated with human awareness? Why is it OK to blow up a boulder but not a beagle? (Snoopy needs some reassurance here.)

In the West, dualism is more prominent than pan-psychism. According to dualists, at least part of the mind dwells in a non-physical domain. If we can't see how some mental activities could be neural, that's because they are just not physical. René Descartes, for example, "restricted consciousness and reason to a distinct realm of immaterial souls whose whole essence was to think."[150] Only humans have souls, he thought, so only humans are conscious. "As he wrote quite unequivocally, a dog may howl pitifully when hit by a carriage, but it does not feel pain."[151] Of course a dualist could say that animals also possess immaterial minds or spirits of some sort.

"Dualism is not the most widely held view in the current philosophical and scientific community, but it is the most common theory of mind in the public at large, it is deeply entrenched in most of the world's popular religions, and it has been the dominant theory of mind for most of Western history."[152] But dualism suffers from several serious problems.

---

[149]Koch is aware of these issues. He notes that his theory "does not invalidate the notion that some bits and pieces of the brain are more important for certain classes of qualia than others. . . . Thus, the quest for the neural correlates of color, sound, and agency remains meaningful" (2012, p. 128). "Another significant challenge . . . is to explain the unconscious" (p. 129).

[150]Van Gulick 2011, p. 141.

[151]Koch 2012, p. 151.

[152]Churchland 1984, p. 7. Sir John Eccles attempted to support dualism

First of all, how can something non-physical interact with the material world without being detected by science? Physical science has been absolutely brilliant at explaining longstanding mysteries. It would seem strange if consciousness, and only consciousness, was beyond the reach of scientific research. And here's another problem. "If there really is a distinct entity in which reasoning, emotion, and consciousness take place, and if that entity is dependent on the brain for nothing more than sensory experiences as input and volitional executions as output, *then one would expect reason, emotion, and consciousness to be relatively invulnerable to direct control or pathology by manipulation or damage to the brain.* But in fact the exact opposite is true."[153]

Some issues about the mind-brain relationship are also troublesome for dualism and pan-psychism. Take the explanatory gap, for instance. If the mind is situated within the brain, it's hard to see why one pattern of neural events would be candy apple red instead of granny apple green. But suppose the mind is part of an immaterial soul. Why then would a particular visual quale be constituted by one *soul state* instead of another? Of course, since non-material entities are so mysterious, dualists can just claim that it is their nature to have qualitative character, so no explanation is needed. This is what philosophers call hand-waving, and it can reach the intensity of aerobic exercise.

Dualists must also deal with the problem of duality. (Dualism and duality are very different ideas, of course, but as it happens, duality poses challenges for dualism.) Conscious experiences seem to have a dual char-

---

scientifically in Eccles 1987.

[153]Churchland 1984, p. 20. But William Lycan (2009) objects to Churchland's premises. "What dualist ever said, or even implied, that the mind is dependent on the brain for nothing more than sensory experiences as input and volitional executions as output?" (Actually some religious dualists do make similar claims.) In the same article Lycan states that even though he is convinced that dualism is false, no one has proven that it is. "This paper argues that no convincing case has been made against substance dualism, and that standard objections to it can be credibly answered. . . . I have no sympathy with any dualist view, and never will. This paper is only an uncharacteristic exercise in intellectual honesty. It grew out of a seminar in which for methodological purposes I played the role of a committed dualist as energetically as I could. That was a strange feeling, something like being a cat burglar for a few months." What splendid objectivity and candor!

acter as *what* we experience and the fact that *we* are experiencing them. It's hard to know how a single brain state could be both of these things at the same instant, but dualism has the same problem. Even if experiences occur within an immaterial soul, each experience needs to include both being aware of something and the "something" that we're aware of. But what if one's soul malfunctions, so that the soul-self believes it is detecting, say, a sharp pain when it is actually detecting a pleasant tingle? What is the real conscious experience, the pain or the tingle?

Levine notes that it is hard to know how *anything at all, physical or non-physical,* could have this dual character. "The duality problem is really a problem about how there can be anything like conscious awareness, which seems to require both unity and distinctness all at once."[154]

Some cope with this quandary by claiming that experiences are "self-intimating." An experience is known just by being what it is. Whenever it occurs, it is automatically apprehended by an experiencing subject. Both physicalists and dualists struggle to say how this could be so, and pan-psychism does no better. Sensory experiences also seem present, in special and puzzling ways. Neither dualism nor pan-psychism explain this mystery, except to say "that's just the way it is." In short, some key aspects of the mind-*body* problem turn out to be **a mind-*anything* problem.** Consciousness is perplexing and paradoxical, no matter what sort of thing it turns out to be.[155] Regardless of whether experiences are immaterial sense data, neural activities, or mystical spirit vibrations, they are incredibly hard to comprehend.

Flawed solutions to persistent enigmas

Now let's briefly consider more recent proposals, starting with the sense datum theory. Around 100 years ago Bertrand Russell and others

---

[154]Levine 2001, p. 173; cf. p. 177.

[155]These considerations tie into Frank Jackson's knowledge argument. "The problem with physical theory is that it is objective, and if dualism is presented as objective in the same sense, then it is as vulnerable to the knowledge argument as physicalism" (Howell 2008, p. 127). Similarly, Carruthers and Schechter comment that even in a highly advanced version of panpsychism, this theory "still wouldn't help us with the mind/body problem. For the explanatory gap would remain in place, untouched and wide open as ever: panpsychism does nothing to close it" (2006, p. 37).

claimed that we are directly "acquainted" with sensory qualities such as colors, pains, and tastes. They called these qualities sense data, and many believed they were non-physical. Russell and his compatriots thought that our direct knowledge of these inner mental states gives us indirect knowledge of external objects.

At roughly the same time, psychologists were studying consciousness enthusiastically. This was "the great period for the mobilization of the methodology of introspection, which will now be presented as scientific and entitled 'systematic introspection' . . ."[156] However because science was making remarkable progress in understanding the universe, many scholars hoped to comprehend the mind as a purely physical entity. They were uncomfortable with odd gizmos such as sense data. As a result, scientists, psychologists, and philosophers increasingly disdained the study of consciousness. John B. Watson confidently proclaimed that *"consciousness is neither a definite nor a usable concept . . . [B]elief in the existence of consciousness goes back to the ancient days of super- stition and magic."*[157]

In 1949 Gilbert Ryle's book *The Concept of Mind* questioned the entire notion of inner awareness. Rather than trying to inspect our own psyches, Ryle suggested we should focus on human behavior, including verbal behavior such as speaking and writing. This sort of philosophical behaviorism had a huge impact on humanities and social sciences in universities all over the world.

Many behaviorists denied that we know things about our own inner lives which others cannot observe. In fact some believed that the only way we can know ourselves is by monitoring our own actions. We don't know we're sleepy till we catch ourselves yawning, and we wouldn't know we were bored unless we noticed ourselves acting bored. Ryle actually makes these claims in *The Concept of Mind*.[158]

---

[156]Vermersch 1999, p. 21.

[157]Jonkisz 2012, p. 55.

[158]Ryle answers the question, "How does a person know what mood he is in?" by saying that "he finds it out very much as we find it out. . . . he does not groan 'I feel bored' because he has found out that he is bored. . . . Rather, somewhat as the sleepy man finds out that he is sleepy by finding, among other things, that he keeps on

Rejecting the idea that we can introspect sensations, Ryle asserted that "if it was correct to say that a person observes his sensations, it would be proper to ask whether his inspection of a tickle had been hampered or unhampered, close or casual and whether he could have discerned more of it, if he had tried. No one ever asks such questions, any more than anyone asks how the first letter in 'London' is spelled."[159] He clearly thought these were silly ideas, but he was writing before the time when psychotherapy had been widely experienced and introspective disciplines such as meditation had become commonplace. At this point many people have practiced carefully attending to emotions, thoughts, and bodily sensations. Nowadays counselors and meditation instructors help people learn to closely attend to physical sensations and mental states. (See, e.g., Eugene Gendlin's classic self-help manual from 1978, *Focusing*.) As a result, it is now trivially obvious that attending to our own mental states can be "hampered" by distractions, "close or casual."

Ryle also claimed that a person who says "I feel depressed" is not reporting an observation. "Nothing would surprise us more than to hear him say 'I feel depressed' in the alert and judicious tone of voice of a

---

yawning, so the bored man finds out that he is bored . . . by finding that among other things he glumly says to others and to himself 'I feel bored . . .'" (1949, pp. 102-03). Seager comments that even though "such a proposal has the advantage of denying any 'magical' kind of self access, it suffers from the rather grave disadvantage of applying very poorly, if at all, to the majority of our claims to self knowledge" (1999, p. 141).

[159]Ryle 1949, p. 207. Ludwig Wittgenstein makes a similar comment. "It can't be said of me at all (except perhaps as a joke) that I know I am in pain. What is it supposed to mean – except perhaps that I am in pain?" (quoted by Schwitzgebel 2014). Not only is it meaningful to say I know I'm in pain, it's meaningful to say that I can know various things about a pain, and I can know these things more fully or less fully, steadily, momentarily, or intermittently.

detective, a microscopist, or a diagnostician." Nonsense. Therapists regularly see people expressing surprise at the moods, emotions, attitudes, and impulses they have discovered by turning the searchlight inward. Evidently Ryle thought we just blurted out reports of our emotions, without first noticing them within ourselves. He writes that when a person says, *"I feel depressed"* this is just "a piece of conversational moping."[160] Sometimes it is, but it may also express an introspection-based *aha*.

I find it quite disturbing that people took philosophical behaviorism so seriously, but eventually its weaknesses became obvious. Geach, for example, comments that Ryle "makes no serious attempt to carry out his programme consistently . . ."[161] And Lycan calls Ryle's arguments that we do not know our own minds through introspection "pretty desperate."[162]

The mid-twentieth century saw the rise of identity theory, which proposed that experiences are identical to brain events.[163] This approach faces the challenge of multiple realization. It seems as if both humans and dogs feel pain, for instance. But if human pain is identical to certain kinds of brain events, and dog pain is identical to very different neural activities, pain cannot be just one kind of brain state.

The identity question is partly about how to use words. Many who reject identity theory still say that the mind is *realized* or *constituted* by brain states instead of being identical to them, and the distinctions among these ideas are subtle. Knowing what my pains have in common with the

---

[160]Quotes from this paragraph are from Ryle 1949, p. 102.

[161]"The mental acts in question are indeed referred to throughout in a highly depreciatory style, as 'itches', 'tingles', 'tweaks', 'agitations', etc.; but this rhetorical trick proves nothing" (Geach 1981, p. 23).

[162]Lycan 2009.

[163]Some identity theorists have thought of consciousness in terms of "inner scanning." "In perception the brain scans the environment. In awareness of the perception another process in the brain scans that scanning" (D. M. Armstrong, quoted by Güzeldere 1995a, p. 345). By the way, physicalism need not insist that we express all truths in the language of physics. Many agree that "describing and understanding reality requires us to use a wide diversity of theoretical, conceptual and representational schemes, many of which cannot be reduced to the language and concepts of physical science" (Van Gulick 2002, p. 42).

pain states of dogs or "Martians" is a more substantive matter, however, and I'm not sure how to solve this problem.

In recent decades *functionalism* has become popular. Functionalists suggest classifying conscious states according to the function they carry out in a mental system, their place in the system's architecture. For instance, we should classify the mental states of a space alien as pains if there is enough functional similarity between the inputs and outputs of these "Martian" states and the inputs and outputs of the states that Earthlings know as pain.

More Details: Functionalism still has many proponents, but it has lost support due to difficult technical issues. "What hamstrings functionalism is its inherent inability to capture the intrinsic nature of consciousness,"[164] writes Jason Holt, noting that color-spectrum inversion is a particularly sticky wicket. Here's an example:

My auto looks blue to me, and let's assume for the moment that my experiences of color qualia are patterns of neural activities in my brain. So when I see a blue car, I experience blue color qualia and these qualia are constituted by a particular pattern of neuronal firings. Then suppose an all-powerful deity alters my brain so that neural activities which constitute blue color qualia are replaced by ones which constitute yellow color qualia and vice versa. Importantly, it also switches the way I *think* about blue and yellow, so that when I have a brain state that constitutes yellow color qualia I think and speak about seeing a blue color (and when I have a brain state that constitutes blue color qualia I think and speak about seeing yellow).

If functionalism is correct, I should notice no difference in the way my car looks. Functionalism defines qualia in terms of inputs and outputs. The "blueness" *inputs* from my optic nerve into my brain haven't changed, and my brain still processes color information the way it did before, right up to the point where I have a conscious experience of the car's color. At that point my qualia are switched, due to divine intervention. But despite this switch, the *outputs* from this qualia state are the same as before. Because a mischievous god has played with my brain, a qualia-state of yellowness makes me think and speak of blueness. So

---

[164]Holt 2003, p. 14.

even though my color qualia have been reversed, *these qualia still play exactly the same functional role.* They still have the same positioning within my brain, and the same function – representing the car's color and making me respond appropriately. My color qualia still receive blueness inputs and cause blueness outputs. They are still caused by blue objects and they still lead me to think about blueness, speak about blueness, and buy blue touch-up paint when my fender gets dinged.

But wait! Aren't qualia *what we experience?* How can my qualia be switched without my noticing? Functionalists say that if there is no change in function, there is no change in experience. I'm still seeing a ding in my blue fender and I'm still going to buy blue touch-up. But if the quale itself *has* changed from blue to yellow, it seems as if I would realize that. Functionalists still haven't solved this problem to the satisfaction of other theorists.

🐞 🐞 🐞 🐞 🐞 🐞

Some philosophers say that experiences are *self-representing.* Most everyone agrees that conscious states can represent things such as physical objects (including our own bodies). Some contend that these states also represent themselves. For instance, "when a person consciously perceives a tree, she is in a perceptual state that represents both the tree and itself."[165] This seems to me like being one's own grandparent, but proponents have tried to explain how it makes sense.

Self-representationalism supposedly solves the problem of duality and avoids the risk of a bewildering mismatch between the way we subjectively experience a quale and the way the quale actually is. Let's say a quale represents an item as being red. Could our apprehension of this quale become so addled that we experience it as green? Self-representation says no, because *there are not two different states here.* One state is both the subjective experience of the quale and the quale itself, and a single state can't conflict with itself.

If this idea seems unclear, you're not alone in finding this matter mystifying. Philosophers are actively discussing this theory, and some

---

[165]Kriegel 2006, p. 1.

plainly think the others are confused. And Michael Tye thinks self-representationalism could indeed encounter the problem of misrepresentation. If a state represents both a color quale and our apprehension of that quale, the *aspect* of that state which represents the quale might represent it as red, while the aspect that represents our experience of the quale might "think" it's green.[166]

Uriah Kriegel is working to develop an account that resolves this problem and others. His analysis is clever and resourceful, and I will be interested to see whether it can work. Kriegel has said that "the self-representational theory is perhaps best cast as a research program . . ."[167] If it succeeds it will indeed be a conceptual breakthrough in philosophy of mind.

In addition to the theories I have listed so far, there are "mysterians" who consider consciousness an insoluble mystery. In *The Problem of Consciousness* Colin McGinn maintains that inherent human limitations make it impossible for us to understand how conscious experience is related to brain activity.[168]

I have omitted three approaches that I'll discuss in more detail – HOT theory, representationalism, and eliminativism. We'll consider one of these now and the others in the next two chapters.

---

[166]Tye 2009, p. 7.

[167]Here is the full quotation, which Kriegel made while responding to critics. "Their commentaries make me think that the self-representational theory is perhaps best cast as a research program: a general framework that attempts to portray the broad outlines of what must be involved in a mental state's being conscious, but many of whose details are still in need of being worked out" (2012, p. 484). In *Subjective Consciousness,* Kriegel discusses other difficult challenges to his theory (2009, p. 99).

[168]McGinn 1991. "Soon, I was being labelled (by Owen Flanagan) a 'mysterian', the name of a defunct pop group, and the name stuck." "I am not against the label, understood correctly, but like all labels it suggests an overly simple view of a complex position. At first the view was regarded as eccentric and vaguely disreputable but now it is a standard option – though one with very few adherents. Its primary attraction lies in the lack of appeal of all the other options, to which supporters of those options are curiously oblivious" (McGinn 2012).

HOT? Or not?

Consciousness seems to involve two aspects:

1. *What* you are experiencing – sights, sounds, tastes, and so on.
2. *Being aware* of what you are experiencing.

Higher-order thought (HOT) theory contends that in order for (1) to be conscious, we need (2). More precisely, something becomes conscious only if we *think about it in a particular way* – by means of a higher-order thought, which I'll explain momentarily. HOT theory was developed by David Rosenthal, who wanted to show why some mental states are conscious and some are not, and it has won many adherents. For similar approaches see this footnote.[169]

For Rosenthal, a conscious experience "is a compound of two things."[170] There is a mental state, which by itself is not conscious, and a particular sort of thought about that state. A mental state that is not in any sense known, attended to, or thought about would not be conscious.

---

[169]Rocco Gennaro's views are difficult to explain briefly, but his 2012 book *The Consciousness Paradox* is quite thorough and can be understood by non-philosophers who don't mind a good mental workout. It includes an excellent discussion of recent neurological and psychological research, including important data about infant consciousness and animal consciousness. HOGS is an acronym for Robert Van Gulick's higher-order global state theory, a sophisticated and promising model of consciousness that Van Gulick is continuing to develop. In HOGS, an unconscious state is transformed into a conscious state when it is "recruited" "into a *globally integrated complex* whose organization and intentional content embodies a heightened degree of *reflexive self-awareness*" (2006, p. 24). "This is not accomplished by re-representing the relevant information again in another module of the mind or brain. . . . Rather, it involves incorporating the original representation into a new dynamic context that integrates it with a larger, richer network of other active states . . ." (2006, p. 25). For more on HOGS see Van Gulick 2000, 2002, and 2006. Finally, HOP theory (Lycan 1987) focuses on higher-order perceptions rather than higher-order thoughts. The "standard objection to HOP theory" is "that, unlike outer perception, no obvious distinct sense organ or scanning mechanism is responsible for HOPs" (Gennaro 2013b, p. 13).

[170]Rosenthal 1997, p. 738.

Here's an example. Unless you have injured it recently, you probably have not been conscious of the way your left foot feels. But now that I've mentioned it, you may have noticed foot sensations. Tactile data from that extremity were flowing into your brain all along, but mechanisms of selective attention had not brought them "into" consciousness. Rosenthal would say that when you became conscious of those feelings, you had a higher-order thought that could be approximately expressed as *I am experiencing how my foot feels.* So a state becomes conscious when we have a certain kind of thought that we are in that state.[171]

In understanding HOT theory, it's easy to fall into a terminological bear-trap. We tend to conceive of thoughts as active conscious states – such as the way you are actively thinking about the word "thoughts" right now. But the HOTs that Rosenthal is talking about are seldom conscious. We don't go around all day being conscious of thoughts such as, "now I am aware that my big toe itches, now I notice a tightness in my forehead, now I realize that my legs are crossed." Some have even questioned whether "thought" is the right word to express what Rosenthal is driving at. The sort of higher-order thought that he emphasizes is an *unconscious* affirmation that our current sensory experiences are a certain way. We are conscious of what we're experiencing, but we are not *conscious of being conscious* of what we're experiencing.[172]

At times, however, a higher-order thought is drawn into the spotlight of awareness, so that you are, for example, conscious of the fact *that* you are conscious of the way your foot feels. In such cases, "one also has a third-order thought about the second-order thought."[173] One could go on with quite a few "orders," as when you are:

---

[171]Rosenthal 2012. We call these thoughts *higher*-order because we think of "primitive" mental events such as sensations as being lower on the totem pole, while intellectually sophisticated cognitions are more upscale. One can also speak of first and second-order mental states. A pain sensation is a first-order state of the brain, and the thought about it is second-order.

[172]". . . the higher-order states must themselves be predominantly unconscious. This is to avoid regress, since conscious higher-order states would themselves require yet-higher-order states, with no end to the number of orders of representation if all were to be conscious" (Beeckmans 2007, p. 91).

[173]Rosenthal 1997, p. 742.

worried
> *that you are wondering*
>> *whether your opinions*
>>> *about the nature of a quale*
>>>> *that you truly believe*
>>>>> *you are now experiencing*
>>>>>> *are legitimate*

That's around six "orders," depending on how you slice it.[174] Did you forget to take your Dramamine?

A higher-order thought must not rely on inference. Suppose you are in a deep hypnotic state in which you feel no sensations in your right arm. You cannot make those sensations conscious just by having a thought about them, such as "I think nerve impulses from my arm are still coming into my brain." For a mental state to become conscious it must cause us to automatically and irresistibly think, "I am in a state of feeling *X.*"

HOT potatoes

Here are criticisms of Rosenthal's theory, starting with some that seem easily corrected. First, HOTs are supposed to be stateable as something like this: "I am experiencing the taste of vinegar." The HOT, therefore, "must refer to oneself."[175] But babies and non-human mammals are presumably conscious, despite lacking verbal skills and well-developed self-concepts. Even so, we could modify this requirement while retaining the general spirit of Rosenthal's approach. Babies and animals can distinguish their own bodies from other parts of the world. If they could verbalize their HOTs they might say something like, "this body feels cold and it's moving toward a warmer location."[176] "Rosenthal

---

[174](1) The quale (red, let's say) is the first-order state. (2) In HOT theory the second-order state is an unconscious thought, something like, "I am visually experiencing *red*." (3) You are *consciously aware* that you are visually experiencing red. (4) You have an opinion about the nature of this quale, perhaps believing that it is a brain state. (5) You wonder whether this opinion is legitimate. (6) You worry about wondering this.

[175]Rosenthal 1997, p. 745.

[176]A related point: For a while Peter Carruthers supported the "rather baroque

is aware of these difficulties," acknowledged Dretske, "and he suggests that . . . the requisite higher-order thoughts need not be conceptually very sophisticated."[177] It seems as if a toddler, a bat, or a senile adult could have the same general sense that you and I do of *"nasty taste on tongue now,"* without a sophisticated self-concept or the ability to speak.[178]

Now we'll confront a serious challenge to HOT theory. We've discussed the fact that when one state of mind monitors another it may fail to monitor it accurately. For example, one might touch ice without knowing what it is, and think one had been scalded. So a higher-order state can misjudge a first-order state. And here's a hypothetical self-monitoring mistake that would be quite perplexing:

Suppose one has a higher-order thought along the lines of "I'm hearing bells," and one is indeed hearing bell sounds. HOT theory says that this higher-order thought *makes the auditory sensation conscious.* But in principle, the brain might malfunction and get stuck, continually HOTting *"THE BELLS, THE BELLS"* – even though the bell-sound experience isn't there any more. The sensation is gone but the higher-order thought lingers on. Rosenthal responds by saying that if we have a HOT about a non-existent perception, then we have a conscious experience of that perception even though it does not exist.[179]

---

conclusion that animal pain cannot really count as pain due to the lack of higher cognitive faculties in animals, and hence it should not be of any moral concern to us, humans" (Güzeldere 1995a, p. 341). He "argued that creatures with only unconscious pains – pains that would lack any subjective qualities, or *feel* – could not be appropriate objects of sympathy and moral concern. But Carruthers has changed his mind." He is now "concerned to show that animals can be objects of sympathy and moral concern because the 'most basic form of mental harm . . . lies in the existence of thwarted agency, or thwarted desire, rather than in anything phenomenological'. . ." (Gennaro 2012a, pp. 232-33). For more on infant and animal consciousness, see Gennaro 2012a, Chapters 7 and 8.

[177]Dretske 1995, p. 111.

[178]For additional concerns about HOT theory see Van Gulick 2006, pp. 13-16.

[179]Rosenthal puts the point bluntly: "The theory says that a HOT suffices only for a mental episode to seem subjectively to occur, not also for that episode actually to occur" (2011, p. 433). "If one has a sensation of red and a distinct HOT that one has a sensation of green, the sensation of red may nonetheless be detectable by various priming effects. But what it will be like for one is that one

Did you do a double-take on that one? So did William Seager, who complains that this is inconsistent with the fact that HOTs are supposed to explain the occurrence of conscious sensations. If we can be conscious of sensations without those sensations even existing, then "no real role remains for the phenomenal properties [e.g., perceptions of sound or color], which become merely a gratuitous metaphysical extravagance."[180] Since we can have an experience just by having a certain sort of thought about an *alleged* experience, we don't need any "first-order" perceptions and sensations at all. Just having the HOT will do quite nicely, thank you very much.

Why does this matter? Because it challenges widespread and deeply held intuitions about what it means to be conscious. It might even mean that experiences are entirely constituted by our thoughts *about* our experiences. But many believe that the truly precious aspects of consciousness include the experiences themselves.

Partly because of these considerations, Ned Block has charged that HOT theory is "defunct." In rebutting Block's critique, Rosenthal and Weisberg admit that higher-order thoughts are not always about actual states of mind. The "object" of a thought is an *intentional object.* (This sense of "intentional" does not mean "deliberate" or "on purpose." An intentional object is the thing the thought is about.) "Conscious states are states we represent ourselves as being in, and so, like all objects of representation, they need not exist."[181]

Block clarifies this seemingly perverse idea. "Weisberg . . . says what is conscious is always an intentional object; however sometimes the intentional object exists and sometimes not. (If any non-philosophers have gotten this far, the intentional object of a mental state is what it is 'about'. Ponce de Leon searched for the Fountain of Youth and so the (non-existent) Fountain of Youth is said to be an intentional object.)"[182]

---

has a sensation of green. Similarly if one has that HOT with no relevant sensation at all" (Rosenthal, quoted by Block 2011a, pp. 423-24).

[180]Seager 1999, p. 78.

[181]Weisberg 2011, p. 439.

[182]Block 2011a, p. 425.

So intentional content is content that is about something. A visual perception of an object is *about* that object. But Block rejects the idea that conscious experiences are merely intentional objects. He denies that we could have a conscious experience of something that does not exist – either in the outside world or as an experienced sensation or perception. "If they say this, they reveal that the what-it-is-like-ness they invoke is fake."[183]

I have tended to agree with Block that every conscious state must actually exist within our minds. If not, the theory of consciousness is fake, just as Block charges. However I have now concluded, much to my own surprise, that there may be a way to make something like Rosenthal and Weisberg's argument work. I'll elucidate later.

Summing up

Traditional religions have often explained consciousness in terms of pan-psychism or dualism, but most philosophers now reject these strategies. Brilliant and determined scholars have tried several other theoretical moves, so far to no avail.

In higher-order theory, a conscious experience combines a mental state, which by itself is not conscious, with a particular kind of thought about that state. But we don't actually need the state that we're thinking about. According to Rosenthal, if we have a higher-order thought about a non-existent perception, we experience that perception even though it isn't there.

We'll now examine another approach called representationalism. Understanding the strengths and limitations of this theory will help us drill down to core issues.

---

[183]Block 2011a, p. 425. Gennaro supports Block's position, and Van Gulick concurs. "Rosenthal's position is certainly one dialectical option, but like Gennaro I find it less than attractive. It is hard to dispel the air of paradox from the claim that there is conscious qualitative what-it's-likeness in the absence of any qualia (or any qualia of the relevant type). . . . It all seems rather puzzling, and the price of adopting Rosenthal's solution to the misrepresentation problem seems high in loss of intuitive appeal" (Van Gulick 2013, p. 56).

Chapter Seven
Representationalism Versus *Swampman*

Walking down the road the Devil and his friend see a man pick up
something from the ground with astonishment. "What has he found?"
asks the Devil's friend. "He's found the Truth" says the Devil. "Isn't
that bad news for you?" says the friend. "Not at all" says the Devil,
"I'm going to help him *organise* it." – Jiddu Krishnamurti[184]

The representational gambit

Since it's hard to figure out how conscious phenomena could be brain
states, how about saying that what we experience is "representational
content," and become a representationalist? For most readers representationalism will be an unfamiliar word, and it's associated with a
bewildering zoo of other technical concepts.[185] Illustrating the terminological confusion that infests philosophy, representationalism comes in
two flavors, internalist and externalist,[186] but some use this term to refer
only to the externalist version. Furthermore Edmond Wright contends that
those who speak of representationalism today often define it in ways that

---

[184]Jiddu Krishnamurti, quoted in Morgan 2012, p. 251.

[185]Philosophers energetically debate the meaning and implications of the
seemingly-innocuous word, "represents." "A representational theory of
consciousness requires a theory of representation. At the moment there are lots
of these on offer but they all seem to lead to real difficulties when coupled to
the theory of consciousness" (Seager 1999, p. 153).

[186]Turausky (2014, p. 224-25) comments on internalist and externalist representationalism. And Gennaro writes, "... unlike many representationalists, I express
sympathies with *narrow* representationalism, which is the view that
phenomenal properties, and the representational properties they are equivalent
to, depend on a subject's internal state, so that molecular duplicates will
necessarily share mental contents" (2013, p. 11).

are virtually the opposite of what it has meant historically.[187] We needn't wade into this squabble. What's important for our purposes is that "externalist" representationalists try to finesse the puzzling features of experiences by saying that they represent states of the outside world. So we will be discussing a brand of representationalism that supports externalism and resolutely denies that introspection tells us about our own states of mind.

Those who appreciate intricate scholarly debates will love this chapter, and if you abhor academic complexities it's fine to skim through this material. But do read the chapter summary. As you proceed, keep in mind Krishnamurti's warning that sometimes the devil is not so much in the details as in the way those details are organized. Should we think of consciousness in terms of representational content, or is that the path to perdition?

Obviously a great many conscious experiences have representational content, in the sense that they represent things about the world. I hear *HISSSS, ROWRR, GRRR,* outside my window, and these noises represent the fact that cats are fighting. My milk tastes bitter, and the content of this sensory representation includes the fact that my milk has gone sour. So far, so good. But those who fly the flag of externalist representationalism claim that every sensory experience can be completely described by saying what it represents about the objects and events that we're perceiving. Non-representational features of experience just do not exist.

What sort of "non-representational" content are these theorists rejecting? Color qualia, for one thing, if we construe those as mental states. Some say that when we see a lemon as yellow, we are not just experiencing what this quale represents about the world. We are also experiencing the quale itself. If our color experiences were switched so that lemons looked bright blue, we would still detect what the lemon experience is representing, the surface of the fruit. But we would also detect the fact that our qualia had been rejiggered. Thus, the argument goes, we would learn something both about physical objects *and about our own minds.*

---

[187]"But with an ahistoric confidence Tye decided to use the term for a theory that is wholly dismissive of the old representationalism" (Wright 2008, p. 3).

Some externalists, it seems, would rather expose themselves to leprosy than say that we access our own conscious experiences *as* experiences. That sounds too much like the outmoded theory of sense data. And externalism has a big advantage. If experiences only show us what our perceptions represent about the world, that explains why they do not seem to consist of neurological goings-on. Recall Michael Tye's famous claim that qualia *"ain't in the head."*[188] I will focus mainly on versions of representationalism presented by Tye and the late Fred Dretske. (Dr. Tye's position has changed in recent years, and his theories continue to evolve.)[189]

Representationalism distinguishes the content of an experience from the vehicle that carries that content. For a simple example, think of a television drama. The content of this drama includes a story about certain characters. The vehicle that carries that content includes moving images on the screen plus a soundtrack. You could tell a story with similar content using a completely different vehicle, such as a long poem.

When we notice our own experiences, do we only notice what those experiences are telling us about the world, or are we also tuned in to features of the experiences themselves? To use Jackson's example, when Mary first sees a red rose, does she learn something about the vehicle that carries her color experiences, a state of her own mind that constitutes redness, or does she just detect the representational content of redness in a new way? Representationalism denies that we can access our own qualia. Instead, qualia "represent properties without having them."[190]

Represents properties *without having them?* Exactly. Suppose I'm looking at a blue balloon right in front of me. According to Tye, all that introspection tells me is that *my mind is now representing* a certain balloon as being blue. I cannot access internal phenomena such as a visual experience of a balloon or brain events that constitute blueness. Those who think we do access such phenomena have supposedly fallen prey to the inner eye illusion.

---

[188]Tye 1995, p. 151.

[189]Showing an admirable open-mindedness, Tye has revised his analysis in a book called *Consciousness Revisited.*

[190]William Robinson notes this claim in Robinson 2008, p. 79.

Think about what you're doing right now, reading words. What a word represents is not typically part of the printed word itself. No matter how long you peer at the word, "squid," you will not find a slithery sea creature wriggling among those five letters. But for those who know how to read English, this word contains "representational content" about an aquatic creature with tentacles.

More Details. The content of this book is conveyed by symbols with certain shapes. Although we seldom focus on these shapes, we are attentive enough so that we might notice an **unusual** typeface. So in reading, we can both *inspect and decipher* verbal representations. We can see words as marks on paper, and we can also access their content, the facts that the words represent.

Is it possible to process information about printed words without having access to information about the letters that make up these words? Sure. A computer connected to an optical scanner could examine a printed page and turn the text into computerized speech, without being able to "comment" on the physical features of the printed text. So it couldn't say whether a word was in serif or sans serif, **bold** or non-bold. Obviously if it successfully turns printing into speech sounds, it is examining the printed text. But it would *lack useful access* to the way the text itself is configured.

For Tye and Dretske, sensory experience is like that. It informs us about the external world, by telling us what certain brain states represent about the world as we perceive it. They admit that we do have access to states of the brain, but deny that we can access them *as brain states*. We can decipher their meaning – Egad! A squid's in my bathtub! – but we cannot inspect them. Thus "one can be aware that one is in a certain state without being aware *of*, without . . . sensing, the state itself."[191]

Dretske says representationalism "likens experience to something like a story. In thinking about a story we can be thinking about: (1) the words that tell the story or (2) what those words mean, the story they tell. Call the first the *story-vehicle* and the second the *story-content*. . . . In the

---

[191]Dretske 1995, p. 109. Moreover, "introspection is *not* a process in which one looks inward" (p. 41).

same way that stories are in books, thoughts and experiences are in heads. What is in the head, of course, are the experience-vehicles, the physical states that have a representational-content. . . . Stories about blue dogs – the blue dog vehicles – are neither blue nor doglike. . . . Just so, what we find by looking in the brain of a person experiencing blue dogs is neither blue nor doglike."[192]

🐛 🐛 🐛 🐛 🐛 🐛 🐛

The myth of total transparency

One powerful argument against the notion that experiences are in our heads is the idea that perceptual experiences are *transparent* to what we perceive. We "look through" the act of experiencing and focus directly on the object. Here's a widely-quoted example by Gilbert Harman. "Look at a tree and try to turn your attention to intrinsic features of your visual experience. I predict you will find that the only feature there is to turn your attention to will be features of the presented tree, including relational features of the tree 'from here.'"[193] Supposedly all sensations and perceptions are transparent to either external objects or states of our bodies. A sound might inform us about a busy woodpecker. A pain might reveal a splinter in your hand. Uriah Kriegel reports that most "philosophers of consciousness think today that conscious experience is indeed transparent in the relevant sense, and supports representationalism." "The transparency of experience . . . has certainly tilted the debate in favor of representationalism, sociologically speaking."[194]

I'm a bit daunted by this alleged consensus, but I'm going to swim against the current on this one. Although some experiences do seem

---

[192]Dretske 1995, pp. 34-36.

[193]Harman 1990, p. 39. Tye agrees with Harman. "The only objects of which you are aware are the external ones making up the scene before your eyes. Nor . . . are you directly aware of any qualities of your experience" (quoted in Kind 2008, p. 286).

[194]Kriegel 2009, p. 71. And David Pitt states that "[t]he main argument for representationalism appeals to the *transparency* of experience . . ." (Pitt 2013). Nevertheless, Roblin Meeks reports that transparency "remains controversial" (2005, p. 151).

transparent to our surroundings, it would be remarkable if the brain's benign self-deception were flawlessly executed. I will contend that even though experiences often seem transparent to worldly objects, there is sometimes a difference between paying attention to what we perceive and paying attention to the *experience* of perceiving it. We can access the vehicle as well as the content that the vehicle carries. The evidence I will offer is disputable, so see what you think. (If this topic is not of interest, just skim along for a few pages till you see ❦ ❦ ❦.)

More Details: If we looked closely at a Truman Show movie set, we might see a little stitching in *that* corner, and a chip of missing paint just off to the left. And if the brain is making a mockup of reality based on sensory inputs, shouldn't we occasionally come across "brainprints" or faint "neural smudges?" Might these sometimes tip us off that what appear to be physical objects are actually highly processed perceptions? If so, then our perceptions are not perfectly transparent to the objects we perceive. We are consciously aware of some things that are in our minds instead of out there in the world. Let's consider five kinds of examples.

1. *Qualia.* Some say that sensory qualia are states of our own minds. They cite the in-principle possibility of qualia switches, representing lemon surfaces with the experience of the color blue or representing pains as tastes,[195] and they try to show that such a switch would make it obvious that we're accessing the way our minds *simulate* these things. That would contradict the claim that experiences are perfectly transparent to worldly objects.

2. *Misrepresentations.* Closely examining our perceptual experiences sometimes reveals details that are not present in the objects we perceive. Visual phenomena, for example, are less stable than they seem at first blush. Since I know that the exterior walls of houses are stable, I may assume that the visual experience of a wall depicts it as holding still. But what I perceive is continually changing as my eyes re-focus on point after

---

[195]"Representationalism has been quite popular . . . but it remains highly controversial and intuitions clash about key cases and thought experiments. . . . In particular the possibility of inverted qualia provides a crucial test case" (Van Gulick 2014).

point.[196] If I pay close attention I notice fuzziness and jittery motion, but when I stop contemplating my experience *as* an experience, the house seems to stabilize again. We may think that vision is transparent to stable objects, but actually our attention is hopping around like a kangaroo with the hiccups.

Feeling intoxicated is another example. One's stream of awareness becomes fuzzy, foggy, floaty, and fun. Is it most accurate to say we are now representing the world as being different than it was when we were sober, or is it best to say that the mind is now operating differently, and that we know this through casual introspection? If we are even the least bit conscious of a change in the mind itself, then we are conscious of the "vehicle" which carries our representations of the world, and externalism is wrong.

Fred Dretske, remember, compared conscious experiences to stories in books. He argued that introspection only gives us access to the story, access to what the mind is telling us about what's so. But perhaps experiencing the world in the unfocused haze of inebriation is analogous to spilling coffee on a page of a novel. If that blots out a few words, the novel may now represent events differently. But certainly the stain has also changed the vehicle that conveys the story. The same will be true if you go out and get blitzed. After the fourth margarita muddles your awareness, your perceptions of the world will change, and your mind will also be altered in ways that you can introspect. (To study this thesis, attend the biennial *Toward a Science of Consciousness* conference in Tucson, which traditionally concludes with an End of Consciousness Party.)

3. *Noise.* Any information processing system generates a certain amount of noise. I'm not talking about the non-music your next door neighbor plays at midnight. By noise I mean *something that does not contribute to the system's functioning.* It's not just a misrepresentation; it's irrelevant. Here's an example: Look at the icon at the end of this sentence for a few seconds, and then quickly shift your gaze to some distant location: ☆

---

[196]David Bourget (2013) has noted that if we examine our own experiences closely we will notice "little irregularities." We may look at a white wall and see subtle colors, for example.

If you pay close attention you'll notice a very brief blurring between fixating on the star and fixating on the distant focus-point. During that instant, visual experience is certainly not presenting the outside world as it is. In fact it's not presenting the world at all. What you're detecting is visual "noise."

Once in a long while I notice a faint but rather explosive sound that seems to be coming from inside of my head. This has occurred for many years and it's not worsening, so I assume it's nothing dire. It is literally noise, and also noise in the sense of being irrelevant data. It seems possible that the brain itself produces this little detonation.

Representationalists can reply that what we experience always represents the world, but sometimes does so incorrectly. This retort may be legitimate, but it can be stretched so far that it becomes *heads I win, tails you lose.* Any conceivable experience whatsoever could be said to represent the world. It makes more sense to admit that we sometimes experience phenomena which represent nothing at all. And in principle, an all-powerful being could create a creature that was just like us except that all of its visual (auditory, olfactory, etc.) experiences consisted of random noise that represented zero, zilch, nada. Although it would be functionally blind, for instance, its visual states would still be "like something." It might, for example, be introspectively aware of times when this visual gibberish sped up or slowed down. It was not *designed* to have experiences that represent anything, its experiences *do not* represent, they are devoid of representational *content*, but they are introspectable nevertheless. That's a tough challenge for transparency advocates.

4. *Attentional shifts.* Here's an argument that I haven't seen carefully discussed, and I welcome reader responses. Introspection shows us that our attention is selective, and sometimes reveals details about these attentional shifts. Hence it is false to say that if I look at an orange Lamborghini, all I will notice is the way the auto appears from where I'm standing. If I zero in on my own experience I can tell when the color of the car is in the foreground of my awareness and the shape of the car is in the background, or vice versa. And when I am focusing intently on some object, the experience is more vivid than when I'm noticing it in an absent-minded manner. Our marvelously flexible minds direct various *levels* of attention toward widely-varying *segments* out of a huge field of

sensory information. If one is determined to completely construe all experiences in representational terms, one can insist that these shifts only change the representational contents of our perceptions, the "story" that our perceptions are telling us about the world. But it surely seems as if these shifts also involve changes within our own minds, and that we are sometimes aware of these changes.

5. *Non-visual phenomena.* As the word transparency implies, scholars often treat visual events as the standard cases of conscious experiences. But although it's easy to think that vision transparently presents objects to us, this sort of transparent presentation does not occur in all perceptions. Does the sound of a trumpet resemble either the horn itself or the sound waves blatting forth from its bell? Not in any obvious way. If we focus more intently on what see, fine details of the object itself may become more evident. But if we focus intently on music, we become more aware of the sound itself rather than the instrument or the sound waves it generates. In fact focusing on the sound may cause us to be *less* cognizant of its real-world causes and more tuned in to its qualities. As Nicholas Humphrey notes, "when your soul is haled by the music of the lute, you can – and often will – remain gloriously uninterested in the vibrations of the gut string stretched across the wooden box."[197]

Externalists claim that no matter how carefully we monitor our own consciousness, we will never introspect anything except how the world seems to be. They want to avoid the possibility that it is sometimes fitting to construe aspects of experience as mental (and/or neural) events. But this is a false dichotomy. People often talk about experiences without thinking of them as either in the mind or in the world. They are classified as just *experiences*. For instance, I think intuitions about tactile sensations would at least be divided about whether these experiences mainly represent objects that we're touching, states of the skin, both of these, or neither one – touch is just *touch*.

We also have weak transparency intuitions about smell and taste. When you taste soup, does it seem as if you've ladled some tastes onto your tongue? Was the taste sitting in the dish before you took the first bite? If something went wrong with your brain so that you couldn't experience a mouthful of food, would its tastes be on your tongue

---

[197]Humphrey 2011, pp. 105-06.

anyway? Again, I suspect that many of us simply classify tastes as *tastes,* so that gustatory episodes are not irresistibly experienced as transparent to the ingredients of our food.

In my opinion many brilliant scholars have been bewitched by visual qualia. They have overgeneralized from the visual case, drawing sweeping conclusions about all perceptual experiences.[198] And even with visual phenomena we can notice non-representational components such as qualia, various misrepresentations, perceptual noise, and attentional shifts. In short, when we notice our own experiences we do more than just "look through" to the physical things these experiences represent. Total transparency is a philosophical myth.

❧ ❧ ❧ ❧ ❧ ❧ ❧

Here's a related problem. When we are conscious of moods, emotions, and similar states of mind, how is that transparent to physical objects (including our own bodies)? Tye explains it as follows. "Suppose you suddenly feel extremely angry. Your body will change in all sorts of ways: for example, your blood pressure will rise, your nostrils will flare, your face will flush . . ." In response to these physical events, you will "build up a complex sensory representation of how your body has changed. . . . The feeling you undergo consists in the complex sensory representation of these changes."[199]

This is an insightful description of anger-related body states, and one could argue that these states form a pattern that literally *is* anger. In fact as a psychotherapist, I have emphasized the bodily nature of emotions, teaching people to notice that certain characteristic sensations accompany strong feelings. Nevertheless, in 50 years of attending closely to my own feelings, the notion that emotions and moods are *nothing but* bodily sensations has never seemed to fit. Others may have different intuitions about this issue, but it is certainly not obvious that externalism wins this volley.

---

[198]"The scientific study of conscious awareness has been dominated by the examination of visual consciousness while the effects of bodily senses . . . on consciousness have been frequently overlooked" (Salomon 2013, p. 17).

[199]Tye 1995, p. 126.

Kriegel suggests that rather than viewing moods as body states, we might construe them "as concerned with changes in the world as a whole, rather than in oneself as a whole."[200] But it seems far-fetched to think that a change in mood alters my perceptions of the entire world in a way that is consistent with the change in mood. If I am depressed, that may not make me think that a child doubled over with laughter looks any less delighted than she would if I were feeling chipper. And it is clearly quite useful to know what's going on in our own minds. Moods help convey this information.

If total transparency is a myth, this undermines one of the greatest attractions of externalist representationalism – but the theory could be correct anyway. We now turn to some crucial problems representationalists must overcome.

Representationalism's vulnerabilities

Uriah Kriegel notes that "representationalism is an initially somewhat unintuitive view, at least to the traditional philosopher. Intuitively, we tend to think of reddish experiences as experiences that do not simply represent red objects, but represent them in a specific *way* – a reddish way. The intuitive outlook has it that the basis of the experience's reddishness is not in *what* the experience represents, but in *how* it represents it."[201]

Dretske responds confidently to this line of reasoning. "The way to shed this prejudice against externalism is quite easy: shed (as almost everyone has) this quaint conception of sense experience."[202] But after implying that virtually everyone has piled onto the externalist bandwagon, he admits that most philosophers take internalism "as plausible enough not to need argument."[203] He acknowledges that he himself feels "the pull of the

---

[200]Kriegel 2009, p. 64. Similarly, William Seager contends that "objectless emotions such as diffuse depression or elation can be regarded as representational 'colourings' of our view of the world. No doubt this will remain controversial for many, but if one can force oneself to swallow the universal representational character of all conscious experience, there are great benefits to be gained from this approach to consciousness" (Seager 1999, p. 134).

[201]Kriegel 2009, p. 68.

[202]Dretske 1995, p. 149.

[203]Dretske 1995, p. 150.

Internalist Intuition" and then echoes a comment that many have made: "The problems about conscious experience are so baffling that one can reasonably expect the right answers – if right answers are ever to be found – will require abandoning *some* deeply held convictions about the mind-body relation. One will have to make a hard choice about what to give up. My choice is the Internalist Intuition."[204]

So Dretske sees representationalism as the lesser evil, but other scholars have claimed that in some cases:

1. Two experiences include different qualia but have the same representational content. In synesthesia, for example, the mind can "say" that an object is shaped a certain way by generating a visual experience of it or by manufacturing a taste experience. In fact one book on synesthesia was called *The Man Who Tasted Shapes.*[205]

2. Two experiences may have the same qualia while representing different things. For instance, we can look at this box and see it as having a frontal plane that faces down and to the left, or up and to the right. Same qualia, different representation. However some say that the box's qualia do change after this shift. What do you think?

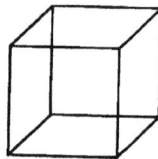

[204]Dretske 1995, p. 151. In the same passage he says he would not have thought to question internalism "but for the fact that unless it is challenged, an even more (for me) obvious fact must be rejected – the idea, namely, that what goes on in the mind – what we think, feel and experience – and, therefore, the qualities in terms of which we distinguish thoughts, feelings, and experiences from one another, are nowhere to be found in the head, where the thoughts, feelings, and experiences are." That's either a triple negative or a quadruple negative.

[205]Cytowic 1993. Dretske "considers whether a blind person, who can tactually discriminate shapes, textures, movements, and so on, thereby knows what it is like to see these properties. Dretske claims that she does . . ." But Lopes responds, "I find this difficult to accept. It seems to me that tactile and visual experiences have distinctive phenomenal characters through and through" (Lopes 2000, p. 445).

More Details: Sometimes experiences mislead us, as in dreams and hallucinations. If I dream about a giant centipede with the face of Joseph Stalin, doing the rhumba, this dream experience represents something about the world. When I awaken I will realize that it was a *mis*representation. In principle the misrepresentation experienced in a dream or hallucination might be experientially identical to a veridical (accurate) experience. But for various technical reasons, many believe that a hallucination cannot have the same representational *content* as an accurate perception, even if they seem to be exactly the same. The two experiences would have the same qualia but different contents.

Concerns about hallucinations eventually led Michael Tye to abandon "strong" externalist representationalism, even though he was a leading advocate.[206]

Swampman lives

Representationalists have struggled to explain representation, and the most promising idea involves *tracking*. "This is Tye's . . . term. Neural events track physical properties if they systematically covary with those physical properties in normal conditions."[207] But tracking is more than just the fact that two states correlate with each other. There has to be some reason for saying that experience A tracks physical property B. So perhaps a sensory perception tracks (and thus represents) something if the con-

---

[206]"I no longer hold . . . that veridical and hallucinatory perceptual experiences share a common representational content. And so, relatedly, I no longer accept strong intentionalism – the view that the phenomenal character of an experience is the same as its representational content" (Tye 2009, p. xiii).

[207]Robinson 2008, p. 80. (Robinson opposes Tye's representationalism.)

nection between the perception and what it tracks has contributed to evolutionary fitness. Our visual system, for example, was evolved to track features of objects such as their shapes. But evolutionary theories of tracking must address the possibility of "rogue consciousness" – "creatures who lack the requisite features to count as *representing* . . . but who seem nonetheless to be capable of conscious experience."[208]

One famous rogue is an imaginary twin of the late professor Donald Davidson, described in a splendidly grotesque thought experiment. Suppose, Davidson said, his own body were pulverized by a bolt of lightning in a swamp. And imagine this same lightning bolt "simultaneously transforming a nearby dead tree into an exact replica of him. Although the resulting 'Swampman' behaves exactly like the original author of 'Radical Interpretation', Davidson denies that the 'Swampman' could properly be said to have thoughts or its words have meaning – and the reason is simply that the Swampman would lack the sort of causal history that is required in order to establish the right connections between itself, others and the world that underpin the attribution of thought and meaning."[209]

For our next thought experiment, picture Swampman invading San Francisco, followed by a phalanx of decidedly *non*-philosophical zombies. Scattering terrified tourists, they stagger relentlessly toward the annual conference of the American Philosophical Association (Pacific Division). Which theorists would they devour first? (I realize that a

[208]Seager 1999, p. 153.

[209]Malpas 2014.

physical duplicate of Donald Davidson would not actually say "RAWR" or attempt to eat colleagues, but I have granted myself a bit of latitude here.)

Externalists tend to claim that Swampman has no conscious experiences. Its mind was not evolved to track anything, since it was not evolved at all. Since it doesn't track, it doesn't represent, and since it doesn't represent, it does not have experiences – and thus does analytical ingenuity triumph over common sense![210]

Tye offers the example of a pod growing on a distant planet which somehow becomes "a microphysical *duplicate* of an active brain – one belonging to a human being who for the same period of time on Earth initially is having sex and then (after 8 minutes) smoking a cigarette and drinking green chartreuse." Does the pod "undergo *any* experiences? It seems to me that the *intuitive* answer . . . is No."[211]

What do your intuitions suggest? Would Swampman (and the pod) lack experiences? I agree with Fiona Macpherson. "While Dretske endorses this conclusion, most philosophers would find this result a reductio ad absurdum of this position."[212] And this is not just a theoretical quibble. It ties into the moral significance of consciousness. Seager imagines the way we might treat Swampman if we were certain that he had no experiences. "Is it just a 'brute intuition', unsupported by any reasonable theory of mind or experience, that leads us to suspect, as the creature screams and writhes as we hold its hand in the fire, that it feels pain?"[213]

---

[210]Dretske puts it bluntly: "What is in heads A and B could be physically indistinguishable and yet, because these pieces of gray matter have had relevantly different histories, one is a representational system, the other is not; one is the seat of thought and experience, the other is not; one makes the person in whom it occurs aware of the world, the other does not" (Dretske 1995, p. 125).

[211]Tye 2009, pp. 195 and 196. "For example, one could hold (as I actually do) that physically identical brains belonging to creatures with very different evolutionary histories and normal habitats could be subject to different raw feelings" (Tye 1997a, p. 970).

[212]Macpherson 2005, p. 136.

[213]Seager 1999, p. 170.

Seager goes on to clinch the point. Swampman's mind "would bear a relation to genuine mental states analogous to the relationship a *perfect* counterfeit dime would bear to a genuine dime, i.e. the counterfeit is identical to the real dime in every respect *except* production history." Because Swampman lacks "the proper external credentials," we deny that he has conscious experiences. "Thus, the issue of . . . Swampman's mental states becomes a merely verbal issue and also, I think, becomes entirely trivial."[214]

One occupational hazard of philosophical inquiry is the risk of chasing a complex chain of premises and inferences right over a cliff, wholly losing touch with what one was originally trying to explain. This seems to have happened with some versions of representationalism.

More (Juicy) Details: The debate over externalism and internalism has become heated at times. In criticizing a paper published in *Journal of Consciousness Studies,* Jack and Prinz write: "In the hands of Noë & Thompson, externalism becomes an eccentric doctrine that locates consciousness outside of the organism. To our minds, this is the kind of philosophical manoeuvring that prevents scientists from taking philosophers seriously."[215]

Noë and Thompson reply by admitting that "externalism about content is compatible with internalism about the vehicles of content," but they suggest that externalism about these vehicles is correct nonetheless. "Behind the purple prose is the ferocity of dogmatic conviction. Jack and Prinz, like many philosophers and scientists, *assume* that the causal

---

[214]Seager 1999, pp. 203-04.

[215]Jack and Prinz 2004, p. 55. On the same page the authors critique externalism by mentioning neurons in the visual cortex that detect the edges of objects. These "edge-detectors qualify as such only because they respond to edges . . . and were evolved to do so. . . . But that does not mean that edge-detectors, if such exist, are not in the head. It means that their identity is . . . relational (compare: a mother is only a mother because she has a child, but a mother is not in her child). . . . Conscious states may have their content in virtue of the features that they detect in the world, but they are still located squarely within the brain. Externalism is a red herring. It has no implications, as far as we can tell, for neuroscientific research on consciousness." Well argued.

substrates of experience are entirely in the head. Perhaps they are right. But the issue is far from settled yet."[216]

❦ ❦ ❦ ❦ ❦ ❦ ❦

In case you aren't worried about the moral status of swamp critters, let's bring the point home by considering what an all-powerful being could do to you. An omnipotent deity, or demon, could redecorate your brain so that you experience new qualia, which occur at random and give you the impression that certain things are happening out there in the world which are not. You could enjoy marvelous sound-qualities, for example, which do not result from any activity in your ears. Despite the fact that they track nothing, I maintain that you would be just as conscious of these novel qualia as you are of current sound-experiences.

If Tye and Dretske are wrong about Swampman, that doesn't disprove representationalism, but it suggests that they have lost the scent of their original quarry, the felt realities of human sentience.

Summing up

Representationalism is a creative way of understanding how consciousness could be a physical phenomenon even though it does not seem to be a brain process. Everyone agrees that sensations and perceptions usually represent things (such as headaches or the coldness of ice). But externalist representationalism says that all we are aware of about our experiences is what they represent about the external world and our own bodily states. We do not access the thing that's *doing* the representing.

I have clarified this subtle idea with the example of reading words. As you read this sentence, you both inspect and decipher strings of letters on the page. Since you can inspect them, you may notice when I **change typefaces.** And if you know English you can decipher their meaning.

Externalist representationalists say we decipher what our experiences represent, but we cannot inspect the experiences as such. So even though we detect our own sensory brain states, and we know what those states

---

[216]Noë and Thompson 2004b, p. 94.

are "saying" about the outside world, we can't detect anything about the sensory states themselves. Conscious experiences do not give us access to internal, mental phenomena.

There are several standard objections to representationalism. Two experiences may include different qualia but have the same representational content. The reverse may also be true. And some conscious experiences may possess no representational content whatsoever.

The Swampman scenario exposes a key weakness of Tye and Dretske's representationalism. Swampman is a hypothetical creature that has states which are exactly like our own conscious states in every way, but he has no evolutionary history. He just appeared out of nowhere. Since he lacks the right evolutionary "credentials," externalists deny that his mental states represent anything. Therefore, they allege, he is not conscious, but that sounds very odd.

It's true that internalism leads to all sorts of complications, but externalist representationalism creates additional tangles. Could it be that neither externalism nor internalism can explain consciousness? Maybe we should just give up and admit that there's no such thing as introspectable experience. We'll consider this option in Chapter Eight.

Chapter Eight
How to Lose Consciousness

There's a very simple way to finesse the deepest puzzles about consciousness. It's called:

Eliminativism

Now say that fast three times: **"E - lim - i - na - tiv - ism."**

This tongue-twisting term means eliminating something from one's list of real things by saying it does not exist. I am, for example, a Zeus eliminativist and a unicorn eliminativist. I don't think either of these are real, so I'm not likely to think about them unless I'm reading mythology or buying statuary.

Eliminativists, also called eliminative materialists, say that worrying about the Hard Problem of consciousness is like thinking unicorns exist and wondering why we can't find any. The Hard Problem is an illusion. "There isn't any further problem. There just seems to be."[217] "Indeed eliminative materialists deny that we have any experiences at all. Instead they claim that talk of 'sensations,' 'experiences,' 'qualia,' and the like are examples of the use of a worn-out vocabulary."[218]

Some wag has responded by suggesting that philosophy, having lost its soul and lost its mind, is about to lose consciousness. In reality, few if any philosophers want to utterly eliminate all consciousness-related concepts. Even the most famous eliminativist, Daniel Dennett, titled his best-known book *Consciousness Explained.* But some do want to jettison troublesome terms such as qualia and what-it's-like-ness.

Descartes dismissed – but is the Theater really dead?

Three prominent eliminativists are Paul and Patricia Churchland and Daniel Dennett. Paul acknowledges that his viewpoint "was widely seen

---

[217]Dennett: http://www.youtube.com/watch?feature=endscreen&NR=1&v=48o14sHasA8.

[218]"Dennett's project is to explain consciousness without explaining phenomenal consciousness." In fact for Dennett "there is *no such thing* as phenomenal consciousness!" (Seager 1999, p. 85).

as a faintly cranky position." He had "set out, in 1973, to foment a revolution in epistemology and the philosophy of science. But I found myself, ten years later, pigeon-holed as a grumpy and hyperbolically iconoclastic philosopher of mind."[219] He and his wife Patricia wanted to replace common-sense concepts such as belief and desire with scientific concepts such as neuronal activation patterns. Patricia eventually came to "rue the day that we called it eliminative materialism." The Churchlands, she said, were mainly interested in revising concepts of mind rather than eliminating them.[220]

In this discussion I'll mostly focus on Daniel Dennett, who rejects some important ideas that date back to René Descartes. For hundreds of years many agreed with Descartes that reality includes two very different constituents, mind and matter. Today most philosophers have abandoned this dualistic mind-body split.[221] But in addition to rejecting the notion that mind is an immaterial substance, some want to abandon the concept of mind altogether, or at least delete its spookier aspects. This was a goal of Gilbert Ryle, and Dennett was one of Ryle's doctoral students at Oxford.

Dennett argued that we have been led astray by a metaphor that he calls the Cartesian Theater. Descartes thought we could examine consciousness in much the same way that we watch a stage production. But Dennett dismisses this metaphor for two reasons:

---

[219]Churchland 1998, p. 901.

[220]Patricia Churchland expressed her regrets in a recent interview. "In the end I think that was a mistake, I'd call it revisionary materialism if I had to do it all over again, I'd call it really nice guy materialism . . . I'd give it a nice name" (quoted by Baggini 2012, p. 70).

[221]Not all philosophers have dumped Decartes. For instance, Edward Feser writes that "there is a long tradition, going back at least to Descartes, . . . according to which the qualia we know directly only through introspection are all we know directly, period: everything else . . . we know only by inference. . . . This is indirect realism, the famous (or perhaps infamous) doctrine of the Cartesian prison-house of the mind, escaping from which has been the central project of modern epistemology. Controversial and even unpopular as it is, this doctrine is, in my view, essentially correct. . . . [Q]ualia are what we know best and are that on which our knowledge of everything else rests" (Feser 2001, pp. 5 and 9). (Paragraph breaks have been deleted.)

1. There's no audience.

2. There's no play.

Some scholars who have abandoned Descartes' dualism still maintain that we can detect inner states via introspection. Dennett condemns this as *"Cartesian materialism"* – giving up Descartes' idea that the mind is an immaterial substance, but failing to discard the image of a Mental Theater in which the inner self perceives sensations and perceptions, observing them as if it were watching a staged drama. So Dan evicts both the performers and the audience.

Dennett's views continue to evolve. In *Sweet Dreams,* he says "I didn't get it all right the first time, but I didn't get it all wrong either. It is time for some revision and renewal."[222] So he has altered some of his views, but in what follows I will address the sort of eliminativism found in the most famous book he's written:

Consciousness Explained

Many philosophers value the first-person perspective. Remember Nagel's remark that in order to understand a bat's consciousness we must include the bat's viewpoint. But rather than beginning with the first-person data of our own experiences, Dennett emphasizes the third-person perspective of science. Sometimes he sounds like a behaviorist, only focusing on observations of behavior (including speech), and he pooh-poohs the idea that we can learn about our minds through introspection. Importantly, Dennett admits that it seems *to him* as if he is aware of an inner world which is richly populated by sensory phenomena. He has the same intuitions about this as other people, but he does not "credit" those intuitions as being accurate, "any more than I credit the sometimes well-nigh irresistible hunch that the sun goes around the earth . . ."[223] We may think there is an inner stream of consciousness that we can discover by examining our own experiences, but we are deluded.

In the Rylean tradition, the Daniel Dennett of *Consciousness Explained* sometimes implies that we have no privileged access to our own mental states, as in this personal example:

---

[222]Dennett 2005, p. ix.

[223]Dennett 2012, p. 88.

I was once importuned to be the first base umpire in a baseball game – a novel duty for me. At the crucial moment in the game (bottom of the ninth, two outs, the tying run on third base), it fell to me to decide the status of the batter running to first. It was a close call, and I found myself emphatically jerking my thumb up – the signal for OUT – while yelling "SAFE!" In the ensuing tumult I was called upon to say what I had meant. I honestly couldn't say, at least not from any privileged position. I finally decided (to myself) that since I was an unpracticed hand-signaler but competent word-speaker, my vocal act should be given the nod, but anyone else could have made just the same judgment.[224]

This is a marvelous story of a moment when Dennett had no more knowledge of his own mental state than did bystanders; all were equally confused. Perhaps he believes that there is no internal stream of consciousness which he could have consulted to know whether he meant to say "Out" or "Safe." One can hear echoes of Ryle's claim that we know we are sleepy only because we catch ourselves yawning. And yet the story is so memorable and amusing precisely because it is atypical. Most of the time people serving as umpires do know what they meant to say. And most of the time we can describe our own states of mind more accurately than others can (except perhaps Mom or a good shrink). Each of us has special expertise, for example, in recognizing the onset of our own pains and pleasures.[225]

Dennett warns us against reflecting upon our own experiences in order to understand phenomena such as color experiences, pains, and pleasures, and he flatly states that "we shouldn't do autophenomenology. It leads us into temptation: the temptation to take our own first-person convictions not as data but as the undeniable truth."[226] Although I don't go all the way to eliminativism, I am glad that Dennett has spilled so much ink trying to show that we make errors in describing our own experiences. I'll empha- size this point in my own account of consciousness.

---

[224]Dennett 1991, p. 248.

[225]Michael Tye notes that "It is widely accepted that we have privileged access to the contents of our thoughts. On this view, we can know what we are thinking just by introspecting without engaging in any empirical investigation of our environments" (2009, pp. 183-84).

[226]Dennett 2005, p. 113.

Dennett realizes that despite his warnings people will continue to "do autophenomenology." He treats first-person reports as important data, data about what we *think* about our experiences. And he has coined the awkward but helpful term, "heterophenomenology," which means using first-person reports to understand what someone thinks about his or her inner life. Dennett is perfectly okay with paying attention to what people say about the yumminess of peanut butter and the yuckiness of spoiled milk, but he denies that peanut butter and sour-milk tastes are introspectable phenomena. Instead, he sees reports about these experiences as a kind of story that the brain makes up about its own sensory activities. (Recall Dretke's similar idea.)

Where do we start?

Here is a crucial dispute. **What is our starting point in understanding consciousness?** What is the basic datum we want to comprehend? Daniel Dennett and Joseph Levine answer these questions very differently. Levine disagrees with Dennett's claim "that all we have access to is our propensity to make judgments."[227] He is concerned that verbal judgments leave out or distort the actual contents of consciousness. Therefore "conscious experiences themselves, not merely our verbal judgments about them, are the primary data to which a theory must answer."[228] Dennett says this is illogical. "If . . . you have conscious experiences you don't believe you have – those extra conscious experiences are just as inaccessible *to you* as to the external observers. So a first-person approach garners you no more usable data than heterophenomenology does."[229]

We have to be careful here because it's hard to state our starting point clearly. As I see it, our starting point in understanding consciousness is not our experiences, as if experiences could speak up for themselves. Nor is it merely a group of bottom-line judgments about our own minds. It is a certain way of thinking about ourselves, *focusing our attention on experiences while thinking of them as mental states and wondering what they are.* Two steps in this process are especially important – pre-verbal

---

[227]Levine 2001, p. 135.

[228]Levine, quoted in Dennett 2005, p. 44.

[229]Dennett 2005, p. 45.

ponderings and verbal articulations. You may have sometimes noticed, in thinking about some complex question, that you first got a "sense" of the answer. You then found ways to put your answer into words. In studying consciousness, several intuitions about core problems have "clicked" so that they made good sense to me – but then I struggled to articulate these intuitions on paper. Try catching your own thought processes in their pre-verbal phase, noticing thoughts that clearly seem correct and yet are not yet verbalized. It isn't easy to notice this important step, but here's an exercise that may help.

✎ *Pre-verbal insights.* Re-read an obscure passage in a book or article. Notice what it feels like to try to grasp the meaning of this passage, and then notice the little "aha!" that occurs when it seems as if you get it. Pause to sense this newfound clarity, and then verbalize what you are thinking. Think back to the way it felt to understand this idea *before and after* articulating it.

As one example, you might go back to the final paragraph of the previous section and think about the meaning of "heterophenomenology." Note what it's like for you to interpret this term, before and after putting your interpretation into words.

More Details: I agree with Levine that *verbal* judgments cannot capture the fullness of consciousness. Fred Dretske concurs, and suggests that we can enjoy much more of "the multiplicity, the richness" of conscious experiences than we can possibly capture in words. He interprets Dennett as claiming that our conscious experiences cannot differ unless our *judgments* about them differ. In reality, says Dretske, "my judgments do not always – perhaps they never – track my conscious experiences of the world."[230]

Believing there is no principled difference between conscious and unconscious aspects of the mind, Dennett offers a "multiple-draft" theory of consciousness. At any given time the brain contains multiple inter-

---

[230]Dretske 1995, pp. 113 and 114. I doubt that Dennett thought that words can capture the entirety of the speaker's states of consciousness, but I am not sure how he would clarify his views about this matter.

pretations of what's currently going on, and these may contradict each other. Some of these manage to control our actions, but a swarm of others keep struggling to seize the reins. Dennett says that no one story about what I'm now experiencing is granted the official stamp of approval and admitted into the grand throne room of awareness. Sometimes one draft dominates, and sometimes another holds sway.

I suspect that this hypothesis is an exaggeration, except perhaps for those who are demented or very, very drunk. Even if there is no precise line of demarcation between conscious and non-conscious processes, the lack of a *precise* difference does not prove lack of a *real* difference. And on grounds of evolutionary fitness, it seems likely that the parts of our brains that control our behavior usually draw upon a well-coordinated sketch of current sensory events. Otherwise our actions would be haphazard. Although Dennett's multiple-drafts theory has merit, at some point we must act in non-multiple ways. We cannot both leap toward the leopard and sprint away from it. For our control mechanisms to work properly, behavior-guiding agencies must be reading from approximately the same script.

❦ ❦ ❦ ❦ ❦ ❦ ❦

The Devil and Daniel Dennett

I've seen Dan take quite a bit of ribbing about his skeptical stance. At one conference he interpreted another speaker as saying that the entire body is conscious. If that's so, he asked, then suppose a person's arm has been severed and is being surgically re-attached. Is the severed arm still conscious? Should it therefore be anesthetized for the surgery? Someone then quipped that if it was Dennett's arm the question would be whether *Dennett* should be anesthetized, since he denies having introspectable experiences of pain! That's quite a simplification, but it got a good laugh.

Other criticisms have been less light-hearted. "Dennett's contribution to the study of mind in *Consciousness Explained* is brushed aside by Nagel as 'Gilbert Ryle crossed with *Scientific American*'."[231] And Colin McGinn says that for eliminativists:

---

[231]Tye 1997b, p. 187.

There is just blank matter; the impression that we are conscious is an illusion. This view is clearly absurd, a form of madness even, and anyway refutes itself since even an illusion is the presence of an experience (it certainly seems to me that I am conscious). There are some who purport to hold this view but they are a tiny (and tinny) minority: they are sentient beings loudly claiming to be mindless zombies.[232]

More Details: This is a classic example of refusing to acknowledge that one's colleagues are competent and sincere. Furthermore McGinn commits a logical error that could be stated as follows:

1. Dennett says our impression of having introspectable experiences is an illusion.
2. This illusion is a kind of introspectable experience.
3. Therefore to be logically consistent, Dennett must affirm that we have at least one introspectable experience, i.e., the illusion of having such experiences.

Dennett would reject step 2, and so would I. The question of whether anything at all is introspectable is the very issue at stake, so a claim that illusions are introspectable cannot help settle this dispute. Dennett is contending that the thought, "I have introspectable experiences," is just that, a thought. Like other thoughts, it could be mistaken. Or could it? Which way would you vote?

🐞 🐞 🐞 🐞 🐞 🐞 🐞

Speaking of the numerous condemnations of his work, Dennett writes, "Here's my favorite of all: *'Daniel Dennett is the Devil.'*"[233] Burton Voorhees made this charge. "For Dennett, it is not a case of the Emperor having no clothes. It is rather that the clothes have no Emperor."[234] "I called him the devil in a rather tongue and [sic] cheek sort of way because of the way he used rhetorical trickery in his book Consciousness Explained to try and swindle readers into buying his claims . . ."[235]

---

[232]McGinn 2012.

[233]http://www.youtube.com/watch?feature=endscreen&NR=1&v=48ol4sHasA8.

[234]Voorhees 2000, p. 56.

[235]Voorhees, http://www.samharris.org/forum/viewthread/9298/P465.

I have noticed, by the way, that representationalists are seldom tagged as eliminativists, perhaps because they accept the existence of experience, introspection, and sensory phenomena. They even speak comfortably about qualia, having shooed away its troublesome connotations by changing the way qualia are defined. But externalist representationalism is emphatically eliminativist about inner experiences.[236] Introspection tells us what qualia represent about the world rather than revealing the qualia themselves. Because they do not label themselves as eliminativists, representationalists such as Dretske are unlikely to be lumped together with the devil and Daniel Dennett. They have managed to eliminate introspectable qualia without being sent to perdition.

The Marilyns mistake

Dennett emphasizes the errors we make in describing our experiences, and an increasing number of philosophers agree. According to Eric Schwitzgebel, philosophy has traditionally affirmed the accuracy "of our knowledge of our currently ongoing stream of experience," but in reality most people "know very little about what might seem to be obvious features of their stream of conscious experience . . ."[237]

---

[236]"Representationalism can be understood as a qualified form of eliminativism insofar as it denies the existence of properties of a sort that conscious mental states are commonly thought to have . . . namely those that are mental but not representational" (Van Gulick 2014).

[237]Schwitzgebel 2011, pp. ix-x, ix.

I agree with Schwitzgebel. While leading psychotherapy groups, for example, I have been amazed that so many people have such limited awareness of their own attitudes and emotions. When asked, "What are you feeling now?" they often say how they have *usually* felt in similar circumstances, how they think they *should* feel, how they imagine *most* people would feel, what they think I *want* them to say they feel, how they have *generally* been feeling in the past few minutes, or what sort of feeling *they think others would applaud*. Few are able to tap into the detailed, second-by-second flow of their own stream of awareness, at least without practice.

Someone might initially say, "I feel sad," for example, but after carefully focusing on her experience she might discover to her own surprise that she was mainly feeling angry. (Perhaps she was taught by her parents that good girls don't get mad.) Her beliefs about how things seemed to her experientially were quite different from her actual state of mind. Incidently, this could be one cause of the placebo effect. When people expect an inert "drug" to ameliorate their symptoms, they often report that it does. This may be partly because they are not competently monitoring their own sensations. They are living more in their concepts than in their own bodies.

Let's apply these ideas to Dennett's example of Marilyns on wallpaper. Suppose you walk into a room that is wallpapered with hundreds of images of the face of Marilyn Monroe. Perhaps you will almost instantly conclude that the entire wall is covered with representations of Marilyn's face. If so, would your head contain clear images of hundreds of Marilyns, neatly arranged just as they are on the wall, as if they've been photocopied inside of your brain? No, says Dennett.

> Having identified a single Marilyn, and having received no information to the effect that the other blobs are not Marilyns, it jumps to the conclusion that the rest are Marilyns. . . . What is not the case, however, is that there are hundreds of identical Marilyns represented in your brain. Your brain just somehow represents *that* there are hundreds of identical Marilyns, and no matter how vivid your impression is that you see all that detail, the detail is in the world, not in your head.[238]

---

[238]Dennett 1991, p. 355.

I'll now rewrite Dennett's passage as I think a fairly competent intro-spector would state it:

> Having perceived a number of Marilyns, and having had peripheral visual experiences consistent with the notion that the other shapes are Marilyns, and knowing that wallpaper tends to be regularly-patterned, I believe the entire wall is covered with Marilyns. But that is an inference rather than a direct perception.

At times Dennett seems to imply that if we realized how often we are mistaken about what we experience, we would end up agreeing with him that we do not introspect any conscious experiences at all. We aren't much good at "autophenomenology," so just forget about it. But if people tend to be sloppy introspectors, they can try to improve – and they can be more careful about basing crucial philosophical doctrines on their own subjective hunches.[239]

Shall darkness descend?

Many have criticized eliminativism for its "dark and silent" conception of sentience. William Seager writes that one "consequence of Dennett's view, I fear, is that all is darkness within."[240] Dennett is undismayed. "But of course! We know that to be true. There is nothing 'luminous' . . . going on in the brain."[241]

---

[239]After reading *Consciousness Explained* I ran some informal experiments in which audience members at a lecture were asked to close their eyes while an assistant and I held up a bed sheet with a floral design. After I asked them to open their eyes, we quickly dropped the sheet so that they saw it only briefly. "Do you think the pattern on this sheet was consistent?" I asked. Most agreed that it was. But when I asked whether they had *seen* the entire pattern or had just seen part of it and guessed that the rest was regular, the group was divided. I suspect that after training in moment-to-moment awareness, a larger percentage would state that they had seen part of the pattern and generalized about the rest of it.

[240]Seager 1993a, p. 126. Compare Chalmers' comment that zombies are "all dark inside" (cited by Cottrell 1999, p. 6).

[241]Dennett 1993, p. 154. Similarly, Papineau writes that some believe in an "additional inner light which illuminates the minds of conscious beings. But this is a mistake. There aren't any such extra inner lights whose emergence stands in need of explanation. There are just the physical states, and that's all" (1995, p. 265).

The worry about Dennett's position could be expressed as follows. Light definitely exists in the outside world, and may or may not also exist in the mind. But since there are no lights inside of the brain, if the mind is just a part of the brain it cannot contain illumination. Admitting this would leave us with a sense of loss. We thought we enjoyed light-experiences, but we were only fooling ourselves. Darn.

We can reframe the issue by saying that experiences of light do not *duplicate* the photons that are zipping all around us. Instead they *constitute* an aspect of inner awareness that we call "light." The light photons that physicists study also exist, but they are quite different from the *experience* that we call light. We need not worry that all is darkness within. The conscious visual states that correlate with retinal photon stimulation *just are* light-experiences. We respond to these experiences, we think about them, we enjoy them, and they are constituted by brain processes.

It is intriguing to see that when Dennett offers a positive account of experience-judgments, he says they roughly resemble the sudden intuition that someone is standing behind us, even though at that instant we have no sensory evidence that this is so. In this analogy, note how the judgment mechanism is cut off from any sort of detection process. Dennett even describes the experiencer as sitting "in the dark."[242]

Will the last person to leave the Cartesian Theater please turn off the lights? *(Just kidding – they've never been on.)*

Let us consider this issue in relation to the famous pink ring of *Consciousness Explained*.

Return of the ring

On the back cover of *Consciousness Explained* there's a donut-shaped pink ring in the midst of a grid of black lines and reddish lines. Closer examination reveals that the paper where the pink ring appears is not pink at all, but perfectly white! A donut-shaped segment of this pure-white paper *appears* to be pink because of an illusory spreading of pinkness around the reddish lines. Since the pink ring does not exist in the external

---

[242]Dennett 1991, p. 364. See Siewert 1993, pp. 98-99 for a helpful discussion of this passage.

world, it may seem obvious that it must exist in the mind. Dennett agrees that people think this is so, but says they are wrong.

An imaginary anti-eliminativist named Otto (who evidently champions "Otto"-phenomenology) then speaks for those who believe in the sort of inner experience that Dennett denies. Otto maintains that there is a crucial difference between *just thinking* there seems to be a ring and there *really seeming* to be such a ring. "Now you've . . . fallen into a trap," replies Dennett. "You seem to think there's a difference between thinking (judging, deciding, being of the heartfelt opinion that) something seems pink to you and something *really* seeming pink to you. But there is no difference."[243] Years later, Dennett re-affirmed this claim. *"The proper way to criticize my view is to develop an independent case for 'real seeming.' A number of people have tried. Nobody has yet succeeded."*[244]

Although I appreciate Dan's desire to delete misleading mumbo-jumbo, I agree with Otto that there is a difference between a subject's "being of the heartfelt opinion that" there seems to be a pink ring and there actually seeming to be such a ring. I doubt that I can convince Dr. D., but I'll try to show that when people believe an experience seems a certain way, they are sometimes mistaken. Since really-seeming-so and thinking-it-seems-so occasionally come apart, "real seeming" is for real.

---

[243]Dennett 1991, p. 364. Nicholas Humphrey, who is also an eliminativist, or leans in that direction, says something similar. If one makes a distinction between what someone's experience *actually is* and "a *description of what that experience is* . . . I would say you have just pulled a fast one on yourself. You have fallen for the tempting idea that there is something conscious experience *actually is* that is separate from what the subject *thinks* it is. . . . But it is not so" (Dennett 2011, p. 19).

[244]Dennett, http://ase.tufts.edu/cogstud/papers/chalmersdeb3dft.htm. Italics are in the original. But Georges Rey disagrees with Dennett even though Rey himself is a qualia-eliminativist. "There seems to me every reason to think there are phenomena of *really seeming* that exist apart from merely the phenomena of merely *judging* one way or the other . . . [M]oreover (*pace* Dennett) things can seem to seem a certain way, and yet not seem that way at all. For example, as against Dennett's (1991) claims about there being no fact of the matter about whether it's the taste of beer or our preferences for it that have changed since childhood, it seems to me this could be settled by investigation of a person's gustation module, about which his superficial introspective judgments are perhaps hopelessly confused, mistaken or undecided" (Rey 2007, p. 119).

Consider Anton's syndrome, a bizarre disorder in which blind people believe they are normally sighted.[245] This is a stunningly mistaken judgment about the way one's experience *seems,* even though Anton's patients are of the "heartfelt opinion" that they can see. And Dennett himself cites "well-studied cases of subjects . . . who become color-blind but don't notice their new deficit, blithely confabulating and naming colors at chance without any recognition that they are guessing."[246] Such exotic syndromes show that even the most passionately-expressed opinion about visual seemings could be disconnected from actual sensory experiences.

Furthermore even normal individuals often learn to notice additional aspects of some familiar experience. One may carefully describe a musical tone, thinking that one has mentioned all consciously accessible aspects of the sound. But after another listener says, "I hear a lot of vibrato!" one thinks, "I was vaguely aware of this vibratory quality all along, but I wasn't focusing on it." One's thoughts about this experience had overlooked an aspect of the way the sound really seemed. In fact, if the vibrato had vanished before we noticed its presence, the sudden change might have led us to realize that it was there *before* it disappeared. Similarly most of us have retrospectively noticed a refrigerator hum immediately after it ceased.

If the eliminativist-in-chief hopes to persuade most philosophers that there is no difference between thinking one is experiencing a pink ring and actually experiencing such a ring, perhaps he should elaborate on his conception of thinking, judging, and having heartfelt opinions. (And perhaps he has.) As these terms are ordinarily used, they mean something very different from *having a perceptual experience.* Again, words may be getting in the way.

---

[245]Metzinger 1995a, p. 19. And Ned Block mentions "a variety of neurological syndromes in which patients confabulate – what they do or experience is at variance with what they think they are doing or experiencing. A prominent example is anosognosia in which blind patients think they see or paralysed patients think they are moving the paralysed arm. In some cases, it appears that the patient is hallucinating, but in other cases the disorder genuinely seems to be a disorder of thought . . ." (Block 2011a, p. 423).

[246]Dennett 2005, p. 98.

Dennett has waged a fine battle, hoping to banish the illusory ring and every one of its introspectable compatriots, but he cannot succeed. Every time we look at the back of his book, the ghostly ring that isn't there will stubbornly return.

Summing up

Daniel Dennett argues that we have been hoodwinked by an appealing idea that he calls the Cartesian Theater. He claims that this metaphor leads us astray, and that in reality our minds contain neither an audience nor a play. Introspection makes it seem as if both exist, but this is an illusion.

Although eliminativists can show that we make many incorrect statements about our own conscious experiences, this does not prove that consciousness is unreal. Nevertheless, when we engage in "autophenom-enology" we should remember that our judgments about our own inner lives are always somewhat removed from our actual experiences.

It's easy to poke holes in other people's accounts of consciousness, but hard to craft a theory that works. In the next six chapters I'll give it a try.

Chapter Nine
Seeing Through Our Useful Illusions

The first principle is that you must not fool yourself,
and you are the easiest person to fool.
— Richard Feynman[247]

Our maddening, magnificent quest

Dedicated scholars have spent decades searching for solutions to the Hard Problem, but this quest for a philosophical holy grail has led us into a maze of competing theories. How can we build upon what has been accomplished and move toward a solution?

Realistically, any accurate theory will probably include some peculiar aspects. As Schwitzgebel suggests, "it became evident in the late twentieth century (if it wasn't evident earlier) that all metaphysical accounts of consciousness will have some highly counterintuitive consequences. . . . *Something* apparently preposterous, it seems, must be true of consciousness."[248] So every horse in this race is likely to look ridiculous, but can any of these ludicrous nags make it to the finish?

In the next few chapters I will suggest an alternative which claims that conscious experiences are brain states, but my approach will be quite different from traditional internalism. At times I will drift close to outright eliminativism, and I expect vigorous reader feedback. Have I stepped over that perilous edge, descending into endless darkness and silence?

In attacking a traditional theory, critics sometimes go to an opposite extreme, in a sequence of thesis, antithesis, and synthesis. Sense data, the inner eye, and the theater of the mind are misleading theses, so various antitheses have been proposed. Some of these, such as the sharp-edged eliminativism of Dennett and the kinder, gentler eliminativism of Dretske and Tye, contain fine insights. But in denying first-person access to inner states, they lose contact with vital realities.

Although the inner eye metaphor is seductively misleading, it does contain kernels of truth. Conscious experiences put us in touch with

---

[247]Cited by Koch 2012, p. 159.

[248]Schwitzgebel 2011, p. x.

sensations and perceptions. When you or I have a visual afterimage, for example, we are aware of something that now exists, discovering an occurrent reality. We can, in some sense, inspect this entity, monitoring it as it changes colors and gradually fades away. But our access is limited by our own cognitive mechanisms. Introspection is not a magical ability that reveals sensory phenomena in their pristine actuality.

Subtle fundamentals

As we begin, here are some key considerations to keep in mind. First, remember the distinctions between current experiences, recollections of experiences, thoughts based on these recollections, statements that express these thoughts, and ways that these statements are understood within some linguistic community. As an example, think of being reunited with a loved one who has been in great danger. This episode involves:

1. What one experiences at the moment of reunion.
2. What we recall a millisecond later about these intense feelings.
3. Thinking about what those feelings were like.
4. Putting them into words: *"I'm just shaking with relief!"*
5. The ways that friends and family members interpret these words.

Whenever we say anything about experiential phenomena, we are already processing information at a certain distance from the episode we are describing. Discussions of philosophy of mind are based on beliefs which we can verbalize, and these beliefs arise out of complex and largely unconscious neural mechanisms. If my own stream of consciousness could talk, it might correct some of the things I say about it, but it cannot stand up for itself and proclaim its own nature.

One more preliminary – keep a sense of mystery in mind as you think about your own consciousness. Remember Daniel Dennett's comment that "we shouldn't do autophenomenology" because it tempts us "to take our own first-person convictions . . . as the undeniable truth."[249] I'm hearing quite a wail from the baby he's tossed out with the bath-water, but Dan is absolutely right to warn us that basing beliefs on introspection is risky business.

---

[249]Dennett 2005, p. 113.

Before I begin sketching my proposed solution, let's recap the question with which we began. *It seems as if some states of mind are "conscious" and others are not. Could these conscious experiences, in principle, be states of the brain?* These questions are especially hard to answer when we deal with sensations and perceptions. Here are six of the most stubborn puzzles about these sensory experiences.

First Puzzle: If consciousness is in our heads, why don't sensory experiences seem like brain processes?

Second Puzzle: Manifest presence. Why do perceptions and sensations seem to be "there?"

Third Puzzle: The explanatory gap. How can we show why a particular experience is constituted by a particular brain event?

Fourth Puzzle: When Mary sees colors, does she learn something new?

Fifth Puzzle: Are philosophical zombies possible?

Sixth Puzzle: Duality and misrepresentation. If *what* we experience and *our being aware of this experience* do not match, which is the "real" experience?

In praise of ruthless modesty

How well do we know our own conscious episodes? Here are four answers.

1. Infallibilism: We always know our experiences just as they are.[250]

2. Weak fallibilism: Our judgments about experiences are typically accurate, but we can make errors due to careless introspection or odd circumstances such as brain damage or strange stimulus conditions.[251]

---

[250]Bertrand Russell thought "that sense data are 'things with which we have acquaintance, things known to us *just as they are* . . .'" (quoted in Tye 2009, p. 97). But C. D. Broad thought that infallibilism about one's own experiences was "a curious superstition" (Rosenthal 1995, p. 368). Psychological and neurological research "suggests that the traditional assumption that the contents of consciousness are given to us directly and immediately must be wrong" (Metzinger 1995a, p. 19). Nevertheless, "we generally regard introspection as telling us the whole truth and nothing but the truth about our mental states . . ." (Baergen 1992, p. 107).

[251]Chalmers, for example, has maintained "that our judgments about experience

3. Strong fallibilism: In at least some cases we make important mistakes about our own experiences, even while paying careful attention.

4. Eliminativism: We are mistaken if we believe we can access an inner world of experiences. When we think we are aware of sensory phenomena, we are merely making judgments. We are not introspecting mental states.

I assume it's obvious by now that wondering whether our beliefs about our experiences are accurate is not the same as wondering whether our beliefs about external objects are accurate. That's another question entirely. If I'm hallucinating, I could correctly believe I am experiencing what looks like the fatal showdown between David and Goliath, but falsely believe that I am actually witnessing that Biblical battle.

Let's also be clear that our minds do not contain two different mechanisms for monitoring conscious states, one for detecting experiences *as* experiences and one for detecting states of the world. We only have one stream of consciousness. But we automatically interpret experiential phenomena as *both* "how things seem to me" and "what's really so." In seeing your mother's face, you know that "what it's like to see her now" does not include seeing the back of her head, but you also have a "what's really so" belief that all of her is there.

I will support a fairly strong version of experiential fallibilism, a "radical modesty" regarding our ability to know our conscious states. Such modesty about our own experience-judgments could, in principle, solve key aspects of the mind-body problem without the need for pan-psychism, dualism, externalism, eliminativism, or mysterianism. **In important ways, incorrect beliefs about conscious experiences lead us to deny that experiences could be brain events.**[252]

---

are accurate by and large, particularly when we are paying careful and patient attention" (1997, p. 37).

[252]Fallibilism does not mean that all judgments about our own states of mind are unreliable. Because we can often describe perceived objects with great precision, we know that our internal representations of these objects are finely detailed and precisely monitored. *Importantly, a monitoring system can reliably register the fine-grained particularity of an occurrence while wholly misconstruing important aspects of this episode.* For instance, one might introspect a particular visual experience in minuscule detail, without having any idea that fragments of this experience are located in dozens of places within the brain.

Many seemingly obvious features of awareness are beneficent illusions, tricks of mental magic. But we are both the cunning trickster and the wide-eyed rube that falls for the ruse. We continually pull rabbits out of our own hats, faithfully falling for friendly deceptions that help us navigate our dangerous world.

In the past 20 years, I have sensed an increasing openness to experiential fallibilism in the philosophical community. We are coming to realize that introspection involves an odd combination of precise access and egregious misjudgments. Many beliefs about conscious perceptions should either be suspended pending further consideration or rejected as seductive mistakes.

I will take a middle path between those who think their intuitions about consciousness are clearly correct and those who deny that introspection gives us any internal access. However an especially hazardous pitfall lies between these two extremes. It would be easy to say that introspection-based intuitions are correct when they support my favored theory, and incorrect when they do not! This is one reason I will value reader feedback.

We need more research and analysis to determine which introspective judgments tend to be on target and which are mostly off-base. For now, it seems likely that we usually do well at *detecting, recognizing, and noticing changes* in conscious sensory perceptions, including particular qualia. Sometimes we also make helpful *comparisons* among qualia. But we often make mistakes about other aspects of our experiences. Here are some errors that are particularly common and pernicious:

1. Confusing our experiences with our judgments about experiences.
2. Thinking introspection reveals the internal structure of experiences.
3. Thinking introspection reveals the essential nature of experiences.

Additions, omissions, and other mistakes

More Details: This section is optional, and not all of it pertains to the main thrust of my argument. But reflecting on these errors has helped me become more open to re-evaluating my own experience-judgments. First, consider some ways that we "see" more in the stream of consciousness than is actually there, confusing our opinions about experiences with the experiences themselves.

Additions; gilding the lily. In Chapter Two we saw that we overestimate the completeness of our own perceptions, especially visual perceptions. We conceptually augment the world of visual phenomena, thinking it contains more than it does. But here's a subtler form of augmentation. Every experience triggers myriad associations, some of which activate imaginative mental states that are overlaid on our perceptual states. We are mostly oblivious to these subtle augmentations because we are busy coping with real-world situations, so we confuse our judgments about an experience with what we actually discover there.

These inflationary judgments can exaggerate the similarities between experiences and physical objects. Then, since the experience is "obviously" object-like, we doubt that it could be neurally deployed. Seeing a tree, for example, may call forth memories, emotions, and impulses. These activate a detailed conception of what this tree is like, *and our concepts expand upon our percepts.* They amplify, and sometimes contaminate, our judgments about what we are now experiencing. For instance, my judgments about my experience of a particular tree is partly shaped by memories of tactile sensations. It is impossible to know how much my thoughts about the way a tree "obviously" looks are influenced by memories of the way trees feel to the touch. Similarly, notice that snow "looks" cold, but to me, the whitish top of a lemon meringue pie fresh from the oven does not.

An especially fortunate conceptual inflation allows us to detect sketchy perceptual information and take that to be a *person*, as in seeing someone's image on TV. As small children we interacted physically with parents and playmates for countless hours, and we remember how people look, act, feel, smell, taste, and sound. We infuse these memories (and project our own bodily sensations) into the persons we currently perceive – a useful mistake, since moving entities that superficially appear to be people typically *are* people.

Omissions. Now consider the opposite source of error. Instead of adding properties that are not experientially present, we may ignore properties that should be head-smackingly obvious. Most of us have noticed "floaters," tiny shreds of semi-transparent tissue in the eye. When a friend of philosopher Edmond Wright got sick, she "noticed them for the first time and attributed them to her illness, having never observed them before although they had been present throughout her life."[253] And E. J. Lowe notes that the visual field contains not one but two transparent images of the nose.[254] Most of the time I am unaware of these ghostly images – and yet when I roll my eyes downward and far to the right or left, an image of my proboscis is smack in the middle of my visual field! I look right through this diaphanous datum without being aware of it.

Other mistakes. In addition to augmenting and omitting some aspects of experiential phenomena, we may simply misjudge them, as when the supposed stability of visual experiences makes us doubt that such phenomena could be brain activities. (See Chapter Seven.) Later I will argue that certain beliefs about the ultimate nature of qualia are not well-founded.

By the way, there is some affinity between my "ruthless modesty" about our ability to know experiences and Colin McGinn's mysterianism. Both of us emphasize cognitive limitations that make it hard to understand inner states. But I think McGinn gets it exactly backward. As I see it, our cognitive limitations make it difficult to *establish* that there is an insoluble problem of consciousness and *clearly define* that problem, rather than preventing us from solving a well-defined conundrum.

❦ ❦ ❦ ❦ ❦ ❦

Importantly, there is no solid consensus about the extent of our additions, omissions, and other misjudgments, or the degree to which these mistakes disguise the true character of consciousness.[255]

The shell game and how to win it

We have seen that consciousness seems to require both being aware of something and the "something" that we're aware of. Take, for example, the flavor you enjoy while indulging in a glazed doughnut. This involves:

---

[253]Wright 2008, p. 18.

[254]Lowe 2008, p. 61. Is this example a conscious experience? What do you think?

[255]Georges Rey warns us that even though "we may indeed have privileged access to certain features of our mental lives, we still may not have privileged access to *just which features it is to which we have such access*" (1995, p. 124).

1. Being aware of the flavor.
2. The flavor you're aware of.
3. And perhaps some combination or blending of (1) and (2).

The flavor mentioned in item (2) is the flavor in our minds, the inner sensory quality. I am not talking about items in the outside world, such as the ingredients that make doughnuts scrumptious.

Earlier, we discussed Joseph Levine's insightful comments about the problem of duality. He says it is "deeply puzzling" that qualia "are simultaneously objects of, and acts of, awareness."[256] The taste of a doughnut, for example, seems to be both a particular quale *and* our being aware of this quale – an odd paradox. This "awareness relation . . . ought to entail that there are two states serving as the relevant relata, yet experience doesn't seem to admit of this sort of bifurcation."[257] Some have tried to make sense of this enigma by conjecturing that qualia are known, disclosed, presented, *by their very existence.* But how could one explain self-presenting phenomena in physical terms?[258] And here's the kicker: "Whenever we are dealing with a representational relation between two states, the possibility of misrepresentation looms."[259]

In Chapter Four, I mentioned this hypothetical case:

---

[256]Levine 2001, p. 174.

[257]Levine 2001, p. 168. And Kriegel writes that conscious experiences are "the *act* of awareness and the *object* of awareness all at once. It is presumably for this reason that conscious experiences are sometimes said to be *self-presenting*" (Kriegel 2005, p. 29). As Rosenthal reports, some have scoffed at this idea. "Being conscious is often thought of as a reflexive property of conscious states, as though such states were somehow conscious of themselves. Ryle vividly captures this idea with his disparaging metaphors of conscious states as 'self-intimating' or 'self-luminous'" (Rosenthal 1997, p. 738).

[258]Of course one part of a complex system could process information about another part of the same system. We humans do this in lots of ways. But it would be strange if an entity literally monitored itself, in the sense that its *being* in state S at time T constituted the act of *monitoring* the very same state S at the very same time T.

[259]Levine 2001, p. 108.

1. A person sees the color red and

2. Perceptually represents this color within the brain in an entirely normal way,

3. But due to some weird malfunction the experiencing subject, the part of the mind that is aware of this sensory experience, is in the same state it would normally be in while perceiving the color green.

In this bizarre state of affairs, *would the quale that one is experiencing be red or green? Or both? Or neither?*

If the quale is realized by an inner state which is the *object* of experience, one would be aware of the quale red while subjectively taking it to be green – and presumably thinking, speaking, and acting as if it is green, as well. To some, that seems ridiculous. But if qualitative character is realized by a state of the experiencing *subject*, the quale in question would be green. In that case we don't even need the object. Just the subject-state will do, and this may also sound silly.

I will later suggest that one of these absurd ideas actually makes sense. Which do you think I'll pick?

The mystery of consciousness is like a shell game, in which we try to say which nutshell hides a coin. Where do we find the *real* experience? We may think it's in *what* we're experiencing, a particular quale that we're attending to. This idea leads to puzzles, so maybe it's under shell number two, the subjective state of being aware of the quale. Still more puzzles. How about a compound-state consisting of both? But two different aspects of this state could slip out of alignment, causing the same problem to pop up again. Finally, out of desperation, we may imagine that the real experience is none of the above. Rather it is *the quale itself.* But that confuses matters further by adding a mysterious extra item. No matter which "shell" we turn over, searching for the real quale, we end up scratching our heads.

Fallibilism suggests a solution: Admit that since it is possible to make extreme mistakes about our own states of mind, one could, in principle, experience the color red, clearly and vividly, while subjectively misconstruing that quale in some highly dysfunctional way – e.g., sincerely believing that one is experiencing the color green.

We normally do know what colors we are experiencing. We're good at that, but the reliability of color introspection may tempt us to think that color judgments can't be grossly mistaken. In reality, people can be delusional about virtually anything. Some people firmly believe that they are dead, or that they have become someone else, or that their leg is not their own even though it is firmly attached to their bodies.[260] Therefore admitting that we can make profound errors about our own experiences helps solve the problem of duality.

But what would the experience be *like* if one grotesquely mis-construed one's own qualia? This malfunction could occur in many ways, and in some instances we may be able to know what the experience is really like. If we can determine that an Anton's Syndrome patient is totally blind, and we are able to rule out hallucination, we can say that what visual experience is like for this person resembles what visual experience is like for a blind person who is aware of being blind. But other cases would be harder to assess. If a traffic light is red, I should perceive it as red, think it's red, and act as if it's red. But I could also:

Perceive it as red, think it's green, and act as if it's green.
Perceive it as red, think it's green, and act as if it's red.
Perceive it as red, think it's red, and act as if it's green.
Perceive it as green, think it's green, and act as if it's green.
Perceive it as green, think it's green, and act as if it's red.
Perceive it as green, think it's red, and act as if it's red.
Perceive it as green, think it's red, and act as if it's green.[261]

If I roar through red lights even though I report that they look red, we would want to repair my cognitive and behavioral mechanisms so that I

---

[260]"There are patients with Capgras syndrome, who come to believe that people who are close to them (or, in one case, the patient's poodle) are imposters. We meet unfortunates with an intense desire to have their own healthy limbs ampu-tated, others who are paralyzed on one side but insist against all evidence that they are not, and, in Cotard's syndrome, people who sincerely believe they are dead" (Gottlieb 2011 p. 12).

[261]These options do not specifically refer to a state of the experiencing subject, but referring to thoughts seemed simpler and clearer than referring to the less familiar concept of subjective experience. In offering this list I am merely illustrating the manifold dysfunctional possibilities of human sensory experience.

respond normally to conscious perceptions. On the other hand, I might keep stopping at red lights that I am *experiencing* as red, even though I *think* they're green, baffled by the fact that I am inexplicably stopping when I'm sure the light says "Go!" In that case we would need to repair both my cognitive responses to my own color experiences and my behavioral responses to what I think. I'd probably want to see a specialist.

In short, at least some examples of the problem of duality can be explained in terms of erroneous judgments. This solution fits our usual way of describing the relationship between an information processing system and the information that it processes. On the other hand, the notion of self-presentation or self-intimation involves an exotic and mystifying relationship between that which detects and that which is detected. Such an extraordinary proposal calls for extraordinary evidence, so those who favor this line of reasoning must shoulder a substantial burden of proof. And as a rule, we should be skeptical of speculations which generate intractable philosophical disputes. If one claims that experiencing a quale requires both the quale as it is and the quale as we are aware of it, that is a fallible judgment rather than something that introspection clearly demonstrates. We can shut down the shell game by admitting that it isn't so.

That sounds good, but I still need to present an adequate alternative. I have argued that it is possible to consciously experience one quale and *think, speak, or act* as if it's another. That takes care of some kinds of misrepresentation. But what if I'm truly experiencing quale-red and yet the part of me that is aware of this experience is truly in the state it would normally be in if I were seeing green? *Which one is the real quale* and which one is the imposter? I'll address this issue in Chapter Twelve, going so far out on a limb that I'm resting on a twig. See if you think it holds me.

Is fallibilism plausible?

For some time after I became an experiential fallibilist, my mind kept re-assembling my old assumption that what experiences are like is just *obvious.* It reminded me of the way a rubber band returns to its original shape no matter how many times I stretch it. Thoughts would pop into my mind to the effect that *I do not "judge," in some fallible fashion, that my experiences are thus-and-so. I know what my experiences are like and that's the end of the matter.* I had to patiently remind myself that this very statement ("I know what my experiences are like") was generated by complex and fallible agencies within my brain.

To accept experiential fallibilism, we must allow our confident assumptions to dissolve into perplexity, admitting that no matter how carefully we focus on an experience, we might make major mistakes in describing its properties. One cannot achieve this perspectival revolution instantly, as if by flipping a mental switch. The brain balks at such a disorienting, vertigo-inducing cognitive shift.

Sensory experience is a deeply mysterious tangle of cerebral activities, out of which certain convictions emerge. To become relentlessly modest about our own experience-judgments, we must be willing to focus upon some current experience and sincerely entertain the idea that a seemingly-compelling belief about this experience may be erroneous.

Even if the brain continues to construct the belief that we know experiences just as they are, we can "look through" this belief and realize that it might be wrong. We can allow our preconceptions about consciousness to blur, to soften, to become flexible and yielding. When part of me still stubbornly maintains that I have near-perfect access to my own conscious processes, I can treat that belief as a mechanical production of the brain's "squadrons of simpletons," and reaffirm the value of ruthless experiential fallibilism.

Summing up

To solve the most intractable problems of consciousness, we can affirm the reality of internal, introspectable states of mind, while admitting that some of our deeply-held beliefs about these states may be mistaken. We can seek a middle ground between the conviction that introspection-based judgments about phenomena are always correct and the eliminativist claim that conscious phenomena do not exist. By maintaining a thoroughgoing and ruthless modesty about our own experience-judgments, we can explain several crucial mismatches between our descriptions of experiences and our descriptions of brain processes.

In general, we do well at detecting, recognizing, and noticing changes in conscious sensory perceptions, including particular qualia. But we also make mistakes such as the following:

1. Confusing our experiences with our judgments about experiences.
2. Thinking introspection reveals the internal structure of experiences.
3. Thinking introspection reveals the essential nature of experiences.

In this chapter we have considered examples of item 1. Items 2 and 3 are mainly explored in Chapters Ten and Eleven, respectively.

Chapter Ten
Shy Synapses and Bashful Neurons

Hide-and-seek inside of our heads

If experiences are brain states, one thing may seem glaringly absent: the brain itself. Why don't experiences seem like neural events? What makes our bashful brain states conceal their identities, donning dark glasses like incognito movie stars?

Many scholars dismiss the idea that introspection literally detects neural structures and activities. It surely doesn't *seem* as if consciousness grants us admission to the nonstop party our neurons are having in our skulls. But let's consider the alternatives. We can say that sensory experiences:

1. Are not brain states.
2. Are brain states but introspection reveals nothing about these states.
3. Are brain states and introspection reveals some things about them.
4. Are brain states and introspection reveals them just as they are.

There are respectable objections to all four options, but the strongest candidate by far is #3. It's especially easy to see this when we think of the *quantitative* aspects of experience. Suppose you dream that you have three hands. You wake up with a vivid visual memory of looking at all three, wondering where that third appendage came from. This series of events has given you access to something quantitative about the way your dream-experience was deployed. In that experience, there were not one, not two, but *three* of those mental configurations that you take to be hands. We can reasonably conjecture that when the brain assembled the hands in your dream, it constructed three patterns of neural activity that had certain relevant features in common.[262]

Even if experiences reveal some things about brain states, it is hard to say whether we can detect brain states *as such*. (It's even hard to say just

---

[262]Of course introspection alone did not show that the hands were brain states. It gave you good reason to believe that three similar states of some sort were occurring. Whether these were mental states, and whether mental states are brain states, must be decided on the basis of introspection plus other kinds of evidence. Later we'll discuss whether such visual representations are *pictorial*.

what it *means* to detect something "as such.") This is tricky terrain, and my suggestions are mostly tentative. But obviously our experiences could consist of brain activities even if we never access any of them *as* brain activities. That would be no more mysterious than looking at a rainstorm or a geranium without detecting the tiny particles of which they are composed. Furthermore it would have been very strange for evolution to shape consciousness so that we naturally and effortlessly take experiences to be brain states. Explicitly noticing our neurons at play would distract us from the outside world. We must be mostly blind to the neural nature of experiences in order for a tiger-perception to actually seem like a tiger.

I do think that in monitoring our own experiences we can sometimes catch signs of construction work in our Truman Show stage sets, but I don't want to overemphasize this idea. In general the brain does a fine job of concealing its own brainishness. It works like a shy stagehand, doing its job tirelessly but staying out of the limelight.

Before I say more about these issues, here are some strategies that have helped me accept the idea that we are consciously aware of our own cerebral processes. In my early explorations of consciousness I systematically practiced thinking of sensory experiences as mental states, and thinking of mental states as brain states. I considered such phenomena from a "giant brain" perspective, imagining myself embedded within that enormous information processing structure. I'll share two approaches that I found illuminating, but eliminativists and externalists may want to add red warning labels to my instructions: *CAUTION: Use of these exercises may lead to belief in a non-existent mental theater.* I am not frightened of this thespian metaphor, but I realize it can easily be abused.

✎ *Made out of mind.* For this experiment you'll need an activity you can carry out alone that involves varied sensory stimuli, such as gardening, jogging, watching TV, or dining alone (or with someone who isn't speaking to you). Focus first on auditory experiences, thinking of each sound-perception, *this is made out of mind.*

You can do the same with what you taste and smell, and your bodily sensations. You can also try this with visual experiences, although this is more difficult. Perhaps start by just focusing on colors. *"Purple of the iris blossom; this too is made of mind."*

✎ *Living inside your mind.* This one requires more concentration, so carry it out sitting, lying down, or walking, in a quiet area. Start by realizing that your current conception of your body is based on what you are now perceiving. You feel the body and you can see part of it. Play with the notion that the body as you perceive it is not your real body. It is an aspect of your own experience. It is like your real body in some ways, but quite unlike it in others. (For example, physical sensations only roughly simulate your skin and your innards.)[263] Then imagine that this body-perception is within your mind, by imagining your mind *surrounding* it – to the right and the left, in front and behind, above *and below* what seems to be "you."

If you wish, you can practice this discipline while entertaining the possibility that it is your brain that surrounds the experience in this manner.

Here are two variations on this theme. If, like many people, you tend to think of yourself as living behind your eyes, realize that this spot where you have imaginatively placed yourself is part of the body-perception. It is just as much a mind-made experience as your experience of seeing the wall in front of you. Your experience of your head is in the same mental "zone" as your experience of that wall. You can also try a mental adventure that I call *brain-walking* – going for a stroll inside of your cranium. Take a walk, noticing your body-perception ambling along through your town-perception and your foot-perceptions treading on your sidewalk-perception. And all of this is (with apologies to Michael Tye) *in your head.*

These exercises can help us see through the transparency illusion, the intuition that sensory experiences directly reveal the world around us. Every perception and sensation is made out of mind. Or so I think. Your experience may vary.

---

[263]For example, I seldom notice sensations in the back half of my lower abdomen, except for the skin in that area and some lumbar muscles that tend to be sore. But if I had kidney stones that region would wake right up.

Even if we practice construing consciousness in mental or neural terms, in several important ways our experiences seem to almost shout that they are *not* brain events. Let's consider one of these apparent discrepancies, a classic mismatch between the way we describe our own experiences and the way science describes the brain.

Clanging bread and the multi-modal finger-snap

One day at the grocery store I tossed a loaf of bread into my shopping cart. It landed with an enormous **CLANG**, and I was nonplused. The sound had clearly come from my shopping basket, precisely as the bread had landed – but bread doesn't clang.

I then realized that the loud noise had actually come from a gong near the cash registers, and was meant to summon additional cashiers. The sound originated thirty feet behind me, but my mind "located" it in the shopping cart beside me. The sight of the bread landing in the cart and the sound of the gong were two simultaneous perceptions, and I automatically judged them to be in the same location. I had fallen prey to the "ventriloquist effect, where a sound is heard to be coming from . . . the most likely *visible* source . . ."[264]

After my bread had strangely clanged, I began to reflect upon our access to the way experiences are structured. If I think of consciousness as an internal, mental process, it seems as if an auditory experience (the clanging sound) occurred at the same mental *location* as the visual experience of bread landing in the cart. Different sensory modalities quite commonly seem co-located. When I hold up my hand and snap my fingers, my visual perception of this action seems to occur at the very same spot as the tactile sensation, the kinesthetic experience, and the sound.

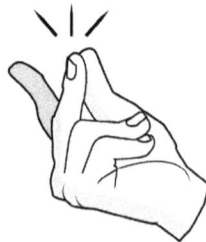

---

[264]O'Dea 2008, p. 304.

When the bread clanged, my experience wrongly represented the sound's real-world location. There is no such error when I perceive a finger-snap. But the four different kinds of qualia associated with the finger-snap – sight, sound, touch, and bodily movement – seem to be situated in the very same *experiential* space, even though science tells us that these four modalities are processed in different regions of the brain. This mismatch makes it seem as if sensory phenomena could not be neural in nature, but introspection-based judgments can be mistaken. In particular, I maintain that *introspection gets an F at detecting the internal structure of perceptual experiences.* It might seem as if experienced sights, sounds, and body sensations are located in the same spot, but we have no reason to believe that we would have evolved this sort of introspective access to experiential structure. In fact just the opposite is probably true, since accessing brain structures could distract us from what's happening around us.

There are other possible explanations of course. Eliminativism dismisses introspection as a little fairy tale that we tell ourselves. Dualism could say that if sensory events seem to occupy the same mental space, then this must be so. But we can also deal with the mismatch between introspection and scientific descriptions by saying that the co-location of sensory modalities is illusory.[265] Furthermore, if four sensory modalities that seem to coincide are instead located in four different brain spaces, then why not in four thousand or four million locations? Indeed science seems to show that the brain's sensory processings "are an inextricable swirl involving complexes of units all over the system."[266] Introspection barely hints at this possibility.

---

[265]In theory of course the brain could channel visual, auditory, tactile, and kinesthetic inputs into a pattern of neural activities that's all in the same brain region. I doubt that this is so, but this is a question for science to resolve. Aleksander and Morton comment on a similar example. "[A]n elemental event in the world such as a small moving green triangle stimulates representational neurons in different parts of the visual cortex: a colour area, a motion area and a shape area. How this integrates to provide a coherent sensation has always been a problem for neurophysiologists. This is the 'binding' problem" (Aleksander and Morton 2007, pp. 21-22).

[266]Kirk 1995, p. 403.

Sliced and diced: introspection detects selected brain states

If it does not seem as if consciousness gives us access to neural events, *what would experience be like if it did?* Think about that and see what comes to mind.

If we accessed the brain through conscious experiences, would we introspect the convoluted shapes of neurons? Would we marvel as we watch ion concentrations flowing across membranes? Would we wax lyrical about our darling little dendrites? Obviously not. An introspection mechanism need not monitor every physical feature of some collection of neurons. If introspection detects brain events, it detects *highly specific neural activities* rather than chunks of nerve tissue. Brain agencies that monitor experiences want to know what's relevant, nothing more. It would be bizarre to access cerebral metabolic processes, the length of neurons, or the links between nerve cells.

So neural activities are sliced and diced before they're put on our plates. We introspectively access selected aspects of neural activities that tell us about the outside world and some of our own bodily conditions and mental states. The rest falls away as if a sculptor had scraped excess material from a block of marble.

Let's take an example that some find difficult to explain. While seeing a light pink shirt and a dark blue shirt, side by side, we are in touch with very different visual qualia, two color experiences that almost seem like opposites. Yet it could turn out that the neural processes which constitute these states are similar to each other. Would this be a blatant mismatch between our descriptions of experiences and what science reports about the brain? Not necessarily. Even if the brain events that constitute our perceptions of light and dark colors closely resemble each other, *introspection need not give us complete access to each of these brain states.* Instead, introspection may mostly disclose ways in which these brain states *differ*, while concealing many similarities.

As an analogy, consider these two bar graphs:

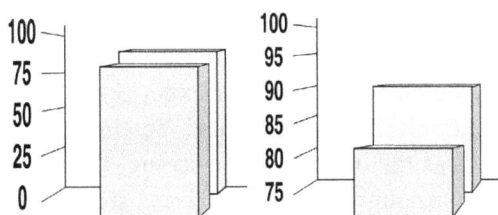

In each graph the front bar is at 80 and the back bar is at 90. But the display on the right hides most of the lower part of each bar, and that exaggerates the difference between them. This slanted presentation is a common propaganda device, and the brain could employ this strategy in benign self-deception. The key point here is that we only access "slices" of neural activity, not whole-hog neuronal complexes as if we were looking through a microscope. No wonder visual phenomena don't seem like neurons on parade.

Raw qualia remain out of reach

So conscious experiences don't appear to be brain states because we lack good introspective access to the physical structure of experiences, and because we detect complex slices of neural activity rather than whole globs of nerve tissue. And here's another problem. When we judge the way sensory experiences seem to us, this judgment is shaped by mental mechanisms beyond our control. For example, even babies are inclined to think of their perceptions as consisting of objects. It would be nice if philosophers could suspend this tendency and introspect their own perceptions "in the raw," but that is impossible. Certain meditative techniques may help to some extent, but our freedom to change the way our minds work is limited.

In thinking about consciousness, we can focus on our own experiences, form opinions about them, and put these ideas into words, but we cannot access experiences just as they are. We may learn more if we repeat the process more carefully, but we cannot know such phenomena in complete intimacy. They maintain a demure distance. We can sense that there is more to consciousness than we can articulate, and sometimes we can gain new insights into these familiar mysteries. But there are mechanical constraints on the way we can conceive of them, and these constraints tend to keep us from construing them as brain states.

Even so, it may be easier to think of experiences as physical if we focus on non-visual qualia such as sounds. We almost irresistibly think of visual experiences as the objects we're seeing. (That's an example of the way the brain creates our reality.) But if one listens intently to sounds, especially instrumental music and other non-verbal noises, they may very well seem to be highly abstract patterns – patterns that are constituted by some underlying medium that continually varies in complex ways. One fine candidate would be patterns of neural activity. In experiencing sounds we may be detecting those patterns.

In making judgments about qualia we must keep in mind the difference between these two ideas:

1. When we notice qualia we are detecting neural activities.
2. When we notice qualia we are detecting neural activities with the clarity and completeness of normal visual perception.

Option 2, of course, is based on the inner eye illusion, the idea that introspection enables us to describe mental states with the sort of detail, precision, and completeness with which we describe objects that we see in good light.

I want to carefully thread this conceptual needle, affirming the fact that we detect our own qualia and that qualia are brain events, while realizing that this detection process is quite different from typical perception and is at this point poorly understood. But once again, we are only dealing with the question of whether we can introspect sensory states *as* brain states. The issue of whether they *are* brain states is a different matter.

With visual perceptions, there is also the question of whether they are imagistic, configured as mental pictures. Perhaps this is an illusion, and our minds are just reading non-imagistic codes that we *think of* as pictorial. Since I deny that introspection gives us good access to the structure of experiences, I can accept this possibility and still say that we experience visual states. But I lean toward a pictorial view, and I'll discuss this issue in the following optional section.

Mind maps and brain maps, pictures vs. words

More Details: Sensory experiences often seem to be map-like. We see things as spread out in space, sounds seem to come from specific locations, and physical sensations map the body. At one time many would have thought it silly to suppose that visual perceptions and bodily sensations are *literally mapped* within the brain. But this is one point at which the testimony of introspection and neuroscience are beginning to coincide. Scientists have discovered many map-like arrays, including perhaps 30 visual maps, and body maps such as the "somatosensory homunculus."[267] The homunculus is very roughly shaped like the human body, and parts of it become activated when stimulated by tactile experiences in the corresponding bodily region. The little fellow in this diagram has been re-proportioned to show the relative sizes of brain areas devoted to sensations from different parts of the body. Evidently he types a lot.

The brain's tactile and visual maps are crude, preserving order but not precisely preserving size and shape.[268] Thus we cannot yet say that when

---

[267]Michael Tye notes the "orderly topographic representation of the surface of the human body that is dedicated to touch. Here adjacent regions of the body surface are projected onto adjacent regions of the cortex" (1995, p. 120). Tye also says that "the fact that the somatosensory cortex is topographically organized and that it is the primary locus of pain raises doubts about the sentential view of pain, because sentences do not have the requisite map-like representational structure. The obvious suggestion, then, is that pains themselves have a topographic or map-like structure. Likewise other bodily sensations and perceptual sensations" (Tye 1995, p. 121).

[268]Güzeldere 1995a, p. 353. "All the regions in visual ventral cortex are mapped topographically to the retina. In early visual cortex (V1) that mapping is

one sees what seems to be a perfect square, there is an activated brain region that is also perfectly square. But it is remarkable that even in these early days of neuroscience we already know that some patterns of brain activity are squarish. Later we may discover how the "slicing and dicing" process we discussed earlier cleans up our experiences, so that the outputs of cellular maps in the brain are experienced as virtually perfect geometric figures.

Even if there are squarish maps within the brain, it's hard to know whether we introspectively detect these physical features. I think we do, but some theorists believe that introspection is just a sort of thought to the effect that certain things are being perceived. Graphic data are translated into a series of 1's and 0's in digital computers, so maybe the brain does something like that too. In that case, what we detect in the brain when we see objects may be entirely non-pictorial. The graphic, shapely features of objects in the world may have been lost. Perhaps when we are experiencing something that seems to be shapely, we are merely in contact with a complex pattern of neural codes.

Philosophers are divided between pictorialists, such as Jerry Fodor and Stephen Kosslyn, and descriptionists such as Fred Dretske, Zenon Pylyshyn, and Daniel Dennett. "This dispute has now festered for almost a quarter of a century, with no resolution in sight."[269] Let's suppose I am looking at a photograph of Mahatma Gandhi. In that case, pictorialists suggest, my visual experience and the photo are both pictorial, spread out in space and arrayed so as to resemble what they represent. The photo resembles Gandhi, and my experience resembles the photo. One of these pictures is in a frame, and the other is in my brain.[270]

_____

precisely point-to-point, but cellular maps become fuzzier as we move to object regions" (Baars 2004, p. 31).

[269]Beeckmans 2007, p. 105.

[270]"Visual phenomenology seems to convey content in a way much more like a picture than a sentence if you ask me" (Seager 2013, p. 46). And of course both "picture" and "sentence" are analogies. Perhaps we need a different metaphor. For a readable explanation of pictorialism and descriptionism, see the Internet Encyclopedia of Philosophy entry, "Imagery and Imagination," by

Dretske said that if we look in the brain of a person who is seeing a dog, we find nothing doglike.[271] Pictorialists could reply that canine shapes are indeed present in numerous brain maps every time we glance at old Spot. Let's say that one seems to see a dog *but this experience is a hallucination.* In that case which interpretation is correct?

Dualism: There is a doglike shape in the mind, but not necessarily in the brain.
Eliminativism: We think we are in introspective contact with a dog-like shape, but we are not.
Pictorialist physicalism: There is a doglike shape in the mind, and the mind is in the brain.
Externalist representationalism: We are in a mental state which represents the notion that we're seeing a dog. But there is no dog image in the brain, and since we are hallucinating, we are not seeing a dog in front of us. In fact the dog shape that we think we are experiencing does not exist anywhere!

Imagistic transduction – how do we see Benjamin? Daniel Dennett uses a DVD analogy to critique pictorialism. DVDs incorporate two different transductions (translations from one informational format to another). To make a DVD we capture spatial and imagistic information from the surfaces of the objects being filmed, and transform that information into digital data. We then transform it back into a spatial and imagistic format which appears on a TV screen.

Suppose you're walking along and notice a small piece of green paper on the ground. Picking it up, you see a picture of Benjamin Franklin. It's a hundred dollar bill. Dennett says we transduce imagistic information about Ben's face into neural activity patterns, but denies that there is a second transduction back into visual imagery.[272] Here's the transduction sequence in more detail:

Amy Kind, which discusses these two theories vis-a-vis both mental imagery and normal visual perception (http://www.iep.utm.edu/imagery).

[271]Dretske 1995, pp. 34-36.

[272]Turausky 2014, pp. 224-25.

Surface features of the $100 banknote (spatial)
Pattern of photons reflected off of its surface (again, spatial)
Retinal pattern due to the impact of these photons (spatial)
Neural impulses traveling up the optic nerve (non-spatial?)
Numerous visual maps within the brain (spatial)
Visual experience of this banknote (spatial?)

I do not know whether optic nerve activity includes spatial/imagistic features, but certainly this is true of the brain's visual maps. So here's the contentious question. If there is a complex of brain-states which counts as a *subjective visual experience of seeing Ben's face,* is this neurally-constituted experience spatial and imagistic?

🐞 🐞 🐞 🐞 🐞 🐞 🐞

I am inclined to think that visual experiences are pictorial. Introspection gives us access to brain states which are (in some fiendishly convoluted manner) laid out in space like pictures. Here is a pertinent thought experiment.

Mending the shattered sunflower

Suppose that when we look at a dog we are accessing many visual maps in the brain, each of which contributes to our experience of seeing Fido. Even though all the information about how the dog looks to us is contained in these visual maps (and allied brain states), some doubt that these widely-distributed neural activities could count as being a visual image of a dog. This is an example of the complexity trap. Since neural activities are very, very complicated, and we think of visual images as being comparatively simple, visual experiences are not pictorial representations. Let's see how we can get out of that trap.

Imagine a 12-inch disk on which a dazzling sunflower has been painted in great detail. A video camera scans this disk and sends data about it to a computer, which prints the flower-image in excellent detail. By using this camera, is this computer able to monitor the entire image? Of course. Now using a glass cutter, we saw the flower in half. And now we have two cameras, each scanning half of the image, and computer software that can stitch them together. We already have technology that can do this quite well. Next, let's cut it into four parts, and use the same approach. Again, re-assemblage is no problem.

Finally, we drop the glass disk onto concrete, shattering it into a thousand pieces. Fortunately none of the disk is lost. In principle, it should be possible to apply the same strategy as before, with a thousand cameras and advanced software. Once again, the computer *would successfully monitor the image.* Similarly, conscious experiences may involve widely distributed perceptual states. Even if a visual perception draws upon a million components, these might be interconnected so that they function as a single state. Does this million-part neural event count as a single visual representation? I contend that it does. It is divided, as the disk was divided when we smashed it. But this complicated assortment of neural events may add up to a coherent image.

Fred Dretske, commenting on hallucinatory images, wrote: "I assume . . . that when a person hallucinates pink rats, the person is not aware of any *object* that is pink and rat-shaped."[273] This is of course true if by "object" one means standard-issue physical items such as rodents. We won't X-ray a brain and find that it's swarming with vermin. But if we acknowledge that images in the brain are deployed in highly convoluted ways, it seems entirely possible that some complex pattern of neural activities does amount to a rat-image. (The rat's pinkness is another matter. We'll consider colors and other qualia in Chapter Eleven.)

Are pictorialists right in saying the brain contains picture-like arrays? Or could the anti-imagistic descriptionists be correct? The jury's still out on this one. The point of the shattered sunflower metaphor is that a visual image could be distributed through the brain in an extremely complex

---

[273]Dretske 1995, p. 180.

manner *and still count as an image.* This removes one important obstacle to the idea that visual experiences are pictorial.

Summing up

I believe that conscious experience consists of brain events and that introspection detects these physical processes. But it's hard to know in what ways we can access brain states *as such.* Introspection is quite different from typical perception and it is not well-understood.

Perceptual experiences do not typically seem like brain states, nor should they. They should present the world rather than our own neuronal configurations. Thus we are mostly unable to detect the physical structure of the brain states which constitute experiences. For one thing, introspection does not reveal gross anatomical features such as dendrites and synaptic connections. If introspection detects brain events, it detects highly specific neural activities rather than chunks of nerve tissue.

In this chapter we have considered introspection-based errors about the way experiences are structured within the brain. Now we will turn to errors about the essential nature of experience. That will enable us to think more clearly about the explanatory gap, zombies, and what Mary discovered when she first saw red.

Chapter Eleven
Black-Box Agnosticism Demystifies Qualia

I appreciate the patience of my readers in waiting for this moment. After ten chapters, we're finally ready to discuss ontology. Sarcasm aside, I actually think you'll find this material interesting, even if you thought ontology was a medical specialty that deals with fearsome diseases.

Ontology, AKA metaphysics, studies the nature of things. What is real, and what are the basic kinds of entities, states, events, processes, properties, and so on? There are many ways of thinking about the true, authentic, essential, deep, really-real nature of things like tumbleweeds, tubas, time, space, statues, scorpions, softball games, quarks, quarrels, clouds, persons, and panic attacks. We can slice up the reality pie in lots of ways, but this chapter will consider one key question. Can we learn about the ontology of conscious experiences – especially sensory experiences – through introspection?

Does introspection disclose the deep nature of qualia?

As you can probably guess, I think the answer is "No." It may seem as if we can directly grasp the essence of sensory experiences, but this is a crucial mistake. Using introspection to make judgments about the ultimate nature of conscious phenomena can be terribly misleading. If we view such judgments with skepticism, while affirming that sensory experiences are real and introspectable, some of the hardest problems of consciousness can be dissolved. That sounds good, but this is not an easy or intuitively obvious pathway. It requires carefully questioning certain beliefs that seem self-evident.

When ancient philosophers wondered about the basic nature of things, they had few resources for dealing with this issue. They could guess that ice and water were made of the same material, since they could see them change into each other. But for the most part they could only speculate. Some believed that everything was made of four basic ingredients – earth, air, fire, and water. We have made progress in dealing with this sort of question, but when we ask about the nature of consciousness we are still, for the most part, in pre-scientific days.

It may seem as if we have direct access to the deep nature of sensory experiences. Some have claimed that when we experience pain, for instance, we learn what pain *really is*. "Qualia wear their content on their introspectively manifest sleeve," write George Graham and Terry Horgan, "in such a way that what you introspect about [qualia] is, essentially, how they are."[274]

Actually it may not even make sense to say we can know what something is "essentially" or "in itself." Many believe that our knowledge is always based upon the way things affect us, or affect things we know about, such as thermometers and weighing devices. Even down at the level of quarks, physicists only know how quarks impact their instruments. Based on those measurements they theorize about how quarks fit into their picture of reality, but they cannot say what one of these subatomic specks *is,* in any ultimate sense.

Regardless of whether things can be known in themselves, there is a less mysterious way of telling what they are. We can sort them into categories that make theoretical sense. We categorize gold and tin as minerals, aardvarks as animals, petunias as plants. So in that more limited way, can we tell what our own experiences are by reflecting on what they seem like to us?

This is an example of the sort of "autophenomenology" that Dennett warns us against, and in this case his warning is well taken. Based upon introspection, people have characterized qualia as:

---

[274]Graham and Horgan 2008, p. 103. Similarly, Christopher Hill notes that when it comes to qualia, some philosophers think that an appearance-reality distinction would be absurd. To them "it seems impossible to draw a distinction between the appearance of a pain and the underlying reality. In the case of pains, it seems, the appearance is the reality" (2005, p. 153). "Chalmers argues that we have a concept of primitive phenomenal properties (such as redness) that we are acquainted with in a way that transparently reveals their intrinsic nature. Others have argued that it is exactly this conception of consciousness that is the trouble" (Brown 2013, p. 118). Galen Strawson (2011) states quite baldly that "we know the intrinsic nature of consciousness . . ." Cf. Strawson 2006: ". . . we can be certain both that there is experience and that we can't be radically in error about its nature" (p. 6). Kenneth Williford, however, finds it "very plausible . . . that consciousness has various sorts of properties that are introspectively inaccessible to it" (Williford 2006, p. 119).

- non-physical[275]
- non-spatial
- unified, in a way that seems physically impossible[276]
- constituted by a spiritual substance[277]
- inherently subjective[278]
- inherently qualitative; impossible to analyze in quantitative terms
- impossible to describe in terms of structure and function[279]

Some also assert that conscious sensory events are part of a cosmic mind, or are "the only true reality."[280] All of these are introspection-based ontological claims, at least in part, *and all of them have been used as evidence that experiences cannot be neural activities.* But such judgments may be highly unreliable. For example, one might be good at knowing precisely when one's experience of pain intensifies but utterly confused about the fundamental nature of pain. Here are five arguments supporting such skepticism:

The first problem is that introspection presents ambiguous evidence about the ultimate nature of experiences. Sensory phenomena do not carry little I.D. cards that announce their ontological nationality. In fact it is distressingly evident that intelligent and well-informed commentators flatly contradict each other about the "obvious" nature of qualia. Virtually

---

[275]Levine (2001, p. 129) cites and disputes this claim, as well as Descartes' contention that mental states are non-spatial.

[276]Michael Pauen states that "one of the fundamental intuitions of dualism" is "the idea that the unitary character of first-person mental experience cannot be accounted for in naturalistic terms, given the immeasurable multitude of neural activities" (2011, p. 95). The noted dualist Sir John Eccles contrasted "the undoubted unity of my conscious experience" with the brain's "neurological events of the utmost diversity and complexity" (Cotterill 1995, p. 290). Eccles' belief in the unity of consciousness was probably grounded in reflections about his own experiences, yet Buddhists and followers of David Hume do deny the unity of consciousness.

[277]This is of course a common teaching of those religions which maintain that human consciousness survives death.

[278]Levine 2001, p. 7.

[279]Chalmers 1997, p. 6.

[280]Noted (but not asserted) by Güzeldere 1995b, p. 32.

all of the ontological claims cited above are controversial. This Babel of conflicting opinions should make us think more than twice about trusting our own intuitions regarding these matters. I agree with Georges Rey that "our understanding of the metaphysics of what we introspect may be as theoretical a matter as any."[281]

Second, in over 20 years of studying consciousness I have seldom encountered a careful and thorough attempt to establish the claim that introspection reveals the metaphysical nature of qualia. Those who think this is so seem to believe it is just obvious, and that no further discussion is necessary. But such an important principle requires substantive evidence and analysis.

Third, there is no obvious reason why we would have evolved the ability to assess the ontology of experiences. What would be the fitness advantage in skillfully detecting the essential nature of qualia? By comparison, it is useful to tell whether a sensory state involves perceiving, recalling, imagining, or dreaming. The evanescence of some dream imagery helps us realize that "it was only a nightmare" and the faintness of most pain-recollections helps us know we are remembering a previous pain rather than being hit with another migraine. But there is little or no survival value in knowing whether introspectable perceptions, memories, fantasies, and dreams are all made of the same sort of "stuff," and what sort of stuff that is. One can believe qualia are physical, mental, or spiritual, or be entirely uninterested in their true nature, and still cope well with everyday tasks. Thus it would be surprising if we were good at introspecting the essential nature of experiences – not impossible, but remarkable.

Fourth, some say that qualia are ineffable, i.e., they possess properties which cannot be expressed or communicated. These ineffable properties are often said to be the same properties that are metaphysically problematic. But how could we make metaphysical judgments about an utterly

---

[281]Rey 1995, p. 127. I admit that introspection is a useful source of ontological hypotheses. If reflection on one's own experience suggests that qualia have some non-physical feature, we should investigate that possibility. But we should not evaluate such hypotheses primarily on the basis of subjective intuitions. Instead, we should base qualia-beliefs upon multiple sources of evidence, including the findings of science.

inexpressible property? If we cannot say anything about some aspect of qualia except to vaguely compare it to other ineffable items, perhaps we don't know much about it at all.

And fifth, the hunch that qualia are ontologically troublesome may be partly based on another hunch that is almost certainly wrong, the idea that judgments about our own sensory experiences are always, or almost always, correct. As we've seen, there is strong evidence that we make mistakes about sensory states, especially when we try to do more than just detect, recognize, and notice changes in such phenomena. Using intro- spection to divine the nature of qualia goes far beyond these practical matters.

I find these five arguments compelling, but what could be said in reply? One could maintain that even though ontological intuitions are of doubtful reliability, introspection does show that qualia are ontologically *special*. When we pay attention to experienced colors, tastes, and so on, we are in contact with remarkable phenomena, mental essences that are different from anything discovered by science. This is one reason the Mary scenario is so persuasive. People often think that in experiencing colors Mary learns something that transcends any possible scientific finding.

I agree that this is how it seems, and I do not dismiss this idea as being silly or incoherent, but I still think it's false for the reasons I have listed. Furthermore, after becoming accustomed to "radical modesty" about my own experience-judgments, I can readily imagine my onto- logical intuitions about qualia being incorrect. I'm not as locked in to them as I used to be.

Students of consciousness are caught in a conceptual tug-o'-war. On the one hand, we may have powerful convictions about the deep nature of sensory experiences. On the other hand, these metaphysical hunches have a miserable track record, and they lead to irreconcilable disputes based upon dueling intuitions. I have chosen to deal with this dilemma by becoming quite skeptical about subjectively based ontology claims, but I respect those who say that this is too high a price to pay. And I find it much easier to believe that we detect qualia without accessing their deep nature than to believe that we do not detect qualia at all (eliminativism), or that they exist only as stories we make up about the external world (externalist representationalism).

In *Purple Haze* Joseph Levine advocates "modest qualophilia." He maintains that qualia are real, but he offers a penetrating critique of "bold" qualophilia. "The bold qualophile believes that certain metaphysical claims can be established on the basis of what is presented in experience. For instance, it is often claimed that qualia couldn't be physical properties, or that they are simple, unstructured properties. . . . Descartes claimed to demonstrate that extension was no part of the essence of a thinking thing, and the mind was indivisible by nature. These are bold, metaphysical claims, and I, as a modest qualophile, do not feel they are warranted by what is presented in experience. . . . it is always possible that what is presented within first-person experience embodies errors of all sorts."[282]

Well said. Qualia are both familiar and mysterious, routinely detected in every waking moment, but not easily understood from the first-person perspective. As I mentioned earlier, an information processing system may monitor something precisely and consistently, without knowing exactly what is being monitored. This is our predicament in knowing qualia.

Are experiences homogenous?

More Details: Let's consider an example of an introspection-based ontological judgment. Some philosophers believe that qualia do not consist of simpler ingredients. In other words, it is impossible to subdivide a quale into anything except smaller units of the same quale. It's homogenous, all the way down. But it makes no sense for homogenous qualia to be a complex cluster of brain events. Even so, any time one thing detects another, it may leave out important details. Look at your carpet. You detect it, but you do not detect its atomic components. Failing to notice protons and electrons does not show that you have encountered a strange nonphysical object. So why should we think introspection can tell whether qualia have tiny sub-components that are actually states of the brain?[283]

---

[282]Levine 2001, p. 129. He also remarks that "when it comes to essences, or natures, we have no special epistemic access even in the case of our own mental states" (p. 138).

[283]As Christopher Hill maintains, "perceptual representations of yellow do not put us in touch with its quantitative and structural dimensions"(2006, p. 271).

Here's my low-budget takeoff on Dennett's pink ring example. Look inside this rectangle and find an area that triggers a uniform color experience, a spot where the paper's whiteness seems uniform.

If your experience of that spot is homogenous, this may seem to show that it could not be a pattern of neural activities. Neural events are extremely complicated, so how could they generate such experiential uniformity? But this is a classic example of the inner eye illusion. It's easy to think that the way this paper "appears" is a datum that is delivered to us by introspection exactly as it is, *directly*, with nothing left out. However when we talk about conscious experiences we are inevitably processing information at some distance from the experiences we are discussing.

It would be nice if we could push aside our thoughts about consciousness and hand our experiences little microphones so they could speak for themselves. And it may seem as if we can reach past our judgments and embrace our own qualia, but the mind doesn't work that way. If we attend to a visual experience and find ourselves believing that it appears to be absolutely uniform, we have little basis for saying that this is correct. Speaking for myself, I am no more inclined to say that color experiences are homogenous, based upon introspection, than I am to announce, after staring at some patch of red paint, that it obviously does not consist of quarks.

❦ ❦ ❦ ❦ ❦ ❦

Here is a striking example of the way a quale can seem to be just one thing, when it actually consists of distinct components. Many believe that pain is inherently unpleasant, so that pain qualia always contain an "ouch" component.[284] If a pain quale didn't include an ouch, it wouldn't be pain, would it? But chronic-pain patients who take morphine (or, in the past,

---

In addition, both C. L. Hardin and Robert Van Gulick have maintained that qualia are "quite complex, structured states" (Levine 2001, p. 95).

[284]For an astoundingly self-confident statement of this thesis see Goldstein 1994.

have received surgical lobotomies) often "say that their pain remains but no longer bothers them."[285] What's even stranger is a rare syndrome caused by strokes called pain asymbolia. "When burnt or pinpricked, asymbolics deny that their experience is unpleasant; and they exhibit no sign even of suppressed urges to withdraw or grimace or cry out. On the contrary, they often smile and laugh. Hence it looks as though their experience is at worst neutral, and therefore as though they are not in pain. Except, crucially, they say they are."[286] They "experience a sensation which they identify as pain even though it is not intrinsically unpleasant . . ."[287]

"Brand and Yancey recalled a surgeon who performed a lobotomy on a woman suffering under extreme vaginal cramps." When the surgeon followed up with her years later, she said the pain "is still there. I just don't worry about it anymore. . . . In fact, it's still agonizing. But I don't mind."[288] Importantly, these patients can identify pain when it occurs and "can distinguish different pains, like pricks, heat, or pinching, as well as rate its intensity and location. . . . These are tasks a true analgesic, someone who feels no pain, cannot master. They are also not rationally impaired: once they realize that permanent damage might occur due to a painful stimulus, they can retract. But it is not the feeling of pain that elicits this reaction. It is an additional cognitive evaluation."[289] Evidently it is quite possible to have a pain without having an ouch.

In short, we should be skeptical of ontological judgments based upon introspection, *particularly when competent theorists disagree.* Since introspection seems pitifully ineffective as a guide to the nature of ex-

---

[285]Bain 2011, p. 172.

[286]Bain 2011, p. 173.

[287]Fink 2011, p. 47.

[288]*Ibid.* "Similar experiences of pain without unpleasantness have been also reported by meditators and those in a hypnotic trance, e.g. during dentistry . . ." (Fink 2011, p. 54). See also Nikolinakos 1994. It is, of course, difficult to know whether the quality of the pain they experienced after treatment is the same as it was previously. What is clear is that these patients testify that they are experiencing states with a painful quality that is the same as or similar to pain states they have had before, and that these current pain states do not bother them.

[289]Fink 2011, p. 47.

periences, we should beware of using introspection-based ontological judgments to baffle ourselves with endless philosophical squabbles.

Although this chapter primarily deals with qualia, skepticism about ontological judgments is a powerful tool for dealing with other issues as well. Consider this diverse list of ontological assertions. Experiences are *non-spatial, unified, inherently subjective, inherently spiritual,* and/or *part of a cosmic mind.* One could make any of these claims based upon introspection without expressing them in terms of qualia, or even while rejecting the concept of qualia as incoherent. But introspection is a rickety foundation for establishing these claims.

Black-box agnosticism bridges the gap

Now let's go back to the explanatory gap that we discussed in Chapter Four. It seems as if we cannot explain how differences among qualia could be constituted by differences among neural activities. In particular, how could we explain why some brain event is one particular quale instead of another, e.g., quale-red instead of quale-green? Joseph Levine emphasizes that the explanatory gap is epistemological rather than ontological. In other words, it has to do with what we know about qualia and how we know it, but it is not intended to prove that qualia are non-physical. He himself thinks that qualia are states of the brain, and that we do not understand how this could be so.

Although Levine and I are both skeptical about knowing the ultimate nature of conscious experiences, my analysis has taken me in a somewhat different direction. If there is, as he says, an unbridgeable explanatory gap, certain properties of qualia must be inherently impossible to explain. But *which properties would these be*, if introspection reveals little about the ontology of sensory experience? If we talk about experiences in ways that do not suggest the existence of ontologically peculiar entities, no explanatory gap appears.

Levine has candidly confronted the possibility that his concerns about the gap are grounded in an outdated model of introspection. He asks whether that which seems to be "unexplained by current materialist theories" may be "precisely those properties in which I claim not to believe"[290]– i.e., properties revealed through a direct, "Cartesian" access to experiences. I will try to show that this concern is well-grounded. It seems as if there is an explanatory gap because we think introspection gives us information that it does not.

Suppose that in the future we know with great confidence that a pattern of neural activity called **NA73** constitutes the quale "red." The human experience of redness is *literally identical* to NA73. We then ask why NA73 is redness instead of, say, blueness. And suppose that in considering this issue, we make no introspection-based judgments about the essential nature of redness or blueness. Then ontologically speaking, from the first-person perspective, these qualia become like black boxes.

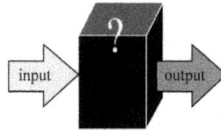

input   ?   output

We call something a black box if we cannot access and investigate its components. We must be mostly agnostic about what's inside, and from this agnostic position we must be skeptical of confident assertions about the box's contents. Of course, some things about our own qualia are accessible to us. I can notice when one quale morphs into another, for example. A spicy taste that lingers for a long time may eventually become unpleasant, so that it seems like a different flavor. *Therefore I am not saying qualia are black boxes in every way. It is the ontology of our own qualia that fits the black box analogy.*

If we think of the experience of redness as a label for something in a black box, something with an unknown nature, several philosophical puzzles just fall away. We only become puzzled if we think we know what a quale fundamentally *is,* or what it is *not* – e.g., "it's obviously not physical."[291]

---

[290]Levine 2001, p. 131. Levine also writes, "I must admit I find it hard to see how qualia could actually be identical to physical properties. Yet, [this] does come into conflict with other considerations that are equally compelling. In particular, it seems to be based on a kind of Cartesian model of access to the facts, one that blurs the line between epistemology and metaphysics" (2001, p. 91).

[291]Despite his doubts about whether we can introspectively access the ontology

Because this point is so crucial I'll elaborate on it, even though this is a rather technical topic. For black-box agnosticism, the following statements are equivalent:

A. We must explain why the experience of redness is constituted by one set of neural processes and the experience of blueness is constituted by another.

B. We must explain why the ontologically indeterminate entity we call "experienced redness" is constituted by one set of neural processes and the ontologically indeterminate entity we call "experienced blueness" is constituted by another.

Statement "A" persuasively implies that explaining color qualia involves a disturbingly deep puzzle. But the puzzle vanishes in "B." Before we decide whether B suggests an explanatory gap, we must say more about the two ontologically indeterminate entities. Otherwise we have no idea what we are trying to *explain*. If we replaced "ontologically indeterminate entity *red"* with "non-physical red soul stuff," there would be no physical basis for the difference between this entity and "non-physical blue soul stuff," but that's because we are saying that these qualia are non-physical soul stuff rather than brain states. We now have an ontological mismatch between color qualia and brain events rather than an apparent, epistemological mismatch. The point becomes "qualia and neural activities aren't the same," rather than "we think they're the same but we can't say why."

On the other hand, if we replaced "ontologically indeterminate entity *red"* with "neural states that constitute the experience of redness," we would not wonder about the physical basis for the difference between this quale and neural states that constitute a blueness experience. The neural state and the experience would be identical in a way that requires no additional explanation. *So the entire analysis of B depends on how we fill in the blanks.* Until we do so, there is no reason to be perplexed.

"A" does not baldly assert that introspection discloses an odd sort of ontology. But in reading that sentence it's easy to inject an unstated ontological judgment, so that "A" becomes, "Since the experiences of

---

of qualia, Levine has not gone all the way to black-box agnosticism. "We are not just labeling some 'we know not what' with the term 'reddish,' but rather we have a fairly determinate conception of what it is for an experience to be reddish" (Levine 2001, p. 84).

redness and blueness *seem to have a special nature that is quite different from neural activities,* we must explain why redness is constituted by one set of neural processes and blueness is constituted by another." Although such ontological judgments are highly suspect, they are insidiously appealing.

More Details: Although some philosophers doubt that their discipline makes progress, I notice an increasing openness to fallibilism about experience-judgments these days, compared to 10 or 20 years ago. Of course I view this change as positive, and I predict that we will continue to move in this direction.[292] Three widely-discussed examples of this openness to fallibilism are Daniel Stoljar's *Ignorance and Imagination: The Epistemic Origins of the Problem of Consciousness*, Eric Schwitzgebel's *Perplexities of Consciousness,* and Derk Pereboom's *Consciousness and the Prospects of Physicalism.*[293] Today those who discuss those books are unlikely to flippantly dismiss them by claiming that the nature of qualia is just obvious.

Pereboom's book[294] proposes the *qualitative inaccuracy hypothesis.* When we think about sensory experiences, "introspection represents phenomenal properties as having certain characteristic qualitative natures, and it may be that these properties actually lack such features."[295] I would

---

[292]In 2001 I submitted a paper to a philosophical journal, in which I argued that introspection-based metaphysical judgments are unreliable. An anonymous referee called my position extreme. But in 2006 a well-known philosopher read my draft paper on Ontological Agnosticism and the Hard Problem of Consciousness. Even though he does not go as far with ontological agnosticism as I do, he agreed that my approach was a defensible option.

[293]Stoljar 2006, Schwitzgebel 2011, and Pereboom 2011. I appreciate Stoljar's analysis, but at one key point he and I go in opposite directions. He suggests that we do not understand how qualia could be physical because we do not understand the physical world well enough. He disagrees with those who say we have "a mistaken conception or picture of experience . . ." (2006, p. 10), and that is exactly what I maintain. Our mistake is not, as Stoljar suggests, a *lack* of knowledge of the physical world, but rather an *overconfidence* in our knowledge of the mental world.

[294]Thanks to Rocco Gennaro for alerting me to Pereboom's *Consciousness and the Prospects of Physicalism.*

[295]Pereboom 2011, p. 3.

put it a bit differently. Some who are philosophically sophisticated believe that qualia seem to have properties that brain states lack. But I do not agree that these beliefs are *mandated by the data of introspection.* That is, I think we can remain 100% faithful to what we find during introspection, without thinking qualia have non-physical properties (or properties that are hard to fit into physicalism). Introspection focuses our attention on current experiences, and we *then* make various judgments about them. We may, for example, say that they manifest some mysterious essence that seems to be irreducibly mental.[296]

Pereboom's *Consciousness and the Prospects of Physicalism* is an erudite and meticulous work that puts consciousness studies into historical perspective. References to Descartes, Leibnitz, Locke, Hume, and Kant abound. Bertrand Russell's speculations also echo through these pages, because Pereboom suggests that we might comprehend consciousness through "Russellian monism."[297]

Rather than advocating one view of consciousness, Pereboom proposes that either (1) experiences seem non-physical because we misjudge them or (2) the mysterious nature of experiences can be explained in Russellian terms. Obviously I applaud option one, and I would love to see him develop a detailed positive argument for his qualitative inaccuracy hypothesis.

❦ ❦ ❦ ❦ ❦ ❦ ❦

---

[296]McClelland explains that for Pereboom, qualia "*appear* to be metaphysically simple properties whose entire qualitative essence is revealed in introspection, but it is an open possibility that this does not reflect the true nature of those properties" (McClelland 2013b, p. 195). If by "appear to be metaphysically simple" he means "are sometimes *judged by philosophers* to be metaphysically simple, based upon introspection," he and I are probably saying the same thing.

[297]Russellian monism maintains that there is some currently-unknown underlying reality which provides the basis for both mind and matter. Some neo-Russellians say this underlying reality is basically physical, some say it is basically mental, and some say it is neither physical nor mental. "Pereboom ultimately encourages the 'protophenomenal' view that those properties are non-experiential physical properties that ground both microphysical properties and phenomenal properties" (McClelland 2013b, p. 198).

Anti-physicalist intuitions may be based on *the special-essence illusion*. Even if we're not sure what qualia are, we're sure they're very, very special. We can contrast two ways of thinking about this issue – qualia as ontologically evident and as ontologically veiled, or opaque.[298] The veiled view of qualia sees them as existing, as being knowable through introspection, and as ontologically obscure. Introspection does not tell us whether qualia are neural activities, sense data, interconnected units of soul stuff, or the entrails of a black hole.

Thinking of experiences as ontologically veiled fits the idea that judgments about qualia are always somewhat removed from what we are experiencing. We reach out toward realities that we cannot fully grasp. In a sense, our first-person knowledge of mental processes functions from the "outside," as it does in our perception of the external world. And just as my firm conviction about the shape of some visible object may be incorrect, my judgments about my own experiences may be both compelling and erroneous.

Ontological agnosticism is a powerful tool for solving several problems of consciousness, and David Papineau mentions one implication of a similar idea. "Maybe the reason zombies seem possible is just that conscious properties seem ontologically extra to physical properties . . ."[299]

Now let's apply ontological skepticism to another famous thought experiment and go . . .

---

[298]In saying that experiences are ontologically veiled I do not mean that an inner eye of introspection sees a veil which blocks our ability to see the experiences themselves. That would suggest that the real quale, the apparent aspect of sensory awareness, is the veil, and that is not what I'm getting at. I am simply saying that we cannot accurately specify the ontological properties of experiences by means of introspection. We access *something,* but its nature is obscure.

[299]Papineau 2007. McClelland notes that Pereboom's approach is similar. In imagining the possibility of zombies, "we are not imagining a scenario that lacks phenomenal properties *as they really are.* We can imagine microphysical duplicates of our world that are stripped of the phenomenal properties that *appear* to be instantiated in our world. However, the claim is that a world like ours microphysically but without the phenomenal properties that they *really* have is not ideally conceivable" (McClelland 2013b, p. 196).

Back to the rose garden

Recall the case of Mary from Chapter Five. When Mary exclaims, "Aha! *That's* what this rose's red color is really like," it may seem obvious that she has new information that doesn't fit the physicalist world-view. But with ontological agnosticism, the mystery vanishes. Ontological agnosticism admits that we may be good at categorizing our experiences. We do a splendid job of telling heartburn sensations from an itchy sunburn and telling the taste of fresh milk from milk that's gone sour. But we may have no idea what color experiences and taste experiences actually *are*. As a result, our qualia concepts act as ontological placeholders, philosophical wild cards, identifying experiential states while "leaving blank" the essential nature of those states.

Before we decide whether Mary's new experience reveals some exotic entity she never knew before, we must consider different ways of filling in the blank. Perhaps her experience will convert her to dualism, so that she fills in the blank by saying, "I am now convinced that redness is a non-physical entity." She therefore claims that there's an ontological gap between this experience and anything physical science could say about the brain. But there is neither a knowledge-gap nor an ontological gap *if she simply remains agnostic about the metaphysical status of her experience.* She will have detected an internal state that she has never introspected before, and that affects her in striking new ways (Wow! So those are colors!!), but that doesn't show that she has encountered a mysterious non-physical substance.

The Mary scenario depends heavily upon the special-essence intuition, the conviction that first-person experience reveals mental states with essential natures that are unusual and perplexing. Since first-person experience is a shaky basis for making this sort of judgment, this thought experiment loses its persuasive force.[300]

That's easy for me to assert, and I am confident that it's true. But it is also counterintuitive. When I see red, or hear a harp, or feel a throbbing headache, it does sometimes seem as if I am encountering phenomena that

---

[300]McClelland discusses a similar idea, quoting Pereboom. "On leaving her monochromatic room, Mary does acquire a new belief that the phenomenal property characteristic of seeing red has that mysterious qualitative nature 'R'. However, '[o]n our open possibility phenomenal redness has no such qualitative nature, so this belief will be false'" (McClelland 2013b, p. 195).

don't fit into the physical world. To solve the Hard Problem we must realize that our impression of encountering special, non-physical phenomena rests upon a flimsy foundation. This realization needs to attain the level of an actual "AHA!" – the kind of clarity a cartoonist would represent by drawing a big, bright light bulb in a thought balloon. If all we can muster is grudging assent – "OK, OK, I get it" – we will find ourselves thinking the same thing tomorrow that we thought yesterday. "Well *of course* Mary learns something new." The rubber band returns to its customary length, and we're back to square one.

Summing up

Several strands of the problem of consciousness grow out of the special-essence intuition. It may seem, for example, as if the sensory quality of turquoise blue is an odd whatchamajigger that could not possibly be identified with what my neurons are doing. But I deny that introspectors are good at assessing the way qualia "really are." For example, we may be good at knowing precisely when we are experiencing pickle tastes, but clueless about the ontology of taste qualia. Hence I disqualify myself from making confident introspection-based judgments about such issues, and I encourage others to do the same. In general, subjective intuitions about the deep nature of qualia should be treated as conjectures rather than dependable discoveries.

Ontological agnosticism enables one to say, "I do clearly and reliably access my own qualia, but I cannot rely upon introspection if I want to determine their nature." To an ontological agnostic, there is no inherent explanatory gap between our understanding of qualia and what science can discover about the brain. It is when we think we know the essential nature of qualia that an explanatory gap seems to appear.

A Fanciful Interlude

In his seminal paper on the explanatory gap Joseph Levine speculated about how the gap could be closed. "There is only one way . . . that I can see to escape this dilemma and remain a materialist. One must either deny, or dissolve, the intuition which lies at the foundation of the argument. This would involve, I believe, taking more of an eliminativist line with respect to qualia than many materialist philosophers are prepared to take."[301] I am proposing another alternative, combining high confidence that intro-spection *reveals qualia* with radical skepticism about whether it *reveals their nature.* This combination of affirmation and skepticism untangles some of the knottiest problems of consciousness. Thus, as Martin Kurthen suggests, we can introspectively identify and label sensory experiences qualitatively, without thinking of qualia as "awesome mental entities oozing with philosophical significance."[302]

Even if this account is accurate it may still seem wrong. Our minds are quite capable of locking out correct theories that contradict habitual beliefs. How then can we extricate ourselves from our own belief boxes? At times I find that metaphorical or even poetic language helps my judg-ment systems relax their stiff-necked resistance. Here are a few examples that pertain to qualia:

Metaphorically speaking, we could think of color experiences as *neural narratives about the secrets of surfaces.*

Experiences of sound *constantly partition the vast vibratory silence that surrounds us.*

Tastes and tactile sensations are experiential wizards, *conjuring the unity of tongue and tabasco sauce, fusing our skin with the texture of silk.*

Scents invisibly decorate the chemistry of air.

And – as you and I experience it – *light is the brain's brand of legible darkness.*

---

[301]Levine 1983, pp. 360-61.

[302]Kurthen 1995, p. 118. Kurthen and I analyze qualia differently, but our motiva-tions overlap.

Chapter Twelve
Hyper-Hallucinations:
The Strange Implications of a Bizarre Thought Experiment

For some this will be the most controversial chapter of *Your Living Mind* and it involves a hardball version of the problem of duality. Let's say you look at a bright light, close your eyes, and see a green afterimage. It may seem natural to assume that having this experience requires two things:

1. The afterimage.
2. A mental state that constitutes *your being aware of the afterimage.*

In general, it seems as if conscious perceptions, sensations, visual imagery, and similar states of mind involve this sort of two-part arrangement. We need both the phenomena that are being experienced and a self or subject who is aware of these phenomena.

This assumption fits the way we talk about consciousness. We say we are *conscious of* something, *aware of* something, and usually this means that we're conscious of things in the outside world. However in being conscious of our own mental states, the same sort of subject-object duality seems to fit.[303] A visual afterimage, for example, is clearly an internal state, and it seems as if we need to have the afterimage *and* to be aware of it. So even with internal states, consciousness seems to be a duet rather than a solo. *What* we are experiencing is singing along with *an experiencing self* that is aware of these experiences. But in thinking about inner, mental states, this two-part requirement lures us into a quagmire of complications. Something's wrong with this picture.

If consciousness is a duet, what happens if one singer goes off key? If the experience and the experiencer are no longer in harmony, which quale are we really experiencing? Suppose that due to some quirky malfunction I am having an experience of the color red, but the part of my brain that constitutes my *self* (the system-of-systems which is aware of my own color qualia) is in the same state it would normally be in when

---

[303]In discussing duality I am talking about experiences in general, not just introspective episodes in which we focus on our own mental states. Thanks to Rocco Gennaro for mentioning this issue. By the way, externalists could claim that after-images are mistaken perceptions of the external world. But some experiences are even more obviously internal, e.g. "seeing stars" after a blow to the head.

I'm seeing green. In this grotesque situation, would the quale I am experiencing be red or green? Or both? Or neither? In Chapter Nine I dealt with some aspects of this difficulty by pointing out that we are capable of extreme delusions, and one could experience redness but think, speak, and act as if it were some other color. But now we will confront a more daunting sort of discord, and this will lead me to a surprising conclusion. *Strictly speaking, conscious experience is a solo, not a duet.*

Admittedly our soloist is backed up by a great big chorus. The mindweaving model suggests that our experiences involve complex interconnections between various conscious and unconscious mental agencies. **But I now claim that a sensory quale is one state rather than a bewildering amalgamation of two interrelated entities. I am abandoning the idea that qualia involve a fusion or a harmonious conjunction of *what* is experienced and what is *aware of* the experience.**

This probably sounds confusing, and it is. We will be wandering through a dense underbrush of subtleties and complexities, deep in the tangled core of the problem of consciousness. And it is appallingly difficult to talk about this topic in ordinary English, because so much of our terminology presupposes a two-part view of conscious experiences. It will be quite a slog, but you've already come this far. Don't turn back!

Well OK, I'll give you a shortcut through the swamp. I'll preview the key issues and how I plan to address them. But I hope you will then follow this journey in detail, perhaps with the sort of curiosity I feel when I watch big machines at a construction site. Even when I'm not quite sure what they are doing, it's intriguing to see them in action. And since the ideas I'll share are recently developed, I hereby mark this chapter:

Under Construction

A quick map of the marsh

Having concluded that the "duet" account of consciousness is hopeless, I will suggest that every sensory experience *is* the act or state of having that experience. So to have a conscious experience, we need just one state rather than two. Importantly, I will be locating qualia within the experiencing self. The self is not detecting conscious qualia. Conscious qualia are *part of* the self. I will show that this paradoxical proposal is actually reasonable, and I will tie this rather abstract issue into the question of why consciousness matters.

To make our journey a little easier, we will mostly focus on sensory experiences such as sensations and perceptions. We could also talk about non-sensory aspects of consciousness, such as your understanding of the words you're reading right now, but that would complicate things unnecessarily and might even send us into quicksand.

Throughout this discussion, remember that terms such as "sensory experience" and "experiencing self," are simple labels for incredibly complex mental and/or neural activities. Even so, I think we can use these terms productively in dealing with the problem of "duet vs. solo."

So let's put on our hip boots, and watch out for alligators. With luck, we may even spot Swampman.

Is hyper-hallucination possible?

It's weird enough to imagine experiencing the color red while believing we're seeing green, but here's an even creepier conundrum. Suppose my experiencing self is functioning exactly as it would be if it were detecting a quale such as redness, but it is not in touch with any color qualia whatsoever. In this (perhaps impossible) scenario, the part of me that is the subject of my experiences – the part that detects, enjoys, and suffers them – is configured just as it would be if it were in touch with the conscious state that we refer to as *red*. And yet (we are supposing), it is not tuned in to any color-state. If this "impossible possibility" occurred, what would I be experiencing?

In hallucinations people think they perceive non-existent objects. But could the experiencing self operate as if we were having, say, a normal visual experience of a butterscotch sundae with two cherries on top, even if it is receiving no sundae-inputs? Let's call this possibility a *hyper-hallucination* to emphasize that it would be a radical step beyond any typical hallucination.[304]

---

[304]Some of the mental states that I call hyper-hallucinations have been called *internal* hallucinations. Although I hesitate to coin new technical terms,

Here is the crucial question: **In this hyper-hallucination, would *what it is like* to be that experiencing self be the same as in a normal visual perception of the sundae?**

Suppose we make a list of all "standard hallucinations," those with typical causes such as dementia, delirium, intoxication and other drug-states, psychosis, stroke, a blow to the head, and so on. I am adding to this list another sort of malady that I'm calling a hyper-hallucination, a malfunction which occurs *only within those brain states that constitute the experiencing self.* (For a more precise definition see this foot-note.)[305] So here are the differences between normal, hallucinatory, and hyper-hallucinatory experiences:

Normal perception: Eyes receive light waves reflected from a real, sugary-fatty butterscotch sundae ➠ Sundae input into visual cortex ➠ Additional unconscious processing ➠ Conscious visual qualia representing a sundae ➠ Subjective awareness of these qualia

Hallucination: No sundae ➠ No light waves from sundae to eyes ➠ Brain generates unconscious representation of a sundae ➠

"internal hallucination" seems confusing since all hallucinations are internal states. Furthermore the word "internal" has been used to distinguish auditory hallucinations that seem to originate within one's head from those that do not. Some drug-induced hallucinations that occur while one's eyes are closed are also called internal hallucinations. See http://hallucinations.enacademic. com/996/internal_auditory_hallucination, and http://www.ncbi.nlm.nih.gov/ pubmed/15145464.

[305]The sort of thing I'm calling a hyper-hallucination could occur in several ways, and different philosophers would conceptualize these possibilities in different terms. A hyper-hallucination takes place when the *last* step in the process of constituting a conscious experience is the *only* step that occurs. Take an experience of redness, for example. Some theorists would speak of the last step in experiencing redness as *being subjectively aware of redness.* In that case hyper-hallucinatory redness would occur in the absence of red perceptual inputs or visual processing, except for the visual processing that finally occurs in being subjectively aware of this color. Other theorists would say that the last step in experiencing redness is *having a higher-order thought* that one is seeing something red. A hyper-hallucination would occur if this higher-order thought existed without any relevant lower-order state.

Hallucinatory visual qualia representing a sundae ⇒ Subjective awareness of these qualia

Hyper-hallucination: No sundae ⇒ No light waves from sundae to eyes ⇒ No unconscious sundae-representation ⇒ No visual qualia representing a sundae ⇒ Subjective experience of visual qualia representing a sundae

This is obviously a very exotic possibility. Why do philosophers think it matters? It matters a great deal because it's about the fundamental nature of consciousness. The possibility of hyper-hallucination suggests that when we think and speak about experiential phenomena, we may be referring to a state of the experiencing self and **not** to the inputs that this self is detecting and responding to. The experience, then, is a solo rather than a duet.

One sort of hyper-hallucination involves the targetless thoughts discussed by David Rosenthal. Rosenthal suggests that when we have a "higher-order" thought about one of our mental states, that state will be conscious. Thus if we have a higher-order thought about a visual experience of a butterscotch sundae, we will actually be conscious of this experience, even if this HOT is the only place in the brain where the sundae is represented. Ned Block, you may recall, found this absurd.

More Details: Let's compare this sundae example with another targetless cognition, the thought I'm having now about a stegosaurus that's sleeping in my back yard. There's no actual dinosaur out there, but I am entertaining a whimsical notion that there is. *I truly have that thought,* even though the thought isn't about something real. In this case having a targetless thought obviously does not make the thought come true. But suppose I have a Rosenthalian HOT that I'm *seeing* a stegosaurus? *Would I truly have that experience* even if it's not there – or even if I'm blind?

Later in this chapter I will side with Block, concluding that HOTs by themselves cannot give us, say, the visual experience of a large and scaly beast. But notice the difference between Rosenthal's targetless

HOTs and my butterscotch sundae example. I am not talking about targetless thoughts. I am talking about *targetless states of the experiencing self.*

Normally, of course, hyper-hallucination is impossible, because normally the experiencing self is forcefully impacted by sensory inputs. For a simple analogy, look at the way these two books lean against each other. Is it possible for one book to be in that configuration without the other? Not without some compensating mechanism, such as wind blowing against the book in a very precise fashion. In the same way, it is generally impossible for the experiencing self to enjoy sensory phenomena unless the self is "leaning against" current sensory inputs, interacting with them in a suitable manner. If a sensory input ceases, the experience based upon this input vanishes. I close my eyes and *poof!* – the world that I was seeing goes away.

Let's toy with the odd idea that a book could appear out of nowhere, positioned just like the one on the right. It would quickly fall, of course, without the "input" of the one on the left. But for a millisecond it would be positioned as if it were leaning on its book buddy. And the same thing could happen with the relationship between:

1. A sensory state that we are experiencing.
2. The self that experiences this sensory state.

Conceivably, 2 could occur without 1, which seems quite strange. That's the problem of duality.

❦ ❦ ❦ ❦ ❦ ❦ ❦

The terrible triplets test

For a stern test of Rosenthal's targetless thoughts, consider an example offered by Ned Block.[306] Imagine triplets, each of whom is thinking, "I am in intense, agonizing pain." One actually is in pain, another is tasting chocolate, and the third is in no relevant introspectable state whatsoever. I'll push this premise to an extreme and say that while thinking, "I'm in pain," the third triplet isn't having any bodily sensations at all.

When Block says these three are thinking they are in pain, he means that they all have the sort of unconscious higher-order thought that, according to David Rosenthal, would normally make an experience conscious. Rosenthal says that if you have a certain kind of unconscious higher-order thought that could be well expressed as, "I'm in pain," you are indeed in pain. And if you have such a thought to the effect that you are tasting chocolate, but you are receiving no chocolate-taste sensory inputs, *it will seem exactly as if you are tasting chocolate.* (Remember, this sort of HOT is a rather special sort of cognition, not just any old thought. He knows you can't reliably summon up the exact taste of a filet mignon or a fine old brandy, just by deciding to think you're tasting those things.)

Block's response zeroes in on the question of why human consciousness matters. "But how can it be that the triplets all have states that matter in *exactly* the same way – in this case three states that are bad in themselves. . . . If what-it-is-like-ness is supposed to *matter* in the same way *whether it exists or not*, that just shows that 'what it is like' is being used in a misleading way." "If a state of being conscious of agony is supposed to matter equally whether it exists or not, the supposed theory of consciousness is worthless."[307]

---

[306]Block 2011a, p. 425. Block's example is based on a similar thought experiment by Karen Neander.

[307]Block 2011a, pp. 426 and 427. Rocco Gennaro's 2012 book, *The Consciousness Paradox* offers a different way of dealing with targetlessness. Gennaro sides with Block in saying that targetless HOTs would not generate genuine experiences, partly because it is unclear how a conscious experience could occur due to an unconscious HOT, without any associated lower-order state. See especially pp. 59-70 and 96-100.

Rosenthal could reply that simply having a higher-order thought about being in agony could *constitute* agony. In other words, if one has this sort of thought, *then agony exists*. So one aspect of the dispute is the question of whether one can have an experience just by having a certain kind of thought.

This is a particularly exasperating version of the "shell game" that we tried to win in Chapter Nine. Under which shell will we find genuine, standard-grade, certified agony? I have spent an inordinate amount of time trying to solve this aggravating riddle, so I'm not surprised that it leads renowned scholars like Ned Block and David Rosenthal to end up at swordpoints. Ned is emphasizing the idea that the target of our introspections should matter, while David seems to situate mattering in higher-order thoughts about the target. How can we resolve this dispute?

The final doorway

Early in this book I said we'd be stepping through several conceptual and experiential passageways. We now stand before the final door. You may or may not decide to go through, and I myself have only put one foot across the threshold. But I'm leaning forward on that foot.

The two-state view of sensory experiences implies a peculiar fusion of that which is experienced and that which does the experiencing. To deal with this problem we can move to a one-state, "single-order" view. Conscious qualia are states of the experiencing self, and not also *other* states that this self is aware of. Thus when we think about and speak about sensory qualia, we are focusing upon one state and not two.

Let's go back to our butterscotch sundae example and make it chocolate this time. A two-state theory of consciousness might sketch normal perception like this:

Eyes receive light waves reflected from a chocolate sundae ⟶ Sundae input into visual cortex ⟶ Additional unconscious processing ⟶ Conscious visual qualia representing a sundae ⟶ Subjective awareness of seeing a sundae

In this five-step model, inputs from unconscious visual systems are bound together into a conscious visual perception, wrapped with a nice ribbon, and handed to the experiencing subject. The subject then enjoys, suffers, or is indifferent to the gift it has received. But I now favor deleting step #4 (conscious sundae-qualia) and going straight to the last step, the visual state of the experiencing subject. We don't need to complicate this setup by inserting another step in between our unconscious perceptual states and what we subjectively perceive. This visual state simply *is* having a subjective experience that seems like a chocolate sundae.

Note that when we're thinking about being conscious of something in the outside world, as in seeing an actual sundae, the subject-object model is completely appropriate. There is indeed an object that we're subjectively aware of. This sort of subject-object duality is not a problem.

After deleting the intermediate step between unconscious processing and subjective experience, we no longer need to worry about mismatches between *what* we experience and what it is like to be *aware* of this experience. And we don't need to wonder whether a quale is in two places at once – the quale *that* you are experiencing and the quale *as* you subjectively experience it. Of course other kinds of misrepresentations are still possible, such as:

❀ A mismatch between unconscious sensory states and conscious sensory states
❀ A clash between subjective experiences and subsequent thoughts about those experiences

But neither of these contradictions are philosophically perplexing.

My hat's off to you if you've slogged along this far, and it's certainly OK to skip to the end of the next *More Details* section. But you may want to read it if the idea that sensory phenomena such as qualia are states of the experiencing self still seems rather vague.

More Details: Conscious experiences are typically available to mental agencies that control behavior. For humans that involves thinking and communicating, including reporting our own current qualia to others. In the two-level view, it may seem as if thoughts and statements about perceptual experiences involve contact with both sensory states that we experience and the subjective state that does the experiencing:

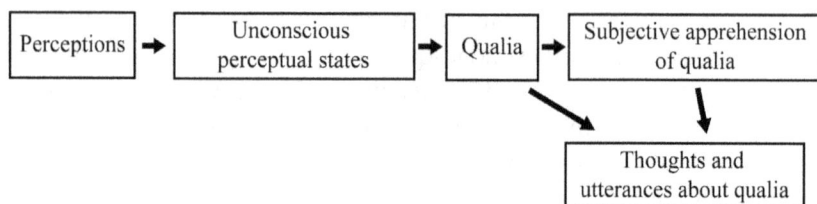

| Perceptions | → | Unconscious perceptual states | → | Qualia | → | Subjective apprehension of qualia |

| Thoughts and utterances about qualia |

In the one-level view, to think about qualia is to think about a state of the subject:

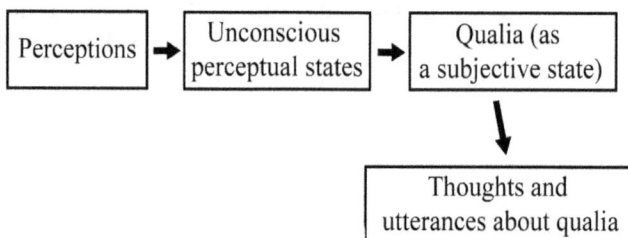

| Perceptions | → | Unconscious perceptual states | → | Qualia (as a subjective state) |

| Thoughts and utterances about qualia |

This rough diagram is intended to show that in the single-state view, when you think about some vivid, right-there sensory experience, those thoughts mainly arise in response to your own current subjectivity. We do not have to befuddle ourselves by thinking experiences are somehow both what they *are* and what they are like *in our awareness of them.*[308]

So when the mental agencies that control our behavior utilize our current experiences, they focus on what these experiences are like for us. We can say something similar about another important characteristic of consciousness, remembrance. The "duet" view seems to imply that memory systems are interested in both the way qualia are and our awareness of those qualia. This is confusing and redundant. The "solo" view says that our memories of sensory experiences are mainly based upon sensory states *as they occur within the experiencing self.* Of course,

---

[308]Various authors, with various theoretical orientations, have expressed similar ideas, as in this comment by Jesse Prinz. "When we experience a phenomenal state, there are not two things in play – the state and our experience of it – but rather one thing: the state being experienced. Experiencing a phenomenal state is simply being in that state" (Prinz 2007, p. 191).

memories are shaped by many other factors, perhaps even including non-conscious sensory states. But we need not say that people remember both a quale that they are experiencing and that quale as the self is aware of it. Having an experience *is* a state of awareness, and it's the experiencing self that is aware.

❦ ❦ ❦ ❦ ❦ ❦ ❦

Do other soloists sing as sweetly?

If this single-state view seems right to me, why haven't I gone all the way through the third doorway? The main reason I have only "put one foot across the threshold" is that other approaches are also worth considering. I prefer mine, but I do not dismiss the alternatives.

More Details: Here are brief comments on competing single-state theories. My theory says that a conscious quale simply *is* the quale as I am aware of it, but here are three additional ways of avoiding the redundancy of duplicated conscious qualia.

1. We could eliminate the concept of selfhood, but somehow retain the notion that human beings experience, enjoy, and suffer phenomenal experiences. Qualia would not be duplicated by being represented within the self if the self does not exist. In Chapter Fifteen I'll explain why we should not abandon our selves.

2. One and the same state could both *be* a quale and *represent* it. I discussed self-representationalism in Chapter Six.

3. We could say that qualia are complex mental states which the self-system monitors, but reject the idea that these qualia are duplicated within the self. Thus the self-system monitors qualia and makes judgments about them, without copying or containing them. I think this option has potential, and it makes good sense to me on alternate Fridays, as it were. But it seems to lose the sense that experiences are *for me*, that they are gifts which I have truly *received*. Even so, I am well aware that many of the terms and concepts we use to deal with this issue are about

as sophisticated as Stone Age daggers – not the best implements for delicate surgery. If anyone has a scalpel, I'd be glad to try it out.[309]

❦ ❦ ❦ ❦ ❦ ❦ ❦

Strictly speaking . . .

Having proposed a single-state theory of consciousness, I'm going to back away from it for a moment. Strictly speaking, consciousness is a solo and not a duet, but we seldom need such technical precision. For most practical and even theoretical purposes we can still use the old subject-object schema that is so deeply embedded in both thought and language. Terms such as "awareness of ___" and "experience of ___" suggest that one thing is detecting another thing, and in some ways this is correct. For one thing, it makes both practical and theoretical sense to say that we are conscious of external objects.

We can also think of mental states in subject-object terms, without becoming ensnared in paradox. There's no harm in saying that suffering a backache involves both something I'm aware of and the act of being aware of it. In this case the duet model works just fine, as long as I don't push myself into conceptual quicksand by imagining that conscious pain-qualia exist both as what I'm aware of and as the act of being aware of them, *as the very same state at the very same time.*

Other examples could be given that are more complex and contro-versial, but my point is that we can often speak of consciousness in subject-object terms without running into problems. In most of this book I speak in "duet" language, rather than using precise, pedantic, and extremely cumbersome single-state terminology. But we do need the single-state "solo" view in dealing with the question of whether a quale is both something that the self is aware of *and* an aspect of what it's like to be this experiencing self, at the very same instant.

---

[309]I don't know of anyone who has developed option 1 or 3 in relation to the problems of duality, misrepresentation, and targetlessness, and I would be interested in examining such analyses.

How to make the "solo" view plausible

Some readers will wonder why I'm making a big deal about abandoning the two-state view. Why is it so intimidating to go through this doorway? So the taste of chocolate is just a state of the experiencing self, and not a weird amalgamation of two interrelated qualia-states. What's the problem? The problem is that scholars such as Joseph Levine are absolutely correct in saying that consciousness *appears* to involve a duality. It does seem as if qualia are "simultaneously objects of, and acts of, awareness."[310]

Even after seeing that a single-state view could work, I found myself resisting it. For many years I had conceptualized experience in terms of both being aware of something and the "something" that I'm aware of. But at some point during my ruminations something flipped, and the one-level view made intuitive sense. Of course! The qualia that I experience are these qualia *as they are for me.* That's what it means to say that they are my conscious experiences.

For obvious reasons, we usually focus on what we are noticing about the outside world and about our own inner states. These salient inputs "get in our face," seizing our attention. Meanwhile the more subtle reality that *we are in subjective states that assert the existence of these outer and inner events* remains in the background. But it is entirely possible to pull a switcheroo, coaxing our minds into a figure-ground reversal. It's a little like what happens when we play with a duck-rabbit image and watch it flip.

---

[310]Levine 2001, p. 174.

Here is a way to reflect on the idea that sensory phenomena are states of the experiencing self, states of *what it is like to be you right now*. This process is similar to the very first exercise in *Your Living Mind*.

> ✎ *Being the subject.* Begin by sitting for a few minutes with your eyes closed, noticing every sound you hear. Choose a simple phrase that means, "I'm noticing how this sound is for me, or in me," a phrase such as, "that's in me," "that's me," "in *me*," or just *"me."* With each new sound, silently repeat the phrase you have chosen. You are imaginatively construing experiences as embedded within you as an experiencing agent. Sense the way these embedded sound-experiences continually change within you. *"That's me, that's me, that's me."*

I suggest repeating this procedure while focusing on bodily sensations, and later on visual perceptions. Experiencing redness, for example, is the registration of redness within you as an experiencer. Eventually you can do this with all sensations and perceptions, just as they arise. For me, the breakthrough occurred when this idea clicked for all of my experiences at once. Then I could sense *everything* I was experiencing as how-things-seem-to-me, purely and completely.

What matters

Now back to the controversy between Block and Rosenthal.

More Details: Rosenthal says that conscious experiences occur when we have a certain sort of higher-order thought to the effect that "I am having such-and-such an experience." This HOT is normally associated with some lower-order state such as a sensory perception, but it need not be. Although it is often said that a HOT *makes* the lower-order state conscious, I interpret Rosenthal as meaning that usually the interaction between the lower-order state and the HOT *helps shape* the HOT. The lower-order state (when it exists) helps determine "what it is like" for the experiencing subject. (In a much more indirect manner, the external objects we perceive help determine what it is like to experience those objects.)

Rosenthal and I agree that targetless what-it's-like states are possible in principle, but I doubt that states of thinking, judging, or believing could constitute vivid sensory phenomena. Instead, I say that sensory phenomena are states of an experiencing self.

Could thinking constitute agony? No doubt an extremely addled individual could be eating chocolate, have an unconscious Rosenthalian HOT that "I'm in agony," and then have a conscious thought along these lines. This belief would cause many of the same effects as actual agony. Someone who was thus deluded would soon be an emotional wreck, confused and distressed at trying to stop a horrible pain that does not exist, ravaged by a sort of phantom-limbic disorder. However I agree with Block that this would not be a typical pain state. Passionately believing "I'm in agony" would not be like actually being in agony – unless this higher-order "thought" is actually a conscious sensation.

❦ ❦ ❦ ❦ ❦ ❦

So thinking I'm in pain is not the same as experiencing pain. But the view I favor is in some ways similar to Rosenthal's. Suppose that instead of saying I *think* I'm in pain, when I'm actually tasting chocolate, we try something like this:

The part of me that constitutes *who I am as an experiencing sub-ject* (the team of neural agencies that enjoys and suffers conscious states of mind) is now in the same state as my identical twin, and the poor fellow is in horrible pain. I, however, have received an anesthetic. My brain contains none of the typical states associated with pain, except for one thing. As I have stipulated, the neural complex that constitutes my own subjective experiences is in precisely the same state as the experiencing self of my twin, and he's in pain. At this moment I'm actually tasting chocolate, but I am not in touch with the sensory processes that should cause me to enjoy this treat. Instead, *what it is like now to be me* is to be in agony instead of enjoying dessert. Rats.

With that sort of revision I think Rosenthal's proposal works, and it may even be what he had in mind.[311] A targetless experiential state could indeed constitute a sensory experience.

I cannot imagine how this could happen in an actual person, short of divine intervention.[312] Our beliefs about our experiences are continually adjusted, due to new perceptual inputs and the brain's extensive systems of checking and re-checking its own sensory states. But the point of thinking about this "impossible possibility" is that chocolate tastes, pains, and all other conscious qualia are situated within the experiencing self. Strictly speaking, conscious experience is a solo, not a duet.

Whew. We're through crossing the swamp. I hope you feel that you've made the journey successfully and are home safe and dry.

In the introduction to this book I said that studying the problem of consciousness has been like wrestling with a zen koan for two decades. Now it seems as if this riddle resembles the most famous koan of all. "What is the sound of one hand clapping?"

I have no idea how one swinging hand could constitute clapping, but I do think that one state of mind could constitute an experience. We don't need to keep going 'round and 'round about the relationship between being aware of qualia and the qualia that we're aware of. *What an experience is like to you or me is, in itself, a conscious experience. Period.*

Summing up

Conscious experiences seem to involve a problematic fusion of that which is experienced and that which does the experiencing. Since this leads to puzzles about targetless subjective states, perhaps we need to

---

[311] If so, I wonder if Rosenthal's account is indeed a higher-order theory, since this interpretation of Rosenthal implies that sensory experiences are constituted by certain thoughts *about* experiences rather than requiring both an experience and a higher-order thought about the experience.

[312] In a different context, Weisberg notes that duality is not a worry that radical mismatches actually happen today. "The real worry is about the theoretical possibility of mismatch. Couldn't God, or neuroscientists of the distant future" make something like this occur? (2013, p. 75).

delete one of these two components. I am now inclined to say that experiences (including qualia) are states of the subject who has those experiences rather than also being states that this subject is aware of. My single-state theory proposes that enjoyments and sufferings are embedded within the self rather than being something that is both separate from the self and somehow fused with it. Thus, strictly speaking, consciousness is a solo rather than a duet. There are, however, several ways in which it is perfectly appropriate to speak of consciousness in dual-state rather than single-state terms, and in the rest of the book I will generally use the more familiar and less complicated dual-state language.

Chapter Thirteen
Presence

Some experiences, especially sensations and perceptions, seem present in a way that is difficult to describe but even more difficult to deny. "Objects, scenes, and events are not merely *represented* in experience," writes Robert Van Gulick, "they are phenomenally *present* to us. They *appear* to us, and we experience them as real and present to us here and now."[313] I have already alluded to this sort of presence, especially in Chapters Three and Twelve,[314] and now we will consider whether this phenomenon could occur within a brain. The issues involved are deep and elusive, suitable for leisurely reflection and sudden insights at three a.m.

Although the manifest character of sensory phenomena seems remarkable, it would be quite surprising if experiences did not seem present. To function as we do, our perceptions and sensations must appear to be real. It's not enough for it to seem *very likely* that my car is leaking orange fluid and my hair is on fire. I must seem to *absolutely know* that I'm perceiving these events. Later I may realize I was dreaming, but even then I would firmly believe that something was "there" in my mind. Although we may have theoretical doubts about this impression of realness, we cannot totally override the brash self-assertion of our own

---

[313]Van Gulick 2006, p. 27. In academic discussions what I'm calling manifest presence is sometimes referred to as phenomenality or phenomenal character.

[314]In Chapter Three I distinguished manifest, phenomenal, "on-stage" experiences from states of mind that are unmanifest, non-phenomenal, and "off-stage." With visual experiences, for example, features such as color, shape, and motion seem phenomenally present, *right-there-now*. But features such as causation are not present in the same sense. Using the example from American football of a pass-rushing linebacker slamming down a quarterback, I suggested that if our minds had evolved differently we might have assumed that the quarterback had drawn the linebacker toward him as if by magnetism, pulling his adversary over on top of him. So we could completely reverse our interpretation of the direction of causation, without changing anything about our experience of color, shape, and motion. This fits the idea that colors, shapes, and movements are experientially present, whereas causation is not present in this way. We also touched upon presence in Chapter Twelve, in discussing the problem of duality. Some people say that in order for an experience to be phenomenally present, it must exist in itself, and it must also be present to the experiencing subject. In theory, there could be a contradiction between the way an experience *is* and the way it is *for us,* the way we experience it. We'll return to this issue later.

sensations and perceptions. It's as if the outside world has climbed right into our minds.

In the external world, objects interact through physical effects, whereas in the inner world, obviously-real-presence provides simulated objects that force us to respond. When a mental image of a rock is mentally hurtling toward the mental image of my head, I'm going to physically duck. How does the brain perform this tour de force, making our experiences seem thus-there-now?

Presence is
  The hard problem
    Of what it's like
      When philosophical zombies
      Gather at the Gap

Those who try to comprehend presence are courting insomnia, but it's hard to avoid dealing with it. Many nagging philosophical questions are satellites of this enigma. For example, the *Hard Problem* involves the question of how a brain could generate phenomenal presence. When philosophers say it is *like something* to be conscious, they are often thinking of what seems present in sensory states. Such presence would be missing in *zombies*. And one important aspect of the *explanatory gap* is the need to explain how patterns of neural activities could constitute manifest experiences.

Although phenomenal presence is hard to define, its connection with these classic perplexities helps us distinguish states that seem present from those that do not. If we think about the states of mind that generate intuitions associated with the hard problem, what-it's-like, zombies, and the gap, those are the states that seem manifestly present. When people say, for example, that the zombie's brain lacks the light of consciousness, light is a metaphor for presence.[315]

---

[315]A related point: David Chalmers' Hard Problem challenges physicalism by questioning the connection between neural states and conscious experiences. But there is an *"ontologically impartial"* Hard Problem that applies to physicalism, dualism, pan-psychism, and other theories. *Even if we explain every other aspect of consciousness, how can we explain presence?* We could close the explanatory gap, comprehend the ultimate nature of qualia, show why

How to lasso this will-o'-the-wisp?

How could experiential presence occur in a physical system (or any system whatsoever)? Are sensory phenomena sprinkled with qualia-sparkles, so they twinkle in the darkness of our skulls? Are unconscious sensory data decorated with these sparkles as a sort of graduation present, when they are promoted into the spotlight of full awareness? I'm poking fun at these ideas, but I can surely understand why people struggle to comprehend this aspect of consciousness.

What do you think? Is presentationality a feature of the experiences themselves, as size, shape, and mass are features of lamps and anvils? Does presence have to do with the way such experiences are positioned in the mind's architecture? Do we say some mental states are present because we just happen to *call* them present, phenomenal, and the like? Or does using these terms convey something truly significant about such states? And once we've successfully unpacked this concept, how would we make it clear to a philosophical zombie?

Some deny that we can ever know how presence is realized within the brain. Since my main goal is to refute claims that consciousness could not be physical, I will respond to their skepticism. The groundwork for these responses has already been laid, and most of my comments will consist of referring back to previous passages. However I also want to at least gesture toward a positive explanation of presence. I acknowledge that this theory-sketch is only a beginning. The link between brain events and phenomenality is notoriously obscure. Part of the problem is that we aren't sure how to think about the relationship between sensory experiences, our pre-verbal beliefs about these experiences, and the words we use to express these beliefs. I sometimes find it difficult to turn my pre-verbal judgments about presence into coherent English, and this in turn makes it hard to critically evaluate these judgments. So like Chapter Twelve, much of what follows is under construction.

---

experiences don't seem like brain processes, and so on, but still find ourselves puzzled about the presentational aspects of these and other issues. Of course, one may simply stipulate that it is the nature of certain entities to be phenomenally present, but one would like to see a more satisfying explanation than, "that's the way it goes."

Here are seven features of sensory experience that are closely entwined with presence. Phenomenally manifest experiences typically
seem to be:

1. *Substantial.* Manifest phenomena appear to be substances of some
sort, entities that occupy time and space. We can mentally "point to,"
examine, and describe some of their seemingly substantial features. We
cannot do these things with most non-sensory states.

2. *Qualitative.* These experiences are differentiated from one another in terms of qualia – *that's a color, that's a sound, that's a funny
smell.*

3. *Interrelated.* Sensory phenomena are coherently interconnected.
They're not just an assortment of disconnected data-dots. Some of these
relationships help perceptions simulate the spatial universe – objects A,
B, and C are at locations X, Y, and Z. Spatiality, of course, helps create
the impression of substantiality. And even phenomena that we don't
think of as spatial are experienced as part of an integrated whole.

4. *Known in an unusual way.* We seem to have a very special way
of knowing manifest experiences. For one thing, they seem to be:

5. *Undeniable.* The presence of conscious sensory states is virtually
indubitable. Without realizing it, we may even assume that such phenomena "deliver their own news," reliably informing us about the way that
they are. "Regardless of what you think about me or whether you even
deny my existence," they seem to declare, "I AM HERE." No wonder
some theorists say we must *start* with phenomena that obviously exist,
the qualia themselves.

6. *Present to an experiencing subject.* Some philosophers interpret
this as meaning that sensory experiences occur in two "places." They are
both real as they are in themselves and real as what they are like in the
experiencer's awareness of them. This confusing two-state model leads
to the problem of duality, discussed in Chapter Twelve.

7. *Ontologically unique.* Manifest presence may seem to be part of
the ontology, the deep nature of sensory experiences.

Look back at this list and see which points seem most closely
connected with presence. Ask yourself what would happen to experiential presence if one of them disappeared.

Some have doubted that these seven alleged aspects of presentationality can fit into physicalism. Let's address these worries, beginning with brief comments about four of the items.

Point #3, interrelationship, can presumably be analyzed in neural terms because the brain is such an astonishingly interactive system. Understanding the specifics of these interactions will be difficult and time-consuming, but there is no reason to say it will be impossible. Item #4, "known in an unusual way," is not especially problematic unless it leads us to affirm #5, "undeniable." In Chapter Nine, I suggested that all or nearly all of our beliefs are dubitable. Even a belief that I now feel an excruciating pain might be false.[316] Regarding #6, I have argued that presence does not involve a fusion of subject and object. (For more, see this technical footnote.)[317] However even if you agree with me about #5 and #6, beware. The assumption of indubitability and the concern about subject-object duality can weasel their way back into our belief-systems long after we think we've tossed them in the trash.

More Details: Item #1, substantiality, requires more discussion. Substantiality implies that something real is present to us – something is "there" – so in that sense it's just a synonym for presence. But substantiality also implies extension in time and space. If we can introspect mental states at all, it seems as if we would note their duration in time. But how could the brain produce the compelling impression that we are encountering something spatial?

---

[316]As we discussed earlier, if the brain malfunctioned one could be convinced of being in pain when that is not so. Even in normal functioning there might be a tiny time lag, so that one could believe, "I am in pain," at the precise instant that the pain ceased.

[317]Thinking of experiences as present to an experiencing self can be helpful, but it can also snarl us in conceptual tangles – an *experience* is being *experienced* by an *experiencer* that is *experiencing* its own *experiences*. In Chapter Twelve I proposed a single-order alternative. The experiencing self is in contact with selected unconscious neural activities that carry perceptual information. Its contact with these neural activities helps shape it into conscious what-it's-like states, e.g., what it's like for you to be seeing this page right now. Thus, conscious perceptions are embedded within the experiencing subject. We can then think and speak about these embedded sensory experiences, sometimes accurately.

In Chapter Ten we confronted the question of whether visual perceptions are map-like. Do they seem map-like because we are in contact with map-like arrays in the brain? (Remember, the brain contains around 30 visual maps.) Or do our cognitive mechanisms read a bunch of non-map-like codes that lead us to *think* of visual experiences as being spatially extended? We can ask the same questions about tactile phenomena, bodily sensations, experiences of sound, and in some cases taste and smell.

I contend that our beliefs about the spatiality of sense-experiences are grounded in their actual spatiality. We think they're map-like because they are. Judgment-mechanisms within the brain are detecting information about conscious sensory states, and they accurately conceptualize the fact that these brain-states are spatially arrayed. They may omit or misconstrue some details about spatiality, but they basically get it right. We need more research and analysis to show that this account holds water, but it does help us physically explain the impression of spatiality. It may seem simplistic to say that the subjective impression of spatiality is linked to the actual spatiality of neural arrays, but sometimes simple ideas are correct.

❦ ❦ ❦ ❦ ❦ ❦ ❦

To deal with items #2 and #7, we move on to our next episode, in which . . .

Ontological agnosticism rides again

To help solve the problem of presence, I'll jump on the same horse I rode to leap over the explanatory gap and rescue Mary from dualism. We make mistakes in understanding experiential presence, and some of our errors are metaphysical misjudgments.

For humans, experiential presence involves qualia, and many believe that qualia are ontologically peculiar. But introspection is a wretchedly unreliable guide to the metaphysical status of conscious experiences. We should be very skeptical of introspection-based assertions about the essential nature of qualia. As long as we admit that we cannot introspect their ontology, the existence of qualia is no threat to physicalism.

In addition to these worries about qualia, some believe that presence itself is ontologically exotic. It's as if every sensory experience announces, *"I am an insoluble enigma. I possess a logically-impossible property that philosophers call phenomenality. No one will ever explain my true nature. Abandon all hope, ye denizens of academia!"* Ontological agnosticism is helpful here as well. We may think that reflection on our own experiences reveals a mystical-twistical thus-there-nowness that cannot be understood in physical terms, but introspection is a fragile foundation for such a crucial claim. For instance, it may seem that "presence itself" could never be found in the brain. But this may be based on the same set of intuitions that leads some to say that physicalism omits "redness itself." In Chapter Eleven I offered five reasons for believing that "redness itself is missing" is an insufficiently-supported ontological judgment, and similar considerations apply to presence itself. Although presence is amazing, this does not prove that it is metaphysically bewildering.

Naturalizing presence

Suppose we discard the notions that manifest phenomena are ontologically strange and that our beliefs about them are undeniably correct. If we also reframe "present to an experiencing self" as I have suggested, this leaves four ingredients. Manifest phenomena are, in some sense, substantial (real things that occupy time and space), qualitative, interrelated, and known in a special way. How do these elements work together in the brain to generate presence?

Without repeating my earlier arguments for internalism, I will assume that in focusing on sensory experiences we are focusing on *the states themselves,* not just what they represent about objects we are perceiving. If consciousness dwells within the brain, we are focusing on aspects of neural states. But we are not gawking at whole biological units, applauding the dramatic spectacle as legions of neurons ferociously fire. We are detecting *highly selected* aspects of neural activity patterns. As a metaphor for this sort of selectivity, imagine a creature that looks at a multicolored ball of yarn and is only able to see the yellow threads. (Perhaps a better analogy would involve a creature that has visual access to only one of the *materials* that makes up these threads.) By contrast, when we think about non-sensory, "off-stage" states of mind, our cognitive mechanisms do not detect details about the neural states themselves in a way that enables us to comment on them.

More Details: So our cognitive systems process information about sensory and non-sensory brain processes in two contrasting ways. Furthermore we could easily build a computer that mirrored this distinction. We could enable it to detect and form accurate judgments about the way some of its internal states are configured. However in processing information about other internal states, it could detect what these states signified but not the way the states themselves are deployed. So it could conceptually monitor concrete details about some states but not others, and this resembles the way our cognitive mechanisms monitor present and non-present mental activities.

Our cognitive access to sensory experiences is fallible and incomplete, but we can try to form judgments about them. Such judgments first occur pre-verbally, and linguistic mechanisms then attempt to capture these judgments in words. At a very basic level, we can assert that "something seems to be *there, right now*, real and present before me." We may also say that sensory experiences seem *spread out in time and space, integrated, and qualitative.* These statements reflect neural realities. Although it would take much evidence and analysis to prove this claim conclusively, I think that in important respects, sensory experiences and similar phenomena **are** temporally extended, spatial, interrelated, and qualitative neural states.

I have acknowledged that the spatial aspect of substantiality is a challenging issue, but I am more confident in saying that qualitative character and interrelatedness are features of neural activity. Sensory states are constituted by neural patterns that are appropriately categorized as qualia (see p. 75). And there is persuasive evidence that experiences *seem* to form an integrated whole because certain neural activities *are* integrated into such a whole. Eventually, science should discover how brain states accomplish such sensory integration and what it is that changes in our heads when integration fails. Recall the stroke victims who can describe an object that's sitting in front of them, but haven't a clue where the item is located in relation to other objects nearby. This radical breakdown in sensory integration is certainly due to a change within the brain.

🐞 🐞 🐞 🐞 🐞 🐞 🐞

Simple, subtle

Let's begin exploring this proposal by using a simple example, comparing an experience that does not seem present with one that does. In Chapter Three, I contrasted manifest, phenomenal experiences and unmanifest, non-phenomenal experiences, and I used the example of hearing your friend George say, "I want to quit my job." Let's say he makes this remark while talking with you in a parking lot. As your brain processes the noises his mouth is making, its linguistic mechanisms interpret the meanings of these sounds. I have suggested that knowing what we think someone said is a conscious experience (interwoven, of course, with various non-conscious states). But it is not conscious in the same way as sensory experiences. For the most part, it is not *manifestly, phenomenally conscious.*

As you and George chat, you notice a bicyclist on the left, pedaling in his direction. You assume she can see him, but you keep an eye on her anyway. This visual episode is a clear-cut example of a phenomenally present perception. It seems obviously real, and you track it in its specificity, just as it happens. You are experiencing "what it's like to be seeing a woman on a bicycle, heading straight for George."

"Watch out!" you cry, and George jumps to avoid the errant rider. (She looks to be the same young woman who was lost in our mental hall of mirrors. Perhaps her ordeal in the labyrinth has left her a bit daft.)

If this had actually happened, what would have been the difference between the non-sensory experience of *knowing what you thought George meant* and the manifest, sensory experience of *watching the cyclist?* Look back at the picture of the bicycle and rider, and think about what it is like to experience this image. Obviously you are detecting something that seems substantial and that has discernable parts. These parts are laid out in relation to each other and integrated into a meaningful whole, within the context of your awareness at this moment. There is an impression of spatiality – a certain shape – and you also notice qualitative features, such as black marks on a white background. So the experience seems to be spread out in space, integrated, qualitative, and present. But for the most part, consciously knowing what you thought George meant does not seem present in these ways.

Clarification: In a way, what is unique about manifestly present phenomena is that they seem obviously real. But in another way, some non-manifest mental states seem obviously real – real in the sense of being almost impossible to doubt. For instance, you can be confidently aware of knowing the meaning of the word *you*, mentioned earlier in this sentence. It would be hard to doubt that just now you consciously experienced having access to what "you" meant in this context. (If not, check your driver's license photo and then call a doctor.) What's special about sensory experiences is not just that we are sure they are *occurring* right this minute. It is that they appear to be indubitably *manifest*; present in a substantial way. With non-phenomenal states, on the other hand, there isn't any "there," there. In consciously knowing what "you" refers to, you may or may not have noticed manifest phenomena. For example, you may have experienced a visual image of yourself or sensations in your own body. But your knowledge of who you are is not mainly based upon such phenomena. It is mostly "offstage," even though it is all but indubitable.

Hold tight to the truth that we do experience some offstage mental states such as consciously knowing what George meant and consciously knowing who you are. Now – *what must we add* to this sort of experience to have experiences that seem present? Is it that we access very *specific* features of the experience? That's close, but it's not quite right either.

Here is an example of a state that isn't manifest but is experienced in very specific detail. Remember Jane from Chapter Three, who is trying to decide whether to buy a Honda Civic. As her inclination shifts from "buy" to "don't buy" and back again, she is conscious of these changes even though they are unmanifest. Her vacillations do not seem present in the way that sensory states seem present, but she is aware of them nonetheless. And suppose Jane has amazingly good contact with these "offstage" mental states, so that at any given moment she could tell you the exact strength of her buy-it impulse, on a scale of 1 to 1000. Even if that's humanly impossible, we can imagine that a creature with this ability could exist. With such precise access, why aren't these impulses clearly and obviously phenomenal?

Two ways to check your oil

Think of the difference between checking your car's oil by using a dipstick versus by looking at a digital gauge that reads, e.g, "-.75" when you're 3/4 of a quart low. When you look at the dipstick, you access both what it indicates ("I'm down most of a quart") and some things about the way the dipstick itself is configured. If someone substituted a diamond-studded dipstick for your standard black one, you might notice. But a trickster could swap in some different wiring for the digital gauge and you wouldn't notice, unless it was reading wrong. The point of this very loose analogy is that with experientially present states of mind, we typically know both *what they indicate* and something about *the way the states themselves are configured*. With non-manifest states, we can know what they signify, sometimes precisely, without having access to anything else about them.

More Details: Ned Block makes a useful distinction between access consciousness and phenomenal consciousness. Access consciousness is available for use in "rationally guiding speech and action."[318] Phenomenal consciousness may be useful in the same way, but it also has "what-it's-like" characteristics. In that sense, phenomenally conscious states are usually *describable*. With non-manifest conscious states, one might have astounding access to details about such experiences, without any ability to describe those details. When Jane says her buy-it impulse is 613 on a scale of 1000, she has splendid *access* consciousness of this state but not *phenomenal* consciousness. Thus she cannot say what this state is like (except for incidental phenomenology that does not fully constitute this impulse).

How to explain the difference in terms of neural activity? Jane's access to her current buy-it impulse results from the fact that the neural activity pattern that constitutes this impulse *causes* her to think, speak, and act in certain ways (or to be more likely to do these things). Jane does not need any introspective access to the way the impulse itself is configured. But with manifest phenomena such as the way this page looks to you right now, our cognitive systems monitor some (though obviously not all) aspects of the sensory states themselves. If experiences are in the brain, then in addition to knowing what perceptions tell us about external objects, we also introspectively access some details about the way these neural states are arrayed.

I am trying to pick out the solid insights of indirect realism without succumbing to the inner eye illusion. Some will respond that in thinking about the way this page looks to me, it is absurd to think I am monitoring

---

[318]Block 1995, p. 227.

my own brain. Clearly what I am monitoring is the *page*. Yes, I am attending to the page, quite partially and indirectly. There is an extremely small but extremely useful overlap between the way the page seems to me and the way physicists would characterize it. But I have offered evidence and arguments for the idea that when we think about our sensory experiences, our cognitive mechanisms are monitoring highly selected, "sliced and diced" neural processes. When these neural patterns change, my beliefs about my experiences tend to change along with them. My belief-generating mechanisms are tracking internal states, moment by moment.

ॐ ॐ ॐ ॐ ॐ ॐ ॐ

One simple way to understand what I'm getting at is to realize that when we reflect upon mostly-off-stage experiences such as conscious thoughts, we can say what those thoughts convey about the world. "I believe Antarctica exists." But with present-seeming, on-stage experiences, we can say what the experience conveys and also describe the experience itself. If you were in Antarctica, you would know that it currently exists and you would know how *you experience* that continent. It looks mighty white and it feels bloody cold.

Here's another analogy. Imagine a group of machines monitoring a hospital patient. Most of the machines, let us suppose, detect the patient's bodily states and use these as a basis for various actions. One machine might alter intravenous nutritional inputs, based on blood sugar levels. Another might "write" words in a log – "9:29 a.m., respiration 18," etc. But one machine doesn't do anything and doesn't write anything. It just displays the patient's heartbeat patterns. It doesn't act. It doesn't interpret. It just delivers the news, second by second. That is analogous to the sort of information we access in being aware of manifest phenomena.

Sensory phenomena are also experienced as part of a sensory world. Non-manifest states are not part of that world, or are much less well-integrated into it. Suppose we heard someone say that her worries about the Calvinist doctrine of divine predestination "have just moved closer to my teapot" or "seem to be oscillating in time to that fire siren." She'd seem a tad eccentric. But we expect this sort of thing with sensory qualia. Thanks to such qualia we may see our hand move toward the teapot, or feel a pain "in" the ears that varies with the loud siren. So phenomenal presence is not just a matter of noticing lots of specific details. It's also a matter of the way these details are mutually related.[319]

In principle, then, it is entirely possible that the brain's judgment-mechanisms access certain aspects of the physical configuration of sensory states, including their spatial, map-like deployment, their inter-connectedness, and the way they are structured into qualitative categories. When we access such information, wouldn't that seem rather different than accessing information without any of these features? **Wouldn't we *notice* the difference between accessing information with and without this configurational data? Wouldn't philosophers find terms to apply to this crucial distinction? How about "phenomenality?" How about "presence?"** These ways of labeling sensations, perceptions, and similar experiences are more than just arbitrary or accidental ways of speaking. *They express something meaningful* about these experiences, based upon what we encounter during introspection.

"But come on, Schriner," you may reply. "There isn't just a meaningful difference between phenomenal and non-phenomenal states. Phenomenal states seem REAL, and you haven't explained that yet."

I have suggested that we conceptually access the way sensory states are configured, not just what they represent about the world and our own bodies. We are accessing integrated and dimensional constellations of neural activities. I find it hard to imagine detecting these features of sensations and perceptions without also experiencing them as real, as *thus-there-now*. But if that answer isn't good enough, then play with this question – *real compared to what?*

---

[319]Of course our "offstage" responses to sensory experiences are also meaningfully related to those experiences. They're all in the same mind. But we do not access them as being part of the sensorium. To the extent that our cognitive and emotional responses to sensory phenomena seem to belong to the same world as those phenomena, to that extent they *are* phenomenal.

Human reality

The brain structures the only sense of reality that we are able to grasp. Remember the example of hemineglect? The brain establishes the left and right sides of perceptual space. When hemineglect disrupts this hard-wired cognitive structure, one's experience of the world changes drastically. Similarly, the brain establishes that sensory experiences are at the core of what we take to be reality. All of our thoughts about qualia start with them as real. *We can't get behind that cognitive stance.* In contemplating qualia, we are attending to a basic building block of what reality is *for us*. We can imaginatively pretend that qualia are illusory, but this only supplements our continuing conviction that they exist. Just as a hemineglect patient finds it nearly impossible to pay attention to leftness, a normal experiencer finds it impossible to stop construing experiences as thus-there-now.

Is the reality-sense of all conscious beings the same? Probably not. Here's a scenario that may or may not be coherently conceivable, but it makes a useful point. Imagine meeting a space alien who knows how to plug the experiencing self of a human being into its own sensory processes, and vice versa. Perhaps a startled human would say, "I'm astonished! Compared to the experiences of my extraterrestrial counterparts, my own sense that qualia are 'present' seems shallow and pale. This creature has sensory states that *truly* seem real. Fantastic!" Or perhaps the shoe would be on the other pedal extremity, and the space traveler would be stunned to discover that its most vivid qualia are no more manifest than the most fleeting and subtle human sensations. We cannot know how this fantasy would actually play out, but we do know that manifest consciousness is our human way of realizing concrete-reality.

I'm speculating about Martian consciousness because I want to complexify the either-or distinction between manifest and unmanifest states of mind. Viewing mental states as *either* on-stage *or* off-stage may reinforce the intuition that phenomenal presence is magical and inexplicable. But even in humans, presence may come in several flavors. Different degrees of consciousness, for example, may involve different types or levels of seeming-realness. Plausibly, a perception may be phenomenally present without our being fully aware of it. I have mentioned watching a TV show about hippos and not noticing when it switched to zebras (p. 22); not noticing one's own nose, even when it's in the middle of one's visual field (p. 157); and having a retrospective sense that a musical tone has changed or the refrigerator has stopped humming (p. 148). Regardless of whether we categorize such episodes as "truly" conscious, they may indicate levels of phenomenal presence. Here's another example:

> In this experiment, subjects are shown a minute long video of a static scene of a carnival carousel in which a large and exceedingly obvious foreground object (the base of the carousel) very gradually changes from red to purple. In these experiments, subjects are asked to be attentive and to watch for any changes, but for pretty much all naive subjects it is very hard to notice that the colour change is occurring. . . . Clearly, at the end of the video subjects are experiencing purple (surprise can be elicited if the scene at the start of the video is immediately shown). Introspectively, subjects report no change in experience. How can this be?[320]

Since the carousel base was so large, it seems likely that the viewers did see it changing. It could be, then, that the changing color of the base was present in their experiences, but not present in the same way, or to the same extent, as a color that we are clearly aware of *as* changing. This implies that phenomenal presence may be a matter of degree, rather than either/or.

More Details: To close this discussion, let's consider once again what is distinctive about presence, and how this could be understood in physical terms. It does seem as if phenomenal presence adds something distinctive and extra-difficult to the problem of consciousness. Pretend for a moment that we have succeeded in explaining every aspect of *non-* phenomenal consciousness. Therefore with a conscious experience that is mostly non-phenomenal, such as your experience of realizing that you know what "embezzlement" means, we now understand exactly how this conscious state is constituted in your brain. *What should we add* to this

---

[320]Seager 2013, pp. 47-48.

account to deal with experiences that are phenomenally manifest, such as seeing a menacing bike-rider?

I conceive of consciousness as a state of an experiencing self, and qualia are embedded within this self. They are "what it's like for me to be in a certain qualia-state now." Our qualia-states cannot describe themselves in words, but our brains contain mechanisms for attending to such experiences and making judgments about them. When we arrive at pre-verbal judgments that feel right, we cobble together words and phrases that we hope will express what we're thinking. Here are some words that I use to speak of presence:

When sensory experiences seem phenomenally present, our cognitive mechanisms are detecting specific details of an integrated complex of neural activities that is extended in time and space and differentiated in ways that we think of in terms such as "qualia."

We can express this theory-sketch in terms of necessary and sufficient conditions. In order for normal humans to be convinced that sensory states are manifestly present, it is necessary for our judgment-mechanisms to access details of the sensory states themselves, rather than merely being linked to those states in a way that influences our thoughts and actions. To enjoy *human-like* phenomena, our judgment-systems must detect these states in terms of integration, spatiality, and qualitative character. When appropriately combined, these ingredients are jointly sufficient to constitute our particular brand of phenomenally present experiences.

🐞 🐞 🐞 🐞 🐞 🐞

Summing up

We have been pondering a physical explanation of the experiential presence of sensations, perceptions, and similar phenomena. I have responded to worries that this sort of presence could not occur within the brain, and I have offered a tentative theory-sketch about why some brain-states are accessed in terms of phenomenal presence while others are not. If this analysis appears to be inadequate, *then what has been left out?* And if you can say what you believe is missing, ask yourself whether this belief is mainly based upon your own introspection-based intuitions. Are you sure these intuitions are well-founded? Perhaps they are, but it can be liberating to climb out of our own belief boxes, look around, and see what we discover.

In the past five chapters, I have sketched ways of dealing with deep puzzles about consciousness. In Chapter Fourteen, I'll sum up this theory and add further clarifications.

Chapter Fourteen
Experience Required:
Solutions, Clarifications, Further Speculations

Three difficult doorways

Throughout this book we have been grappling with the question of whether conscious experiences could, in principle, be states of the brain. I have answered *yes,* with a high-octane version of experiential fallibilism, a "ruthless modesty" about our ability to know our minds from within. Certain crucial misjudgments have made it much harder to comprehend consciousness, and to correct these errors I have taken us through three rather intimidating conceptual passageways.

We moved through the first of these portals just by realizing that many judgments about our own experiences are off base. This involved saying goodbye to the inner eye illusion – the assumption that knowing experiences is closely analogous to perception, and is as accurate and complete as normal vision seems to be. I agree with Papineau that this view of consciousness is "inspired by some misplaced visual model, in which we are able to peer in at some immaculately illuminated scene."[321]

Although experiencing qualia is a poorly understood process that may embody all sorts of errors, we needn't go to the opposite extreme and deny that we have any access at all. We generally do well at *detecting, recognizing, and noticing changes* in sensory episodes, but we overlook

---

[321]Papineau 2006, p. 102.

or misinterpret many features of our experiences or imagine we detect features that we do not. These errors exaggerate the apparent differences between conscious states and brain states. For instance, we may think introspection should reveal the structure of conscious experiences, and then wonder why the structures that they seem to possess do not match those of the brain. Resolutely rejecting the inner eye illusion helps put those fears to rest.

Next came door #2 – admitting that attending to qualia gives us little insight into their ontology (Chapter Eleven). Then in Chapter Twelve we confronted a third daunting doorway, the possibility that conscious phenomena such as sensations and perceptions are not *what* the experiencing self is detecting. Strictly speaking, they are states *of* the experiencing self. Thus I have gone through the third, and for me the most difficult doorway, and I am learning to feel at home in this reluctant realization.

This exuberant lad has stepped out of the final doorway, thinking, "I'm so thrilled to have dazzling new insights into consciousness." Or perhaps, "I'm so relieved to be done with the truly gruesome technical sections." In any case he should pat himself on the back for his persistence, even if he's skipped every footnote.

Solving the six puzzles

In principle, each of the following riddles can be solved by showing that they are based on mistakes about conscious experiences.

First Puzzle: If consciousness is in our heads, why don't sensory experiences seem like brain processes?

Experiences don't seem like what we read about in science books, but we were not born with a microscope in our minds or equipped with an app for high-res brain scanning. Subjective experience does put us in touch with brain states,[322] but it detects highly specific neural activities rather than chunks of nerve tissue. Since brain agencies that track sensory states are only "interested" in what's relevant, it would be bizarre for consciousness to display anatomical features such as neurons or dendrites. Such promiscuous physiological access would burden and distract us. In fact, we should be absolutely shocked if our descriptions of sensory experiences *matched* the way science describes the brain.

Second Puzzle: Why do perceptions and sensations seem present?

Some conscious experiences, especially sensations and perceptions, seem mysteriously present. In Chapter Thirteen I discussed ways that errors about our own experiences make us doubt that a brain could generate this sort of experiential manifestation. I also sketched a physical account of presence. Sensory phenomena are monitored in ways that "offstage" mental processes are not. They appear to be spatial, qualitative, and integrated into a unified sensorium, because we have introspective access to patterns of neural activity that are aptly described in these terms. The brain uses these aspects of consciousness to convince us that we are in direct contact with the world. Such phenomena *constitute reality as we know it.* Situated as we are, within our own brains, our thoughts and beliefs about such phenomena treat them as thing-like and radically real. We cannot completely circumvent this impression of substantiality.

Third Puzzle: The explanatory gap. How can we show why a particular experience is constituted by a particular brain event?

Many believe it is impossible to explain why some brain state would constitute one particular quale, such as redness, rather than another, such as blueness. It may seem as if comparing qualia to brain states is about as sensible as comparing letters of the alphabet to numbers, but this is due to the special-essence intuition, the belief that sensory qualities have a very

---

[322]As I mentioned in Chapter Ten, it is hard to know in what ways we detect brain states *as* brain states, or even to say exactly what this would mean.

special nature that we access by looking within. In Chapter Eleven I offered five reasons for concluding that introspection is a poor source of information about the metaphysical nature of conscious phenomena. Our experience of the quale *bright red,* for example, does not give us solid evidence for denying that bright redness could be physical. Experienced redness may or may not have a perplexing ontology, but we can't tell that by looking within.

If we become skeptical of introspection-based ontological judgments, then the names we give qualia such as redness and blueness serve as philosophical wild cards, labels for phenomena that we do not deeply understand. Since introspection doesn't disclose the nature of qualia, there is nothing puzzling to explain. There was no explanatory gap to begin with, so there's no need to close it.

A similar analysis solves the **Fourth Puzzle: When Mary sees colors, does she learn something new?**

If we have no solid basis for saying that color qualia are very special entities whose nature seems to be non-physical, then Mary's discovery becomes philosophically trivial. Her seeing red for the first time is no more ontologically discombobulating than if she had seen some particular shade of gray for the first time. She would have had a different emotional reaction to red than to yet another shade of gray, but this doesn't show that she's encountered something metaphysically remarkable.

Fifth Puzzle: Are philosophical zombies possible?

A philosophical zombie is an atom-for-atom duplicate of a person such as you or me, that behaves just as we do but is not conscious. In Chapter Five I offered reasons for believing that this notion is not coherently conceivable. Furthermore the core intuition that consciousness seems non-physical is partly based upon several other intuitions – experiences do not seem like brain processes, we doubt that brain states could constitute "present" phenomena, and it seems impossible to explain qualia in terms of physical states. These concerns are addressed in regard to puzzles one, two, and three, above.

Sixth Puzzle: Duality and misrepresentation. If *what* we experience and *our being aware* of this experience do not match, which is the "real" experience?

As Joseph Levine has noted, qualia seem to be "simultaneously objects of, and acts of, awareness."[323] But if they are in both of these "places," there could be a mismatch between my awareness of qualia and the way these qualia actually are. If so, which side of this duality would count as the real qualia? To solve this problem we can adopt a single-order, one-state view of consciousness. Strictly speaking, sensory phenomena are states of the experiencing self, not states that the self is detecting. The qualia that I experience are the way these qualitative states seem to me. Some believe that we also need an extra state that is *being* experienced, but I think it's time to drop this needless duplication.

SOFAR, so good?

It's handy to label theories in ways that are easy to recall. Rosenthal has a HOT theory, Van Gulick tends HOGS, Gennaro espouses WIV, and Tye spreads PANIC.[324] I advocate a single-order fallibilist approach that affirms the reality of introspectable experiences – **Single-O**rder **FA**llibilist **R**ealism, which I hereby christen **SOFAR**. This term is easy to remember, and it implies that we are *now in the process* of understanding the mind-body relationship. We are not perpetually stuck at the starting line, as discussions of the hard problem and the explanatory gap often suggest. *Your Living Mind* states where I have come, so far, in probing these mysteries.

I will now consider some possible concerns, including the relationship between SOFAR and eliminativism, and the question of how we know our own experiences.

Fallibilism versus fictionalism

Because I have rejected some commonly-held ideas about conscious experience, my proposal may seem like eliminativism in disguise, but there are important differences between fallibilism and eliminativism.

---

[323]Levine 2001, p. 174.

[324]PANIC stands for the idea that qualia consist of poised, abstract, non-conceptual intentional content. See Tye 1995, pp. 137 ff. For comments on HOT, see the last part of Chapter Six. A footnote in that chapter discusses HOGS and WIV.

Although I have emphatically eliminated qualia as ontologically quirky whatchamajiggers, in doing so I have reframed them, not deleted them. It seems far easier to imagine being mistaken about the essential nature or the constitutive structure of qualia, for example, than to imagine being entirely deluded about our ability to detect experiences of sights, sounds, tastes, smells, and bodily sensations.

By now you can see why I appreciate the work of both Daniel Dennett and Joseph Levine. Both Dennett's eliminativism and Levine's "modest qualophilia" capture important truths, but each sees flaws in the other's analysis. Levine and his allies are right that the first-person perspective provides important data that the third-person approach ignores. Dennett and his cohorts, on the other hand, have seen that subjective hunches about our experiences can harden the problem of consciousness by fostering almost irresistible delusions. But in warning us against these seductive mistakes, Dennett has fought several battles that were not needed to win the war. He has suggested, for example, that we lack privileged access to our own experiences and that there is no dividing line (either precise or fuzzy) that differentiates conscious from unconscious mental processes. Dennett seems to have moderated some of his most controversial views,[325] but people are still irked and intrigued by the brusque eliminativism of *Consciousness Explained*. Nevertheless, we can profit from Dennett's insights without accepting his eliminativist conclusions. In understanding consciousness we don't need fictionalism; fallibilism will do.

Consciousness leads us to believe things about both our minds and the outside world, and we can legitimately doubt that these beliefs are true. In fact we can legitimately doubt the existence of the entire universe. I

---

[325]For example in discussing the many-Marilyns thought experiment (Chapter Eight), Dennett denied that the brain "fills in" missing information. Scientists quickly cited evidence that the brain does fill in missing visual data with what it "guesses" is there. That's one reason we don't notice a blind spot where the optic nerve comes into the retina; the blind spot is filled in with more of what's nearby. According to Roskies and Wood, "neurophysiological evidence clearly contradicts his account. There are cells in the primary visual cortex that represent the region of visual space corresponding to the blind spot. . . . Clearly the blind spot is not neglected, as Dennett suggests" (Roskies and Wood 1992 p. 48). In *Sweet Dreams* (2005, p. 148), Dennett seems to concede that some sort of filling-in does occur.

cannot hop out of my brain and hob-nob with physical objects in their nude actuality, nor can worldly objects smuggle themselves into my skull. But the consistency and coherence of my beliefs about what's going on around me makes it extremely probable that there's a universe out there. I'd guess that each of us has accessed at least *trillions* of data-bits regarding external reality that fit together quite well.

Even though we cannot know the outside world with absolute certainty, it is reasonable and appropriate to say the world exists. Thus we should not be world-eliminativists. We can apply similar logic to qualia and other contents of consciousness. Even though my beliefs about introspectable experiences mislead me in some ways, in other ways they have much the same coherence and consistency as my beliefs about physical objects. *Since we are not eliminativists about the outside world, I see no reason to eliminate the inner world of consciousness.* Just as some of our beliefs about what's so may turn out to be false (alas, no elves or fairies), some aspects of our inner lives may also prove illusory. But that is fallibilism, not eliminativism. An adequate theory of consciousness requires a non-eliminativist account of introspectable experience.

Click! Or clunk? How we know we are conscious

In this section I'll expand on my proposal by asking how we know we are conscious. I'll first bite what I think is a fairly digestible bullet and admit that a conscious state which I have at 1:22.704 a.m. may not constitute knowing that I *am* conscious at 1:22.704. But an instant later I can know that I *was* conscious an instant ago, if a certain series of events occurs. Here's a simple example. Suppose I watch the second hand of a clock for one minute, noting every five seconds whether I believe I am experiencing something. These visual experiences are states of my experiencing self. I am *getting* what the clock looks like to me now, now, now . . .

After one minute, I stop and recall what has happened. I then have a belief that I can express aloud: *"I've been having a series of experiences."*

Here's the click-trick. If my memory systems and cognitive mechanisms are working correctly, it will be obvious to me that the series of episodes in which I kept looking at a clock face *fits* what I just said aloud. This stated belief "clicks," generating a solid sense of rightness, confirming the fact that I am having conscious experiences. Something similar happens implicitly, all day long, whenever we're awake, and this is one reason it's so obvious that we are conscious beings. If I try to deny that I've been having experiences, that causes a clunk instead of a click. Something in my mind immediately waves a red flag – *that's ridiculous! Of course I'm having experiences!*

Our confidence in our own consciousness also involves a sort of experiential inertia. Sensations and perceptions tend to "hang around," persisting in short-term memory. This generates perceptual continuity as fresh perceptions arise amid the echoes of recent experiences. (To see that this is so, simply wave your hand in front of your face a few times and notice the extended blurriness of its motion as perceptual inputs from the recent past persist into the "extended present.") Since every experience is temporally extended, our beliefs about each moment of awareness draw upon inputs spread out over at least some small duration. Kenneth Williford suggests that "an episode of consciousness is the 'child' of its predecessor. Its other parent is just the new information folded into the ongoing replicative process. In effect, it is the reincarnation of its parent *as modified by new input.*"[326] Or as Bob Dylan sang in Mr. Tambourine Man, *"I'm ready for to fade into my own parade."*

If we didn't repeatedly have conscious experiences, or remember having them, or think about those memories, we might not believe, "I am having experiences." But we do all of these things, and thus we know the

---

[326]Williford 2006, p. 134. Sensory experiences, then, are partially shaped by the echos of just-previous experiences. As Marvin Minsky comments, "[e]xistence seems continuous to us not because we continually experience what is happening in the present, but because we hold to our memories of how things were in the recent past. Without those short-term memories, all would seem entirely new at every instant, and we would have no sense at all of continuity or, for that matter, of existence" (Minsky 1985, p. 257).

mind's aliveness. At a very basic level, that's why we are confident that we are not zombies, and that's why most of us cringe at eliminativism.

More Details: The same sort of "click" that tells us we are conscious also enables us to know what we are conscious *of.* If I am hearing Mick Jagger belting out a Rolling Stones hit, here is how I might know I'm having that experience:

1. My experiencing self is in a specific what-it's-like state – what it is like to have an auditory experience that sounds like Jagger's voice.
2. I have thoughts about being in that experiential state.
3. I express one of these thoughts aloud: "I'm hearing Jagger."
4. I am explicitly, phenomenally conscious of the sound of those words.
5. I am implicitly conscious of what those words mean.
6. Various mental mechanisms compare 1 with 5, and I realize that 5 accurately expresses 1. "Yes, I'm hearing Jagger."[327]

❧ ❧ ❧ ❧ ❧ ❧ ❧

Now I'll move to a more speculative mode and ask . . .

Do "offstage" experiences matter?

Some conscious experiences seem "present" while others (such as some of our thoughts) do not. I've used various terms to contrast these present and non-present experiences:

Sensory - non-sensory
Explicit - implicit
Manifest - unmanifest
On-stage - off-stage
Phenomenal - non-phenomenal

Many believe that phenomenal states such as sensory qualia are the only things that have intrinsic worth. William Seager, for instance, has written that qualitative consciousness "makes up the way it feels to be

---

[327]This sequence, of course, involves higher-order states. Item 2 is a HOT about 1, 5 HOTs 4, and 6 HOTs 1 and 5.

alive" and that qualia "are, I am sure, the ultimate source and ground of all value."[328] I used to agree. But I now emphasize the importance of that which *is* conscious – the experiencing self – which is mostly conscious in the implicit, "off-stage" manner we discussed in Chapter Three.

Sensory qualia are merely the tip of a gargantuan iceberg, a visible fragment of the conscious experiences we cherish. Qualia are important, and many of us could greatly benefit by becoming more keenly aware of the rich texture of sensual awareness. Even so, I am inclined to think that what matters resides primarily "off-stage." In case you want to explore this controversial suggestion, here are:

More Details: In Chapter Three I defended the idea that knowing what words mean is a conscious experience – not present in the same way as sensations and perceptions, but genuinely conscious nevertheless. Other implicitly conscious experiences include making judgments about:

- ❀ What is happening now
- ❀ Why one is doing something
- ❀ Why one is feeling a particular emotion
- ❀ Whether one is feeling positive or negative

All of these are hugely important aspects of what matters to us about the living human mind. Neil Levy has recently made comments that support this stance. He notes that phenomenal consciousness is the "kind of consciousness that is usually held to be valuable," but he argues "that a great deal, if not all, of what we value in life and makes beings valuable can be explained by other kinds of consciousness."[329]

❀ ❀ ❀ ❀ ❀ ❀ ❀

---

[328]Seager 1999, pp. ix-x. Seager also "claims that pleasure, as invoked by Bentham, and happiness, as it figured in Mill's utilitarianism, are phenomenally conscious states" (Levy 2014, p. 134). "It is sometimes claimed that phenomenal consciousness is a necessary condition of anything mattering to an organism. Kahane and Savulescu . . . claim, for instance, that only a phenomenally conscious being has 'a point of view, a subjective take on things'" (Levy 2014, p. 132). Of course various writers define "phenomenal" in various ways, and that can lead to misunderstandings. But there is certainly a strong tendency to say that present-seeming states are what truly matter about consciousness.

[329]Levy 2014, p. 129.

Could consciousness be purely implicit?

Here's a rather out-there speculation. Imagine an individual whose brain malfunctions in a way that eliminates all sensory experiences and other phenomenally "present" states. Even her most vivid memories, fantasies, and mental images are drained of qualitative phenomenology. If she thought about the most dazzling sunrise she had ever seen, she could describe it in detail, but no visual qualia would accompany her recollections. In a very real sense, everything has gone dark and silent. *Would this complete absence of sensory qualia eliminate consciousness?* One could argue persuasively that there is nothing it is "like" to be this person. But in another sense could she still be having experiences?

Some would say no. ". . . Siewert thinks that . . . if I were transformed so that I no longer had qualitative experiences, I would no longer exist."[330] But my own conjecture is that this individual actually would be conscious, and that it would still be *like something* to be this non-sensual mind. She would continue to be aware of beliefs, desires, and impulses, even though these cognitions would not "show up" in the way that sights and sounds show up, and would no longer be accompanied by sensory phenomena or sub-vocal speech. And, like the thoughts of the infamous philosophical zombie, these states of mind would bear several of the standard hallmarks of consciousness. They would be available for use in guiding her actions. She would know that they are occurring. They would be remembered at least briefly. They would be at least partially reportable.[331] We could not say these things about genuinely unconscious states.

If this person did express her thoughts verbally, she would not perceive these words as manifest vocal phenomena. Furthermore, since humans were evolved to function with explicitly conscious, implicitly conscious, and unconscious mental states interwoven, being deprived of

[330]Levy 2014, p. 132.

[331]Many disagree with the idea that consciousness could be purely non-phenomenal. Nicholas Humphrey, whose ideas I discuss later on, asserts "the obvious psychological fact" that "*if I do not feel, I am not.* Your core self comes into being only as and when you have sensations" (2011, p. 91). But it would be interesting to find out which aspects of "having sensations" Humphrey would consider phenomenal and which he would consider non-phenomenal – particularly since Humphrey views phenomenal consciousness as illusory!

manifest sensory states would be disorienting, distressing, and even tragic. But I still think that her non-sensory consciousness would *matter*.

Again, these are speculative comments, and thinking about such an unusual scenario will call forth conflicting intuitions. I made these remarks to highlight my conviction that non-sensory, "off-stage" mental states can be genuinely precious. This doesn't make qualitative states insignificant, but it underlines the way they are interwoven with non-phenomenal aspects of mind.

Coming back to our senses

Let's take a break from these abstruse conjectures, and go to a car show. We'll put ourselves in the mind of a fellow named Tony, who is now having a striking visual experience. He's looking at Ferrari 458 Italia, which we can visualize in an arresting shade of red called *Rosso Scuderia*. If we could know what it's like for him right this second, what would his consciousness include?

As Tony's eyes dart from point to point, several times a second, his visual field includes a continually shifting array of relatively clear and relatively fuzzy regions, in complex gradations. His current visual inputs are plumped up by "perceptual inertia," as recent perceptions are briefly held in memory. He tends to think that he sees everything in front of him, clearly and simultaneously, but he is mistaken about that. He also tends to disregard subtleties like shadows cast on the car by surrounding objects and faint reflections in its shimmering paint.

The complex interplay of foreground and background phenomena involves all of his senses – murmuring voices, the scent of new leather, and the lingering taste of this morning's coffee. He is also emotionally aroused, and his imagination is enthusiastically engaged. Soon he's conjuring up a self-guided test drive, flipping the paddle shifters, roaring through the countryside near Maranello.

Numerous thoughts pop in and out of mind. "That guy's blocking my view. I'm thirsty. I should move on soon. My foot hurts. Later I'll change hotels. Does the new hotel have a gym?" All of these brief cognitive episodes involve interwoven sensory and non-sensory aspects of experience plus lots of unconscious processing.

And that is just a tiny taste of what it's like to *be* Tony, salivating over that red Ferrari Italia.

Summing up

This chapter applies the SOFAR theory to the six key puzzles we have wrestled with throughout this book. If I have made progress in dealing with even one of these issues, it will be easier to see how conscious experiences could turn out to be brain events. In my opinion, there are no absolute and insurmountable defeaters that make this impossible.

In the next two chapters we will consider some topics that are closely entwined with the problem of consciousness and apply SOFAR to these issues.

Chapter Fifteen
The Cerebral Self and Its Silicon Cousins

There was a young man who said, "Though
It seems that I know that I know,
    What I *would* like to see
    Is the 'I' that knows 'me'
When I *know* that I know that I know." – Alan Watts[332]

So who are you now?

Discussions about consciousness refer to the self, the subject, the first-person perspective. But what is this self that we speak of so easily? There are perhaps as many puzzles about selfhood as there are about consciousness, and some of these debates are mainly terminological. People argue about which aspects of our minds, bodies, and/or souls, we should *consider* the self, and what terms we should use in discussing it. Shall we say that "I" am a part of my brain? My whole brain? Brain stuff plus soul stuff? Only the soul? Am I my entire body? My body plus the tools that I use, such as tire gauges and computers? And if the self is in the brain, is it a single brain system, or should we use a team model in which the self consists of several systems, working (most of the time) in brilliant coordination? I favor the team model, but there are lots of ways to slice this pie.

We have side-stepped these controversial details by focusing on the experiencing self, the aspect of each person that enjoys life or suffers, that takes it all in. We could expand on this idea by wading into a morass of competing self-models, but instead I will just say that each of us is the experiencing part of ourselves plus additional components that provide a greater context for consciousness. These context-creating components would at least include our memories, our anticipations, our beliefs about what's so, our desires and priorities, our action plans, and the motivational propulsion that mobilizes this agenda. If the self is, as I think, a brain process, this cerebral self probably consists of an enormous number of interconnected parts. It is a complex system of systems, not a single

---

[332]Watts 1972, p. 50. If I know that I know that I *introspectively* know some current quale, higher order theory pegs the last level of knowing as a fifth-order state. Just experiencing a quale without explicit introspection involves two orders, the quale and the higher-order thought about it. Then we know that we know that we know this experience.

point. But even a million brain modules could still count as a single entity if they work as a unit. Perhaps we will eventually replace the idea of selfhood with two, three, or several entities. Nevertheless, *something* within each of us has conscious experiences.

Socrates' challenge to "know thyself" will never be half-completed in any human lifetime. The self is too complex to track itself in real time, and too close to itself for objective evaluation.[333] Our consciousness of self is mostly implicit (non-phenomenal), but clues about ourselves often show up in sensory experiences. When I hear a rousing jazz solo, my emotional reaction may include clearly introspectable phenomena, so that I notice myself smiling and tapping my foot. These clues reveal things about the mostly-hidden me, gazing out of my intricate darkness.

I'll say more about selfhood before moving on to the other theme of this chapter, the possibility of building a conscious machine.

The no-self alternative

Some very wise individuals have suggested that selfhood is a superfluous notion, unhelpful or even destructive. Buddhism declares that there is no abiding self, and many Western philosophers have agreed. "For my part," wrote David Hume, "when I enter most intimately into what I call myself, I always stumble on some particular perception or other, of heat or cold, light or shade, love or hatred, pain or pleasure. I never can catch myself at any time without a perception and never can observe any thing but the perception." In our own time, Thomas Metzinger asserts that "no such things as selves exist in the world. Nobody was or had a self."[334]

---

[333]Harry Frankfurt pulls no punches on this point. "We don't know our own desires, we don't know our own selves very well, so representing ourselves as telling the truth about ourselves is bullshit because we don't know the truth about ourselves" (quoted by Baggini 2013, p. 61). (Frankfurt's noted essay, "On Bullshit," formed the basis of a book that graced the *New York Times* best-seller list.)

[334]Hume and Metzinger were quoted by Taylor 2012, p. 237. Some who agree with Hume's comment are thinking in terms of phenomenal aspects of consciousness. Because I view selfhood as mostly implicit (non-phenomenal, "offstage"), I am not worried about the fact that I have never introspected a com-

Psychologist Robert Ornstein's *Multimind* proposes a many-minded model of personhood, suggesting that each of us is more like a committee or a congress than a single Big Boss who runs the show. Andy Clark says something similar in his essay, "A Brain Speaks." "I am not one inner voice but many. I am so many inner voices, in fact, that the metaphor of the inner voice must itself mislead, for it surely suggests inner sub-agencies of some sophistication and perhaps possessing a rudimentary self-consciousness. In reality, I consist only of multiple mindless streams of highly parallel and often relatively independent computational processes. I am not a mass of little agents so much as a mass of non-agents . . . [which] yield successful purposive behavior in most daily settings. My single voice, then, is no more than a literary conceit."[335]

Clark's elimination of the self is supported by his decentralized view of the brain, and Dennett mates this fragmented model of mind with his project of deleting introspectable experience. "A good theory of consciousness *should* make a conscious mind look like an abandoned factory . . . full of humming machinery and nobody home to supervise it, or enjoy it or witness it. Some people hate this idea. Jerry Fodor, for instance: 'If . . . there is a community of computers living in my head, there had also better be somebody who is in charge, and by God, it had better be me.' . . . But that is the beauty of it! In a proper theory of consciousness, the Emperor is not just deposed, but exposed, shown to be nothing other than a cunning conspiracy of lesser operatives whose activities jointly account for the 'miraculous' powers of the Emperor."[336] He also remarks that "one of the most fascinating bifurcations in the intellectual world today is between those to whom it is obvious – *obvious* – that a theory that leaves out the Subject is thereby disqualified as a theory of consciousness . . . and those to whom it is just as obvious that any theory that *doesn't* leave out the Subject is disqualified."[337]

---

pletely manifest Schriner-self.

[335]Clark 1997, p. 225. Similarly, Georges Rey writes that "we project an enduring object that corresponds . . . to our personal concerns. . . . But, as Hume and Parfit . . . have argued, there is no 'suitable' thing that corresponds to these projections, nothing that's an appropriate object of our reactions and concerns for them or for ourselves" (quoted by Levine 2001, p. 145).

[336]Dennett 2005, pp. 70 and 71. Some paragraph breaks have been removed.

[337]Dennett 2005, p. 145.

I used to side with self-eliminativists.[338] In one lecture that I've presented several times, I have pretended to be an interstellar anthropologist reporting on the strange Earth-notion of personal identity. How odd that Earthlings think their "self" is *separate from the world around them, endures through the passage of time, and is internally consistent* (at least in those with good character). I have enjoyed these presentations and it has felt daring to deconstruct selfhood, but I now realize that this concept points to something important that I no longer wish to reject. It seems quite appropriate to call something an *entity* if it is an enduring arrangement of parts that functions in well-defined ways over time, and that ceases to function in those ways if it is substantially disassembled.[339] The self may well be such an entity.

Some who deny that selves exist could just as soundly deny the existence of squirrels, snapdragons, and the moon. And some do. To them everything is just a collection of interacting particles, so no "thing" exists. The sea, for example, is nothing but droplets of water, so how can we imagine that there's a Pacific Ocean? I am no longer impressed with this approach. I suspect that at times it's just an inexpensive way to confuse ourselves for our own amusement.

A more fluid view of selfhood

Since I think selfhood's obituary has been prematurely penned, I will march out onto a limb that seems fairly sturdy and say that there is some cerebral complex of which it can truly be said, *"This is who I am."* Everybody's gotta be somewhere, and this is where I live.

When we investigate the brain's complex machinations, we discover all sorts of interactions – neural states responding to other neural states, and other states responding to those, *ad infinitum*. Where am "I" in this orgy of synaptic interplay? If we cannot pinpoint some brain complex as the self, should we dismiss this notion as a bedraggled relic of "folk psychology?" If we do, we may be falling into the complexity trap. The

---

[338]I discuss the following ideas more fully in Schriner 2009.

[339]It is difficult to build a bulletproof definition of "thing" or "entity." Without attempting to prove the point, I am siding with those who think entities exist.

fact that some entity is incredibly complicated is no reason to say that it does not exist, or that it is philosophically mysterious.

Let's consider two other reasons for rejecting selfhood and see if they hold up. First, we could claim that there is no self because we are not coherent or consistent, even for brief periods of time. On a non-conscious level this may be true, but competing interpretations of what's so usually sort themselves out by the time we are aware of the winners. Recall the ways that two different parts of the visual cortex interpret the illusory triangle shown in Chapter Two. We don't notice both interpretations because one of them muscles the other one aside at an early stage of visual processing.

Perhaps right now my unconscious mind contains dozens of divergent thoughts and perceptions, all of them trying to claw their way into consciousness. But as I argued in Chapter Eight, a person's view of reality tends to be coherent at higher levels of mental processing. I am not waffling about whether there's a monitor in front of me, a keyboard beneath my fingers, or a worrisome pain in my right wrist. I believe all of these things without reservation.

In theory some secret mental agency might usurp control of my thoughts and actions by leading me to see my keyboard as a small alligator. That "draft" of what's-so-now would get an A for creativity, but unless someone has slipped me some mescaline I doubt that my brain will assemble such an oddball perception. Most of the time our mental processes fall into familiar grooves, and there is not much need for the "multiple drafts" that Dennett emphasizes. Yes, I may experience various impulses about whether to adjust my seating position, and I may wonder if that faint noise was the doorbell, but standard concepts of consciousness and selfhood can easily accommodate these ambiguities.

Another objection to selfhood emphasizes the way we vary from moment to moment, and this is a more credible threat. As a psychotherapist, a student of psychology, and an incurable introspection addict, I am convinced that most people grotesquely overestimate their own consistency. This is a major mistake about selfhood, but it does not undercut the fact that an experiencing self exists whenever we are conscious. I am a very different person when I'm in the dentist's chair than I am while soaking in a hot tub, but in each situation some "I" is suffering or savoring sensory inputs. When the dentist's drill stabs a nerve, there's a *me* that is in pain. My left ankle is not in pain, nor is my liver or my whole brain. A portion of my brain, a finite set of neural complexes, suffers this sensation, and it's perfectly legitimate to call this an experiencing self.

In spite of these intra-personal inconsistencies, I – at least the "I" who is now choosing to type these words – see our self-states as enduring and relatively consistent. Why? Partly because of my reflections on the challenge of deliberate personal growth. So often we are appallingly resistant to change. Certain emotional and behavioral patterns repeatedly assert themselves, in spite of one's wish that they would vanish. They seem nearly as solid and persistent as standard household furniture. But each of these psychological and behavioral patterns is only in charge for a while. Then some other familiar pattern re-asserts itself.

How then shall we think about this combination of change and continuity? One way that works for "all of my me's" is to imagine myself as a sequence of beads on a string. If you think of this day as a string of moments, the states of mind you will experience today are like beads threaded onto your life-string, one at a time. Right now you may be feeling curious, the next minute confused, then interested, then irritated, then amused. Each of these attitudes uses different parts of your brain, as different beads slide into place on the long strand of time.

Becoming aware of these mind-shifts challenges the illusion of personal uniqueness. When I'm angry, my state of mind probably resembles your experience of anger more than it resembles the way I feel when I'm not upset. That's obvious, if we think about it, but it has radical implications. For one thing it spotlights our close kinship with others. But just as many necklaces can be assembled from the same box of beads, your *pattern* of self-states is special. It is your psychological, behavioral, and experiential signature, the configuration that makes you *you*.

Is there anything constant amid these shifting sub-selves? Possibly. Perhaps whenever we are conscious there are systems within our minds that (1) keep track of what's happening, (2) decide what to do, based on the relationship between what's happening and what we hope will happen, and (3) instigate actions to implement those desires. So regardless of whether I'm feeling tense or relaxed, happy or hostile, healthy or sick as a dog, these three mental processes are active.

Although the notion of selfhood may eventually be replaced by other concepts, *something* within us enjoys or endures our current experiences and at this point I call it the self. But could we ever synthesize this experiencing subject?

Artificial consciousness

How do you feel about the possibility that we will someday build a machine that has truly conscious experiences? Does that sound disturbing? Does it threaten our special status? Why, or why not? Would creating a machine-person provide us with an intelligent companion? Is the prospect exciting? Or does the whole thing just seem silly?

We've worried for a long time about whether machines will be better than we are. Back in 1996 a cover story in *Time Magazine* reported a battle of human versus machine that sounded like John Henry's duel with the steam hammer. "When Gary Kasparov faced off against an IBM computer in last month's celebrated chess match, he wasn't just after more fame and money. By his own account, the world chess champion was playing for you, me, the whole human species. He was trying . . . to 'help defend our dignity.'" The rapid progress made by computers underscores "the generally dispiriting drift of scientific inquiry. First Copernicus said we're not the center of the universe. Then Darwin said we're just protozoans with a long list of add-ons . . ."[340] And now neuroscience seems to say that the mind is a cerebral computation system, and a rather slow one at that. But even if computers are faster than we are, processing speed isn't the only key to consciousness. Think about the chess-playing automaton, Deep Blue. Even if you linked it to a camera so that it "saw" the chessboard, few theorists would say that it's having visual experiences.

At one time few scholars endorsed the possibility of machine consciousness.[341] Others have anticipated that when information processing

---

[340]Wright 1996, p. 50.

[341]In 1995 Birnbacher wrote that most scientists and philosophers have believed "that consciousness in machines is . . . impossible in virtue of the laws of the physical world" and that this belief could "almost be regarded as part of scientific common sense" (1995, p. 498).

devices become sufficiently complex, consciousness will spontaneously arise out of their elegant subroutines.[342] I find this puzzling. If consciousness is just a matter of complexity, one could argue that computers are already conscious, and that the internet is ultra-conscious.[343] But many complex brain processes are wholly unconscious, and adding a mouthpiece won't help. A conscious entity is not just a good data processor that broadcasts sentences about its internal operations. I agree with Christof Koch – "Surely, it's not just the amassing of more and more data that matters, but the relationships among the individual bits of data."[344]

In 1992 *Longevity* magazine reported the predictions of Hans Moravec of the Robotics Institute at Carnegie Mellon University. "You can mark on the next century's calender when machines will outstrip humanity in intellectual ability: sometime around the year 2030." By 2010, "machines will act like dogs capable of learning tricks and responding to punishment and praise." Here are a few more of his predictions, as stated in the article. "Around 2030, robots will . . . be the equivalent of immortal human experts in such fields as medicine, biological science, chemistry and possibly even poetry. The machines . . . will be essentially equivalent to us. . . . They'll get a kick out of helping us. 'On average' he predicts, 'they will have rather nice personalities.'" Moravec also proposed that we will turn our brains into computer programs, thus becoming potentially immortal. "During the procedure, a multi fingered robot will delve under our skulls and scan the top few millimeters of brain surface. Then it will write a program to model the electrochemical behavior of that part of the brain."[345] After that it will delete those now-unneeded layers and scan and copy the layers

---

[342]O'Regan and Noë believe "that awareness comes in degrees" and thus "to the extent that machines can plan and have rational behavior, precisely to that same extent they are also aware . . ." (O'Regan and Noë 2001, pp. 191-92).

[343]Christof Koch speculates that "the Web may already be sentient. By what signs shall we recognize its consciousness? Will it start acting on its own in the near future, surprising us in alarming ways by its autonomy?" (Koch 2012, p. 132). But even if consciousness were to arise in some information processing system, I don't see how that would endow the system with an internal agenda. Unless a system has action priorities, it would be unlikely to surprise us with its autonomy.

[344]Koch 2012, p. 124.

[345]Williams III 1992, p. 22.

underneath, till there's nothing left of the brain and everything in that brain is now in the computer.

Obviously inner portions of the brain would not continue to function normally after the outer parts have been destroyed, but that's just one of the bizarre aspects of this scenario. Moravec assures us that we will become accustomed to this sort of thing, but to me this "immortality" procedure sounds like the murder of one person and the attempted creation of another.

Standard equipment for conscious machines

I used to be skeptical about prospects for artificial consciousness, doubting that an advanced computer could ever see colors and hear voices. I don't think that way today.

Here are some capabilities that I believe a machine must possess in order to be conscious, in roughly human terms, of sensory phenomena such as qualia. There may of course be other sorts of sentience that omit some human abilities or add additional features. In composing this list, I felt uncomfortable using terms that seemed inappropriately human, so evidently on some level I still resist the idea of synthetic minds. Sometimes I have used scare-quotes, as when I say the entity is "thinking."

To be conscious of sensory phenomena, a machine would need:

1. *Sensory inputs,* using receptors that detect things such as light particles, sound waves, airborne chemicals, and the movements of its own robot body.
2. Some of these inputs would become configured in ways that *parallel human qualia.* For example, its visual representations of the surfaces of objects might be structured in ways that resemble human color perceptions. The machine must find it virtually effortless to process information about such data in terms of recognition, similarity, differentiation, change, comparisons to remembered phenomena, and relationships to other current phenomena. It must be easy, for instance, to distinguish colors from textures.
3. *An "experiencer,"* i.e., a mechanism or complex of mechanisms that monitors some of the machine's sensory states and is analogous to a human self.

4. *A sense of its own identity.* The machine must regard itself as an enduring entity and know that it is "thinking" of itself in this way.

5. *Attentional systems.* These would make selected sensory information available to the experiencer and render some of the machine's cognitive processes "introspectively" accessible. For example, the experiencer might have access to the fact that it is now attending to auditory inputs and is wondering why there are rustling sounds in the bushes.

6. *An action-oriented agenda.* Based on this agenda and currently-selected sensory inputs, it must try to make some things happen and prevent other outcomes (such as its own destruction).

7. *Memory.* Recalling sequences of its own sensory perceptions and internal processes would help the robot know that it has a particular history and a particular point of view. Long-term memory would also provide an informational backdrop for current sensory data. When the machine sees the front of an approaching auto, it would treat the rear of the car as virtually present even though it is not visible.

At any given moment I, as a conscious human, carry a backpack full of memories and a suitcase full of anticipations. These forcibly shape my present concepts, aligning my *now* with their *thens*. A conscious robot would carry similar luggage.

I hope these seven requirements make it obvious that consciousness involves far more than multi-terabytes of computational capacity. An intelligent machine would have to be configured in particular ways to be appropriately considered sentient. Looking back at this list, does it seem possible to have all of these capabilities without a human-like inner life? If so, what is missing? And which aspect of humanness would be most difficult to design into a machine?

I admit that manufacturing a device that mimics human awareness may be too difficult to ever accomplish. The machine would have to enjoy the sound of a Chopin prelude, the sight of a sunrise, the taste of blackberries, the touch of a handshake or a hug. And it would sense its own perceptions in the rich and complex way that we do. If a breeze blew across its artificial skin, it would be *aware* of something like feeling a breeze. External objects and events would seem vividly real, as if the outside world had climbed right into its mind.

Quite a challenge, indeed. Yet we know of no physical obstacle that would prevent us from building a machine that noticed and commented upon its internal operations in a way that parallels the conscious processes of humans. Perhaps we will discover inherent barriers to the creation of consciousness in machines made of standard industrial ingredients such as metal and silicon, but there's no reason to give up now.[346]

Still skeptical? Do you think that since we are flesh and a computer is made of silicon chips, the two cannot operate in similar ways? Can a "wet" brain be conscious, but not a "dry" silicon system? If not, why not?

For a deliciously disturbing twist on this topic, read Terry Bisson's "THEY'RE MADE OUT OF MEAT." As the story begins, two nameless space aliens are exploring our galaxy searching for intelligent life. For clarity, I'll call them A1 and A2 in this excerpt. These space travelers, we soon realize, are machines. Their mission requires them to contact and welcome "any and all sentient races." After visiting Earth and studying humans, A1 tells A2 the astonishing news:

"They're made out of meat." A2 is incredulous, and asks whether contact has been made with Earth's intelligent machines. A1 replies that on Earth certain meat-beings are in *control* of the machines. "That's what I'm trying to tell you. Meat made the machines."

A2: "That's ridiculous. How can meat make a machine? You're asking me to believe in sentient meat." A2 then asks whether humans have a brain.

A1: "Oh, there's a brain all right. It's just that the brain is made out of meat!" . . .

A2: "So . . . what does the thinking?"

A1: "You're not understanding, are you? You're refusing to deal with what I'm telling you. The brain does the thinking. The meat."

A2: "Thinking meat! You're asking me to believe in thinking meat!"

A1: "Yes, thinking meat! Conscious meat! Loving meat. Dreaming meat."

A2: "Omigod. You're serious then. They're made out of meat." . . . "They actually do talk, then. They use words, ideas, concepts?"

A1: "They talk by flapping their meat at each other. They can even sing by squirting air through their meat."

A2: "Omigod. Singing meat. This is altogether too much."

---

[346]In a recent survey, three quarters of professional philosophers "believed that a robot with a replica human brain could feel love" (Holtzman 2013, p. 32).

Recoiling from the thought of encountering these meat-creatures, one of them shudders in disgust, "[W]ho wants to meet meat?" To find out what happens next, read Bisson's whole story.[347]

If you find it bizarre to imagine that a machine could be conscious, consider the possibility that our flesh-and-blood mentality might seem disturbingly counterintuitive to another sentient being.

Should future computers suffer? Should future humans?

Even if we can create consciousness, there are serious moral questions about equipping machines with positive and negative sensations and emotions. We mortals struggle to cope with our own ability to feel and to suffer. Should we create a form of consciousness that is potentially immortal, that feels pain and experiences distress?

I've suggested that a conscious machine would need an agenda, so that it tries to make some things happen and prevent other outcomes. But having preferences is not the same thing as having pleasant and unpleasant states of mind. Here are some ingredients that would contribute to a machine's *being in pain:*

1. A self or self-analogue that detects internal states, including . . .
2. Sensory inputs that it categorizes in terms of sensory qualities . . .
3. Some of which represent undesirable conditions and cause avoidant behavior, while . . .
4. Other qualia would help constitute the machine's "emotional" reaction, along with feelings of activation, exertion, and mobilization.

The machine could have sensors on its surface, enabling it to detect a dangerous level of pressure against its exterior. Such pressure would be represented by internal states that its self-system could detect. As a result, the self-system would be configured into "what it's like for me to feel intense pain." If it realized it was at risk of being crushed or disastrously penetrated, it would become totally mobilized to deal with this threat, just as our minds and bodies are mobilized with a jolt of adrenaline in similar circumstances. It would experience an overwhelming surge of activation,

---

[347]http://www.terrybisson.com/page6/page6.html. On this site, Terry suggests that if readers "enjoyed this little piece, give a dollar to a homeless person."

as if every bit of its being was suffused with DANGER – DEFEND! If something pressing upon it began to damage its components, it would need to be "subjectively" aware of intense, off-the-chart, MUST-STOP-THIS-FEELING-NOW states.

Importantly, both pain qualia and the desire to get rid of these sensations are required. Without pain qualia a high level of mobilization would involve the expenditure of energy but no sensory discomfort. Without the irresistible compulsion to make the pain stop, the machine would be like humans with pain asymbolia – feeling pain without being bothered by it. True suffering requires both being aware of unwanted qualia or qualia-analogues and having an intense desire to get rid of them.

If you doubt that an artificially-created consciousness could suffer in this way, is that because you doubt that its inner states would qualify as real sensations? Do you think it would lack a self that would have such experiences? And would your objections apply equally well against the idea that a brain could suffer?

What if we built a machine that felt pleasure but never suffered, that was happy but never sad? In that case its pleasures would be very different from our own. For us, pleasure usually involves attachment, and this causes suffering when we can't have what we're attached to. Pleasure, attachment, frustration, and suffering are part of the same package. To make a mechanical person, we would have to install this attachment package in its circuitry, re-creating the poignant predicament that Gautama, the Buddha, identified thousands of years ago.

Gautama discovered that *the craving side of pleasure is what drives us into pain.* Our life is an endless parade of little cravings and big cravings, cravings we can fulfill and cravings we cannot, cravings that are good for us and cravings that destroy us. I wonder about the morality of creating a machine with the excruciatingly delicious yet frustrating combination of pleasure-plus-craving that is such a central part of who we are.

Perhaps if we created a machine with high motivation to achieve good outcomes, but that was utterly devoid of unhappiness, we would have created the first being on Earth whose life is unambiguously worth living.

And even if it was programmed to protect itself skillfully, it would be entirely unafraid of dying.

Fifty years ago Hilary Putnam speculated about the value of sentient machines. "I have referred to this problem as the problem of the 'civil rights of robots' because that is what it may become, and much faster than any of us now expect. Given the ever-accelerating rate of both social and technological change, it is entirely possible that robots will one day exist, and argue 'we *are* alive; we *are* conscious!'"[348]

This may not become a significant issue unless machines feel positive or negative sensations and/or emotions, either by accident or by design. But what if we carefully avoid building pleasure or pain into a device, and it contends that it *does* experience such states? Should we believe it?

Danger: When people evaluate the ethical worth of beings other than normally functioning adults, they are often illogical and insensitive. "Just over two decades ago surgery with neonates was commonly performed with little or no anaesthetic or analgesic intervention." This was partly because such medications can be dangerous for newborns, but it "was also motivated by the belief that the neonate was too immature to experience pain."[349] In assessing the possible consciousness of machines, we should bear in mind this troubling track record.

Woody Allen has caricatured this tendency to think that our own precious experiences are more sophisticated and valuable than those of others. "What a wonderful thing, to be conscious! I wonder what the people in New Jersey do."[350]

---

[348]Quoted by Metzinger 1995, p. 467. British AI specialist Geoff Simons has written a book called *Are Computers Alive?* According to Birnbacher, Simons suggests "that a future evolution of thinking, feeling and sensing computers is not only possible but highly probable. . . . There will be no alternative, according to Simons, to recognizing computers as new 'life forms' over and above the known biotic life forms and to ascribe to them the same rights to protection that we now ascribe to higher animals" (Birnbacher 1995, p. 497).

[349]Derbyshire and Raja 2011, pp. 233-34.

[350]Allen 1991, p. 118.

Summing up

Although it is difficult to precisely define "self," it seems legitimate to say that some agency or combination of agencies "gets" our experiences – noticing them, enjoying them, and suffering them.

An entity with human-like consciousness would need to be more than just a good data processor that broadcasts sentences about its inner life. It would need to have states and components that legitimately count as sensory receptors, qualia, memories, beliefs, an experiencing self, a sense of identity, systems of selective attention, a set of goals and values, and an agenda for realizing them. We might also program such a machine to respond emotionally and feel pain and pleasure, but there are serious moral questions about whether to do so.

In trying to duplicate the human mind in a machine, it may be difficult to imitate our abilities, but almost impossible to duplicate our exquisitely human limitations.

Chapter Sixteen
Consciousness and Freedom

When people talk about human freedom, they often mean the ability to decide what we want to do, to act voluntarily. Some people also equate freedom with a more controversial idea called "free will," which we'll discuss later.

Consciousness and voluntary action seem to go together. As Susan Pocket explains, "[m]ost persons living in Western cultures in the twenty-first century would identify the 'I' who wills and carries out their voluntary movements with their conscious minds. . . . we believe that our consciousness is what causes the voluntary components of our behavior."[351] But many now question this assumption. "[W]hat role does consciousness actually play?" asks Neil Levy. "What is really happening, when you consciously weigh reasons? Each reason, in favour of or against a course of action, has a weight independent of our deliberation . . ." This weight "is assigned unconsciously, or at least independently of consciousness. The fact that you will miss your family and friends matters more than the fact that the job will offer you exciting challenges (say). You do not *decide* that the first matters to you more than the second; the weight of our reasons is simply assigned to them, by subpersonal mechanisms. . . . Consciousness cannot assign the weights; it receives the news from elsewhere."[352]

Daniel Dennett chimes in with a similar idea. "We have to wait to see how we are going to decide something, and when we do decide, our decision bubbles up to consciousness from we know not where. We do not witness it being *made*; we witness its *arrival*."[353]

I wonder if Levy and Dennett are "half-consciously" exaggerating, to make a point that is important but counterintuitive. Clearly the conscious aspects of decision-making can be crucial. We all know that focusing attention on some issue by mulling over the pros and cons can influence

---

[351]Pockett 2004, p. 23.

[352]Levy 2005, p. 72.

[353]Dennett 1984, p. 78. But on the contrary, it is common for people to notice a painful internal conflict, focus their attention on alternatives, find themselves preferring one or the other, and feel relieved that their conflict has been resolved. This is surely an example of "witnessing" a decision being made. But Dennett is right that we do not witness unconscious aspects of this process that are quite significant.

subsequent actions. In psychotherapy this sort of concentrated introspection provokes striking insights, some of them life-changing. Focusing on currently-felt emotions, which are accompanied by intense visceral qualia, can produce especially dramatically results. So it's obvious that *some* of what we experience helps shape our choices. In fact this is an implication of widely accepted ideas such as the global workspace model and even Dennett's own metaphor of fame in the brain. Conscious thoughts, feelings, and perceptions take a center-stage role in guiding our lives.

When Levy says that the weights of our valuations are assigned unconsciously, this glosses over the fact that these valuations have been shaped by years of vivid and complex personal experiences. We have processed information about these experiences on many levels, both conscious and unconscious. But Dennett and Levy are right to emphasize that many aspects of the decision-making process bubble up from *terra incognita*. We need not devalue consciousness in order to acknowledge the interweaving of conscious and unconscious processes.

Is there liberty after Libet?

Discussions of voluntary action and free will often cite experiments conducted by Benjamin Libet. Libet attached EEG electrodes to the scalp of experimental subjects. In a series of trials, the subjects were asked to push a button whenever they decided to do so (within a certain length of time). The time when the button was pressed was recorded electronically. The subject was also asked to note and remember the position of a dot on a clock-like timing device at the exact instant when he or she chose to push the button. The experimenters wanted to compare the time when people *thought* they decided to push the button with brain activity that seemed related to this decision.

The subjects' reported time of consciously deciding to act was, on average, about two hundred milliseconds (1/5 of a second) before they actually pushed the button. Thus their actions closely followed their perceived decisions. But EEG recordings showed increased brain activity prior to this conscious decision. Some have contended that this "readiness potential" was an *unconscious decision to act,* and it commonly occurred three hundred milliseconds before the time which was reported by subjects as their moment of decision.

These studies "have had an enormous, mostly negative, impact on the case for human free will, despite Libet's view that his work does nothing to deny human freedom. . . . Indeed, Libet himself argued that there was still room for a veto over a decision that may have been made unconsciously over 300 milliseconds before the agent is consciously aware of the decision to flex a finger, but before the action of muscles flexing."[354] Some say that the existence of a readiness potential merely indicates an "engagement with an activity" rather than an unconscious action-instigation.[355] Furthermore there may be time discrepancies between deciding to push a button, realizing that one has made this decision, and noting the position of the timer.

Libet's research may be less important than the way people respond to it. Many of us have begun to doubt the extent of our own freedom, partly as a result of realizing how unconscious processes influence our decision-making. Fortunately we can expand our freedom by realizing the importance of systematically influencing the unconscious mind. Psychotherapy, psychoactive medications, and various spiritual and meditative disciplines alter unconscious processes quite effectively. Even so, I am going to claim that one particular type of "free will" that has been extensively analyzed by philosophers and theologians simply does not

---

[354]Doyle 2014.

[355]"Judy Trevena and Jeff Miller of the University of Otago reworked the experiment, asking participants to decide whether or not to move after hearing a tone. Their results showed that the readiness potential was always present, detectable before the tone, and indistinguishable between cases where the subjects decided to move and those where they refrained. They conclude that the readiness potential indicates engagement with an activity, but cannot support a case against free will" (Fox 2012, p. 8).

exist. In fact this rather traditional view of freedom is incoherent and even self-contradictory.[356]

Free will is an oxymoron

The "will" in free will means choice, volition, making up one's mind, but it's easy to ensnare ourselves in logical tangles about whether we are truly free.[357] People often cope with this complexity by thinking about free will until they reach a stage of confusion that seems reassuring, and then stopping right there. That is an excellent strategy if one's goal is to feel comfortable.

The sort of free will that I think is illusory requires two things:

❂ *Free-will choices must be our choices.* If a person makes a free choice, that individual was the one who chose. Free will involves exercising our own volition, deciding for ourselves.

❂ *Free-will choices must liberate us from causal determinants.* To at least some extent, our decisions must transcend prior influences, including our genetic makeup, our habits, our psychological conditioning, and external influences such as custom and social pressure. According to the traditional notion that I think is misguided, our decisions must transcend these influences in a way that contradicts the idea that the universe is deterministic.

Determinism is the theory that every event is determined by prior causes. If we fully understood the laws of the universe and knew everything about what has happened in the past, in principle we could accurately predict everything that will happen from here on out, including our own actions. Most of us assume that typical mechanical systems such as automobiles operate deterministically. If an engine stops working right, we look for what caused the problem. Suppose a mechanic says, "This

---

[356]The following material draws upon Schriner 2009.

[357]Philosophers don't help matters by focusing on technical minutia. "Much of the contemporary literature on free will . . . is saturated with discussion of the tactics of argumentation, and meta-comments on the strengths and weaknesses of various *moves*, to the point where the reader may begin to suspect that the combatants would hate to see a resolution to the controversy since it would bring their sport to an end" (Dennett 2012, p. 94).

may sound strange, but your motor blew a head gasket for no reason at all." We would think the mechanic was speaking loosely or making a joke. Even if we don't know what caused the malfunction, surely there is *some* deterministic explanation for the blown gasket. But when a human being "blows a gasket," is there a deterministic cause?

Throughout this discussion, bear in mind that the sort of free will that I think does not exist requires:

(1) A personal choice that (2) does not result from causal determinants

Without personal choice we are not exercising *our* will. And without at least some freedom from determinants, our will is not free in a sense that certain theologians and philosophers think is important. For this sort of free will, we need both (1) and (2).[358] I believe that eventually this anti-deterministic idea of freedom will be rejected by most well-educated individuals, for several reasons:

First, the notion of free will is being gradually and inexorably worn down by our increasing ability to predict people's actions.

Second, more and more people are thinking about the mind in terms of the brain and its neural machinery. As a result we are becoming accustomed to thinking of ourselves in terms of causes and effects.

Third, it is becoming increasingly obvious that conscious mental processes are interwoven with unconscious processes. Choices are not made in the full light of awareness.

And fourth, the traditional concept of free will is self-contradictory, like the idea of a square circle or a married bachelor. I will now discuss

---

[358]Some philosophers define free will in a way that makes free will and determinism compatible. These "compatibilists" focus on freedom from compulsion rather than freedom from past determinants. If no one is holding a gun to my head, hypnotizing me, or coercing me in other ways, I can exercise free will. A physically and mentally normal individual who is not being forcibly restrained may freely decide to stand up or sit down. Even if the decision to stand right *now* could have been predicted since the beginning of time, compatibilists say the person is freely choosing. Koch states that this is "the dominant view in biological, psychological, legal, and medical circles. You are free if you can follow your own desires and preferences" (Koch 2012, p. 93). For the sake of simplicity I will disregard compatibilism. My concern is with the idea of free will that contradicts determinism.

this contradiction for those who wish to delve more deeply into a point that's somewhat off-topic. (In fact, the rest of this chapter is only loosely related to consciousness studies, but many who are interested in consciousness are also interested in this subject. It also ties into our recent discussions of selfhood.)

More Details: To see why free will is a self-contradictory idea, let's assume for the sake of argument that determinism is wrong. Let's say that the universe is indeterministic, meaning that at least some events are not completely and predictably caused by the past. If some of our choices are indeterministic, even an all-knowing god could not predict our decisions in advance. But would that give us free will? No, and here's why.

Indeterministic events involve a certain degree of randomness. Should I be pleased to hear that my choices may be influenced by the random movement of tiny particles in my head, staggering this way and that as if they've had too much tequila? If there are uncaused events in my brain, then it's as if something has come loose in there, rattling around aimlessly. Why would I want that? Would an MLB pitcher want randomness in the way his throwing arm functions? Would he think that gave him more freedom or less? And if the mind is in the soul rather than in the body, would we have more freedom or less if the states of our souls were subject to random, uncaused fluctuations?

(Randomness is not the same as indeterminacy, but for our purposes they can be treated as equivalent.)[359]

Crucially, indeterminism would not help people act as responsible moral agents. In fact, it's just the opposite. "If my arm randomly jerks

---

[359]Here's an example of the difference between indeterminacy and randomness. Hypothetically, all non-deterministic events that influence consciousness might alter it in some particular direction. They might consistently make conscious experiences more vivid and compelling, for instance (or less so). These factors would be non-deterministic and not precisely predictable, but they would not be random because they would always have the same general sort of effect. Nevertheless, the same analysis applies – such influences would not give us the sort of free will that anti-determinists want. So for practical purposes we can treat "random" and "non-deterministic" as synonyms.

and strikes someone, that is just the kind of thing that *excuses* me from moral responsibility."[360] So writes Roy Weatherford, and Dennett makes a similar observation. "Random choice, as blind and arbitrary as the throw of dice or the spin of a wheel of fortune, does not seem to be any more desirable than determined choice."[361]

This leaves free will advocates in a difficult spot. They want a kind of freedom that contradicts determinism, but indeterminism doesn't give them what they want either. Remember that the sort of freedom we are talking about requires (1) a personal choice and (2) a break from past determinants.

With determinism there is no break with the past. All events are caused by previous events, so determinism negates requirement (2). But what if the universe is partly indeterministic so that some things happen out of the blue, without being entirely caused by what has happened previously? This would give us a certain sort of freedom – the freedom of an open universe that could unfold in many different ways. But this openness would not be due to our personal choices. Indeterministic events would just happen, rather than resulting from our intentions. It would be absurd in such cases to speak of "exercising" free will. So indeterminism negates requirement (1).

❧ ❧ ❧ ❧ ❧ ❧

---

[360] Weatherford in Honderich 1995, p. 293.

[361] Dennett 1984, p. 2. And Ned Block says quite bluntly that the traditional idea of free will "not only doesn't exist but can't exist, because it's incompatible with both determinism and indeterminism" (http://www.closertotruth.com/vid eo-profile/Do-Humans-Have-Free-Will-Ned-Block-/1626). When Daniel Dennett and Ned Block actually agree on something, one suspects that it must be true! Christof Koch does point out one advantage of indeterminism, however. "Although indeterminism has little to say about whether I can make a difference, whether I can start my own chain of causation, it at least ensures that the universe unfolds in an unpredictable manner" (Koch 2012, p. 102). This might be reassuring to those who tend toward metaphysical claustrophobia, afraid of being trapped in a suffocatingly predictable cosmos. Even so, others might dislike the idea of cosmic unpredictability.

It may seem as if we are free to break with the past through a personal choice that could not be predicted even by an all-knowing deity. But when we think carefully about this sort of free will, I think it disappears. **It is an oxymoron, a self-contradictory idea, because "free" contradicts "will."** To the extent that my choices are free from the person that I am at this moment, those choices do not express *my* will. Instead, such choices are freed *from* my will. The self-contradictory concept of free will requires a choice to *issue from* my will, while being *disconnected* from my will. We can't have it both ways.

Let's consider an example of a decision that is clearly mine and that is clearly *not* made through free will. Suppose I'm walking across the street and I notice a truck hurtling toward me. I jump aside to escape obliteration. Was I acting freely? In a very real sense I was not. I am thoroughly motivated to value survival. Avoiding the truck was dictated by my own psychological makeup. Since I was not feeling the least bit suicidal, I had no option other than to hurl myself out of the way. Nevertheless, the choice was up to me, in the sense that nobody was pulling my strings like a puppet. If I had been feeling self-destructive I might have let the truck smoosh me. Again, that would have been *my* choice.

When it comes to freedom, there's good news and bad news. The bad news is that we lack the super-special freedom that goes beyond both determinism and indeterminism. I call this the magical idea of freedom, because to me it is fantastic and impossible. The good news is that we can enjoy the alleged advantages of free will even though we don't have it.

Practical freedom

Determinism does not threaten what I'll call practical freedom. This term has been used in various ways, but to me practical freedom involves at least four components:

1. It requires the ability to act. (Cars can move.)
2. These actions must be self-initiated. (Cars don't drive themselves, at least not yet, so they don't have practical freedom. But a person can drive them.)

3. One must be able to select among alternatives. (A driver can select a destination.)

4. One must be able to *choose to change one's future choices,* modifying one's action priorities. (A driver can decide to switch routes.)

These four kinds of ability are only found in self-altering information processing agents such as human beings. Those who believe in free will want components 1-4, but they add the extra requirement that our choices must contradict determinism. And yet determinism can actually enhance freedom of choice. It establishes the solid connections from one moment to the next that ensure that my decisions are really *my* decisions. In this sense, determinism can help set us free.

There is a paradox here. *We can think of a "chain" of causation as binding us or as empowering us.* We create desired outcomes by relying on dependable patterns of cause and effect. From this perspective, the reliable laws of causation are our friends. They connect us with the past and engage us with the future.

If we understand that we are creatures of cause and effect, we may be more likely to guard against the influence of irrational determinants. Our ignorance of these influences fosters the illusion that all of our opinions are rational. (How odd that other intelligent people disagree with us religiously and politically!)

Ironically, one of the biggest barriers to fully enjoying practical freedom is the illusion that we can simply choose to be free. If we think we can instantly decide to be better persons without taking practical steps to do so, we are likely to fail. We make better choices by developing good choice-making habits, and these habits operate through cause and effect, not through "poof! I'm all better." Therefore one good way to expand practical freedom is to stop relying on super-special free will.

Another reason people want to believe in free will is to protect human dignity. We don't want to view ourselves as a bunch of billiard balls jostling against each other – cause and effect, cause and effect. The billiard ball metaphor makes it sound as if we are victims of forces beyond our control. But we are not victims, and this is crucially important. In fact, if I can communicate just one idea about human freedom, this would be it:

"Determinants" are not just outside forces that push us around. We are also determinants. We are also forces, causes, sources of new action.

This is a subtle point but it is worth contemplating until we see it with 100% clarity. *Yes, we are part of the great cosmic game, and we play by the rules of that game. But we do get to play.*

When we are making decisions, our thoughts, emotions, and impulses are causal forces that influence the process. *Thus we ourselves are part of the active potency of the cosmos.* Without realizing it, we may be setting up a false dichotomy – ourselves versus the universe, as if we were not part of the whole. So we evict ourselves from Reality and then feel pushed around by this huge, alien, deterministic machine that is outside of us.

If we tell ourselves that our choices make no difference, we have (irrationally) mobilized a new determinant that undermines effective decision-making. If we tell ourselves that we make our own decisions and our decisions do make a difference, we have (rationally) influenced our decision-making in a helpful way.

Real freedom starts now

If I think about my past decisions, I am, in effect, looking in a rear view mirror. From that perspective I have neither magical nor practical freedom. Everything is over and done with. But if I focus on the options that are available now, I find the steering wheel in my hand. *Right this second* I am acting, creating, making the difference I decide to make. The way to play my part in the great cosmic game is to focus on what I'm choosing now.

Suppose I look back and think about a time a truck was coming toward me, but I dodged it and survived. Since that event is past, it's no longer part of the game. We can mentally revisit past decisions as if we were entitled to a do-over, but that doesn't work. Whatever I did vis-a-vis the truck is finished. But if I see that lethal lorry hurtling toward me right this second, it's game-on. Time to boogie!

I think a person either does or does not "get" this key insight into present-moment practical freedom. When I myself lose track of this insight, I sometimes remember the analogy of staring into the headlights of an oncoming Peterbilt. Would I rather dodge this rolling reaper, or not? Less dramatically, shall I proofread the paragraph I've just written? Yes, I will . . . and now I've corrected an error.

Here's a comparison between non-deterministic, "magical" free will and practical freedom, focusing on both the past-time and present-time perspectives:

Magical freedom, past tense: My free choices have helped bring me to where I am at this moment. Can I change those choices? No. They are forever fixed. There's nothing I can do about them.
Practical freedom, past tense: My prior choices have helped bring me to where I am at this moment. Can I change those choices? No. They are forever fixed. There's nothing I can do about them.

Do you see the dramatic difference? Right, there isn't any.

Magical freedom, present tense: At this moment I have various alternatives. Which do I choose?
Practical freedom, present tense: At this moment I have various alternatives. Which do I choose?

In making choices right now, there is no practically significant difference between magical and practical freedom. I cannot change the past, and I have the present-time power to choose among alternatives. That is exactly what I need.

Certain ways of understanding selfhood work especially well with determinism (or determinism plus a dash of randomness). For example, we can understand ourselves as grounded in the present, perhaps by focusing on the notion that each of us is born anew each moment, continually arising in the midst of our former selves. Although it may not be possible or even desirable to hold this view consistently, it is sometimes quite useful.

Buddhism offers ways of developing this right-now emphasis, utilizing a principle known in Japanese as hon'nin myo, "from this moment on." From the born-anew perspective the question of whether my past selves had free will is trivial. The central issue is always: *here I am; what shall I do?*

Having discussed freedom of choice in terms of both past and present perspectives, what about the future? Are you concerned that deterministic factors will limit your future options? Well, there are dozens of ways to enhance the flexibility, creativity, and overall effectiveness of your decision-making processes. If you want more freedom, you can get it. Note that at this very moment, either you want to change yourself or you don't. If you want to change yourself you can find ways to do that without believing in free will. And if you don't feel motivated to improve yourself, you don't need free will. So if you're motivated to change, you can change. If you are not, there is little point in wondering whether you are really free. It is ironic that some people are quite upset by the suggestion that we lack magical freedom, but do little to expand their own freedom in any sense of the term.

Is it better to fool ourselves?

I abandoned magical freedom in favor of practical freedom decades ago, and I am generally comfortable with a deterministic world-view (or determinism plus a dollop of indeterminacy). But psychology has taught us the importance of individual differences. Some people may wish to avoid dwelling upon the fact that magical, non-deterministic free will is self-contradictory. Others will have no problem with this realization. Similarly, some people get the jitters if they look out the window of a passenger plane while focusing on the fact that this ponderous people-mover is riding on air, and rather thin air at that. Others contemplate the diaphanous foundation of their flight and remain unperturbed.

Among those who despise determinism are people I deeply respect. Immanuel Kant called efforts to make free will compatible with determinism a "wretched subterfuge."[362] Christof Koch notes that this issue "is no mere philosophical banter; it engages people in a way that few other metaphysical questions do. It is the bedrock of society's notions of responsibility, of praise and blame, of being judged for something you did, whether good or bad." "Personally," Koch writes, "I find determinism

---

[362]Kant, http://praxeology.net/kant4.htm.

abhorrent. The idea that your reading of my book at this point in time is inherent in the Big Bang evokes in me a feeling of complete helplessness."[363]

Here's another problem: *Sometimes the truth can act like a lie.* An idea that is 100% accurate may lead us to think in ways that are inaccurate.[364] Thus a person could discover some new truth, and as a result of that discovery become confused about another issue. For instance, people who rightly reject the traditional idea of free will might wrongly conclude that they also lack practical freedom. Paradoxically, then, learning a new fact would cause a new error. Rejecting magical freedom would cause them to make practical mistakes.

Dealing with this issue is so difficult that it sometimes even trips up eminent philosophers. I admire John Searle's work, for example, but I have doubts about this comment. "Our free will is ineliminable in that we cannot even *think* it away. You go into a restaurant and they give you the menu and you have to decide between the veal and the steak. You cannot say to the waiter, 'Look, I'm a determinist. *Que sera sera,*' because even doing that is an exercise of freedom. There is no escaping the necessity of exercising your own free choice."[365]

Do you see where this argument becomes vulnerable? Being a determinist does not mean giving up one's ability to choose. In fact we could imagine an intelligent machine that could read a menu and make a selection. Perhaps it's at the local Restaurant for Robots, and it craves some high-grade 30-weight. Even if we know without doubt that the machine operates deterministically, it would seem like a peculiar glitch if it told the waiter, "I'm a determinist. *Que sera sera.*" On the other hand, saying "Penzoil Synthetic, please," would be an appropriate use of practical freedom. The device was free to choose Red Line Racing Lubricant instead, if it had been feeling frisky. It was not constrained by

---

[363]Koch 2012, pp. 91-92, 99.

[364]"Some beliefs, even if they are both true and rationally grounded in the evidence, may serve only to undermine our deepest, most identity-constituting projects and thus to undermine our very being in the world" (Taylor 2007, p. 151).

[365]Searle and Freeman 1998, p. 733.

outside forces or internal malfunctions. It acted according to its own nature, manifesting a kind of freedom that is well worth wanting.

Here's another confusion: Some people have excused bad behavior by essentially saying, "my brain made me do it." This rationalization involves the confusion between "I" and "my brain." If I am (roughly) the same as my brain, saying that my brain makes me do things is as silly as saying, "My excuse for committing murder is that I made myself do it," or even, "My excuse is that I did it."[366]

Summing up

The sort of free will that I think is illusory requires two things. (1) *Free-will choices must be our choices.* (2) *Free-will choices must liberate us from causal determinants.* This is a self-contradictory idea, because "free" contradicts "will." Insofar as my choices are free from the person I am at this instant, such choices are freed *from* my will. Fortunately practical freedom provides us with most or all of what we hoped we would gain from non-deterministic free will.

We are only alive in the present moment. From this right-now perspective, the forces that have made me who I am are part of the overall interplay of determinants that has brought the cosmos to its current state. So here I stand, in the midst of it all. What shall I choose to do? Whatever I choose, I hope reliable determinants will enable my choices to bear fruit as I anticipated.

New truths can cause new confusions, so we need to think clearly and carefully if we reject magical freedom. But in general it seems best to live in alignment with truth rather than to engage in benevolent self-deception. We do not need to play tricks with the laws of cause and

---

[366]Those who affirm practical freedom can understand praise and blame in ways that don't contradict determinism. People who are not constrained by outside forces or extreme psychological compulsions can choose to improve their future decisions. When they receive positive or negative input, they can decide whether to heed such feedback. Therefore when we want their actions to change, it makes sense to address them as responsible agents. They are, literally, *able to respond.*

effect as if we could go back in time and become our own grandparents. We are here and we are real and we have real creative power.

Our starting point at any moment is as a person with values, with an agenda, with aspirations. *It is already our nature and destiny to reach toward our varied potentials. We are not static organisms that stay as they are, like lizards or grasshoppers. We are dynamic organisms who were born in motion, born changing, as if we were birds born on the wing.*

Chapter Seventeen
Your Living Mind

Message in a bottle

In its hidden home, my mostly unknown and unknowable self sends out a message and hopes for a response. Like a castaway corking a note inside a bottle and hurling it into the sea, something within me sends a signal into the roiling ocean of sensuous phenomena – "I'm here. I exist. *I am a living human mind."*

Rapidly, reliably, this message floats back to the one who sent it, for the sender is also the intended recipient. Moment after moment, the same thing occurs. By repeatedly tossing tokens of my existence into the volatile currents of manifest awareness, I come to know myself in ways that fig trees, waterfalls, and laptop computers cannot.

The tokens of selfhood that I eject and re-discover are fleeting and fragmentary, but they are evidence enough. My hidden mind has been saved from the frightening darkness. It will not be left marooned in endless isolation. It knows that it exists. It knows that it lives. The message in the bottle has safely come home.

❈ ❈ ❈ ❈ ❈ ❈ ❈ ❈

In this final chapter I will consider the relationship between consciousness and human values. I have already emphasized the importance of "off-stage," non-sensory aspects of consciousness, but I want to say more about the value of vividly manifest sensations and perceptions. I'll begin with a prosaic and partial translation of the metaphorical passage you just read.

The experiencing self is an elaborate configuration of interconnected mental processes. Although this self is "where we live," most of it is not introspectively evident – at least not in the attention-grabbing manner of sensuous phenomena. Fortunately the off-stage operations of this largely-hidden self are interwoven with overtly introspectable experiences. *Sensations* give us clues about bodily states and emotions. *Perceptions* tell us where in the world we are and what challenges we're facing. *Subvocal speech* helps us know our own thoughts and clarify them further. Awareness of our *movements and bodily positions* can tip us off about what we think and feel. (If I feel myself making a fist, perhaps I'm angry.) So the mind's off-stage machinations send fragmentary evidence of itself into the spotlight of manifest awareness. This continuous stream of up-front phenomena helps ground us in right-now reality, keeping us from getting lost. It's a built-in navigation system, guiding us through our lives. It helps us feel that the world around us (and our inner, mental world) is present, understandable, available, and for the most part re-assuringly familiar. What a gift!

Humphrey's beautiful dust

Nicholas Humphrey's *Soul Dust: The Magic of Consciousness* offers fine insights into the relationship between consciousness and human well-being. As Alison Gopnik explains, "Humphrey points to a feature of consciousness that has been surprisingly neglected. 'The bottom line about how consciousness changes the human outlook – as deep an existential truth as anyone could ask for – is this: *We do not want to be zombies,*' he writes."[367] We *value* the fact that it is "like something" to be a living person. Thus Humphrey puts a philosophical spin on the fact that most of us prefer to be awake and alive rather than dead or comatose. Furthermore he also speculates that the main benefit of consciousness may not be "to *enable* you to do something you could not do otherwise but rather to *encourage* you to do something you would not do otherwise . . ."[368]

Humphrey suggests that "consciousness – on several levels – makes *life more worth living.* . . . The added *joie de vivre*, the new *enchantment* with the world they live in, and the novel sense of their own *metaphysical importance* has, in the course of evolutionary history, dramatically increased the investment individuals make in their own survival."[369]

One charming example of this enchantment with the world involves apes rather than people. In Tanzania, scientists observed a chimp named Golden beside a stream "drawing her fingers repeatedly through the rippling water, transfixed, it seems, by the delicate play of light, sound, and touch on her body. Other chimps began to copy her, and within

---

[367]Gopnik 2011, p. 19.

[368]Humphrey 2011, p. 72.

[369]Humphrey 2011, p. 75.

months this kind of water play had become a family tradition." According to Allan Fallow, "Golden finds time to sit on a rock with her hand immersed in the water, overturning stones on the streambed" every time they cross that creek.[370]

No doubt the enjoyable aspects of consciousness do motivate many of us to watch our diets and get regular checkups. But I see this as a secondary benefit of consciousness rather than as its primary contribution to evolutionary fitness. In understanding consciousness I emphasize the continuities between humans and "lower" animals. Humphrey says he isn't sure that fish are conscious at all,[371] but I'll bet sharks typically fight just as hard against attackers as we do. They lack some of our specifically human motivations for clinging to life, but the drive to survive has deep biological roots.

Most of the survival value of consciousness, I believe, is that it provides us with a complex, flexible, and highly usable inner simulation of the outside world and our own mental processes, and of the relationship between the two. But even though "added *joie de vivre*" is of secondary importance, in specific situations it can make a crucial difference. Humphrey also thinks consciousness is valuable in a more subtle way, and here I found his argument persuasive. Our perceptions often represent both external realities and our responses to those realities, in a way that seems to fuse what we perceive with the ways that we react to it. This sometimes creates problems, as when we project our emotional responses onto our surroundings. Thus the people we dislike may look especially nasty, because we're focusing on their most unpleasant features and facial expressions. But Humphrey points out one marvelous consequence:

"It is as if, when you see and hear and touch and taste things, some of the magic of your phenomenal sensation is rubbing off onto the things as such. And this has the extraordinary result of making it seem to you as if *the things themselves possess phenomenal qualities.* As if things out there in the world have an extra dimension of subjective *presence.* Maybe even as if *you have a private line to them,* as if they are imbued with *your*

---

[370]Humphrey 2011, p. 84.

[371]Humphrey 2011, p. 93.

subjectivity. "[372] "Borrowed phenomenality transforms the world into an awesome place."[373]

"Borrowed phenomenality" – what a wonderful concept. Atoms may be devoid of color, but the world as we experience it is lavish with vivid hues. Beauty may be only in the eye of the beholder, but our human rendition of reality spreads beauty everywhere. This is another sort of "message in a bottle," sent out and safely received. We project phenomenality out into the world, but it seems as if we have received it *from* the world.

Thus consciousness "is not just about the joy of living but about the *point* of living too. . . . Because the externalization of value that results from projecting sensations onto objects . . . provides a whole new basis for believing that life has meaning. If it is good to be alive, then it is even better to be alive in *a good world.*"[374]

The quality of life

As Humphrey and others have noted, evolution is guided by the amoral reality that whatever replicates itself effectively sticks around. Thus we have humans, and thus we have bubonic plague bacilli. And thus an extremely large ecological niche is occupied by creatures that feed upon others. In fact one could build a good case for the claim that without the need for effective predation – and the need to protect against predators – we would never have evolved consciousness.

So there is an ominous underside to our wonderful sentience. But during the course of human cultural evolution, our ability to reflect upon pain and pleasure, happiness and distress, led to a shift in our personal agendas. Some of us now aspire to systematically maximize our own well-being and that of others. To do that we must cut ourselves free from mere amoral self-replication. We must actively rebel against many of the urges and obsessions that evolution has etched into our psyches. Many of us see that ego, greed, hostility, and the desire to dominate diminish the

[372]Humphrey 2011, p. 111.

[373]Humphrey 2011, p. 118.

[374]Humphrey 2011, p. 121.

quality of our lives. We want to go beyond these limitations, limits, re-routing our energies toward meaning and value.

Biology programs our brains to generate endless cycles of craving and suffering, but we can retrofit these motivations, using them to construct a new behavioral compass. As Henry David Thoreau wrote, "It is something to be able to paint a picture, or to carve a statue, and so to make a few objects beautiful; but it is far more glorious to carve and paint the very atmosphere and medium through which we look, which morally we can do. To affect the quality of the day, that is the highest of arts."[375] And of course the "atmosphere and medium through which we look" is *conscious experience.*

Some say that understanding consciousness in physical terms undermines our efforts to create value. Let's consider this charge.

Consciousness diminished?

Hundreds of years ago when Galileo affirmed Copernicus' theory that Earth is not the center of the cosmos, the clerics of his day fought bitterly against this idea. It challenged their place at the center of creation, but eventually the Copernican view prevailed. We have been trying to push ourselves back onto center stage ever since, and science keeps knocking us out of the limelight. Darwin showed that our bodies are an integral part of the natural order. Freud taught us that human reason is often over-powered by unconscious drives. And today we are undergoing a new Copernican revolution in self-understanding. "I" am learning to see myself as the shifting activities of systems within the brain. Unsurprisingly, many resist this notion. Their reactions echo the traditional resistance to Galileo, Darwin, and Freud – same tune, different verse.

Saying consciousness is in the brain may seem to undermine our dignity, reducing us to "mere" machines. Thus we see sad-looking robots on the covers of books about mind and brain. Look at the dust jackets of Jean-Pierre Changeux's *Neuronal Man* and Michael Tye's *Consciousness Revisited,* amazingly similar even though they were published a quarter

---

[375]Quoted in *Hymns for the Celebration of Life,* Unitarian Universalist Association, 1964, Reading #395.

of a century apart.[376] Both depict a human head with the brain exposed. Both faces seem passive and morose. Both are rendered in gloomy grays and purples. Tye's robotic fellow is lying face-up, his bright red eye staring blankly, his visible brain filled with sequences of ones and zeroes. Who would want to be like *that*?

These robotic images could serve as Exhibit A for Harold Morowitz, who warns us that "the way we respond to our fellow human beings is dependent on the way we conceptualize them in our theoretical formulations. If we envision our fellows solely as animals or machines, we drain our interactions of humanistic richness."[377]

But not everyone thinks machine analogies are degrading. Douglas Hofstadter asks, "Why don't you let the word 'machine' conjure up images of dancing patterns of light rather than of giant steam shovels?"[378]

Without knowing it, we may allow ourselves to be manipulated by negative metaphors, discouraged by downbeat poetic imagery. ***Beware of depressing poetry disguised as philosophy.***

Physicalism need not rob us of life's richness and beauty. On the contrary, it can both retain and reframe conscious experience, including

---

[376]The cover of *Neuronal Man* was subsequently changed, but it still expresses a disturbingly robotic vision of humans-as-physical. And for a recent example of a mechanistic view of humanity, see the issue of *The Philosopher's Magazine* on "building better humans" (Third Quarter, 2013). Look at the cover (http://www.exacteditions.com/read/tpm/3rd-quarter-2013-36259), and ask yourself whether this "better" human seems like an improvement over *homo sapiens* – and would you want to meet that thing in a dark alley?

[377]Morowitz 1981, p. 41.

[378]Hofstadter 1981c, p. 86.

the experience of wonder itself. I feel not the least bit diminished in moving from "Wow, it's magic!" to "Wow, what an amazing brain!" Hilary Putnam makes a similar point: "I think the traditional dualist says *'wouldn't it be terrible if we turned out to be just matter, for then there is a physical explanation for everything we do.'* And the traditional materialist says *'if we are just matter, then there is a physical explanation for everything we do. Isn't that exciting!'*"[379]

This is another example of a correct idea that can lead us into illusion. It may turn out that we are machines, in the sense that we are physical entities that function according to certain laws. But when we hear the word "machine," what comes to mind are familiar devices such as cars, computers, and food processors. As we saw in Chapter Two, this is grotesquely misleading, because the brain is not like any machine that has ever existed. In reality we are like nothing else that we have ever encountered except . . . human beings.

Back to the beach

Now let's apply what we've discussed in this book to the three examples of conscious experiences mentioned in Chapter One. (If you chose examples of your own instead, you can plug them in here.)

In our first scene you're barefoot, strolling in the surf at Waikiki. You are blissfully aware of the water splashing your ankles and feet, the salt spray, the lulling sun, the sounds of people at play. For these delights you may thank perceptual receptors in your skin, eyes, nose, and ears. Signals from these receptors continually flow into your brain where they're sliced, diced, shaped, and sculpted. A small army of neurological gatekeepers makes some of these inputs consciously available to you as an experiencing subject. Since perceptual inputs are integrated into your knowledge of the world, and you already know you're in Hawaii, the sunshine and salty air fit your current conceptual context. And having read this book, you think, *"How nice to have such phenomenal qualia!"*

Your experience of the beach is far more complex than anyone could possibly articulate. You glance out to sea and notice boats, birds, and surfers. It may seem as if all of them are clearly and consistently visible,

---

[379]Putnam 1980, p. 137.

but careful introspection would show that various regions, points, and patches within this scene are clear, semi-clear, fuzzy, or absent, in complex gradations. Your perceptions of sounds, smells, and sensations also involve many levels of attention and inattention, sometimes sharply focused and sometimes barely-noticed in the background.

And who is this "you" who is sauntering in the surf? It's your body, in one obvious sense. But in another sense it's your experiencing self. After all, this beach-bum reverie might be an especially vivid dream, while your sleeping body shivers at midnight in Minnesota.

Admittedly the idea of selfhood is murky and contentious. We lack even a loose consensus about what is and is not part of the self. Even if we agree on some specific definition, we have little evidence about how such a self-system is deployed within the brain, and only the sketchiest notions about how thoughts and statements arise in connection with its experiences. But if we are persons who enjoy and suffer our own experiences, and we are physical beings, then this enjoying and suffering self is embedded in our heads.

In Hawaii, you are intensely aware of "phenomenally" conscious mind-states such as sounds and tactile sensations. You are also aware of what these perceptions and sensations represent, such as the squish of sand underfoot and the annoying *yawp* of a seagull. When the seabird squawked and selective-attention machinery ushered that auditory perception "into" your awareness, was this audition already wearing the bird-sound label? Or did it enter your awareness as an anonymous noise that you then (almost instantly) blamed on a bird? Regardless of which view is true, you would typically be conscious of both the sound and your belief about its origin, even though this belief would not be "present" in the way that sensory states seem present. And both sensory and non-sensory conscious states are interwoven with unconscious machinations, such as the unconscious associations triggered by a seagull squawk.

So what is this stuff? What is the *experience* that seems like luscious, squishy sand between your toes? Could it, in principle, be a cluster of neural activities? If you've at least poked your head through this book's three difficult doorways, I hope you will agree that this could be so. There are still many issues to be addressed, but there are no absolute showstoppers that grind our quest to a hopeless halt. One might claim that those squishy toe-skin qualia are *purely* qualitative and could not be quantities of anything at all, but introspection is a fragile foundation for building this case.

Now on to the second scenario from Chapter One. You're dining out with good friends, showered with sensuous inputs – sounds, sights, scents, tastes, and other agreeable stimuli. Perhaps you've just made an especially witty remark, and a tablemate laughs in appreciation. Imagine the way her face might have looked at just that instant. Once again we have:

❀ Phenomenal experience: a "thing-like" visual experience, manifestly present and spatially arrayed.
❀ Non-phenomenal experience: consciously believing that you're seeing a friend's face.
❀ Unconscious mental states: faithful neural servants that process visual data into what you take to be a face-like shape, and interpret her expression as appreciation instead of derision.

Throughout dinner these three levels of mentality play their secret game of tag, bouncing off of each other in a resonating, echoing interaction that none of us can track no matter how we try. At dinner your belief that "I'm feeling tipsy" could show up at any or all of these levels – sensory and/or non-sensory awareness plus unconscious processing. You may also be aware of psychological and social subtleties that are barely hinted by explicit sensory cues, and some of this information processing also takes place outside of conscious awareness. For instance, you may be non-consciously cognizant of feeling insecure with your dining partners and trying to impress them. This sub rosa realization could influence your actions even though you might absolutely deny that you feel this way. Thanks to unconscious information processing à la Sigmund Freud, this covert knowledge about yourself might surface that night in a troublesome dream. Then the belief that you were feeling ill at ease might be promoted into full consciousness.

In Chapter One I mentioned one more classic conscious episode – a painful toothache. The brain uses this pain as a lever to press you into action, prodding you to get it to stop. Like other sensory experiences, pain qualia are typically available for use by the mind's mechanisms of behavior control, are constituted within an experiencing self, are remembered at least briefly, are at least partially reportable, and seem "present." And pain often tells you things about both external objects and the way your mind represents those objects. You know something's wrong with that tooth, and it was pain qualia that tipped you off.

In all three of these situations, sensory phenomena and our subjective experiences of those phenomena are muddled up in a maddening mix that makes tenured professors turn to strong drink. To deal with this awkward duality, I have proposed that when you think about a conscious state such as a glimpse of a laughing countenance, your thoughts are directed toward that visual perception *as a state of the experiencing self.* She's smiling. Got it!

Looking back, looking forward

Now that we're close to the end, I'll review some key ideas, principles, and implications of *Your Living Mind,* and speculate about what lies ahead in consciousness studies.

❀ Although philosophers are criticized for not making progress, the difficulty of solving ancient enigmas actually underlines the importance of this discipline. Philosophers are dealing with topics that are very, very hard for humans to address. If you want to develop more respect for this profession, try writing a book about consciousness.

❀ We can learn a lot from the giant-brain perspective, viewing the brain as a very big place in a very small space. And remember that in at least some ways, you dwell *within* this mental metropolis.

❀ Complexity confuses us. Don't fall into the trap of thinking that something can't be true just because it's too complicated to understand.

❀ All statements about conscious experiences are a few steps removed from the experiences themselves. It would be nice if sensory qualia could pipe up and tell us all about themselves, but they aren't wired for sound.

❀ Our minds intermingle three kinds of processes, woven together with exquisite intricacy: phenomenal ("on-stage") aspects of conscious experience, non-phenomenal ("off-stage") aspects, and unconscious mental states. Although conscious qualia are very important, what matters most to us as humans may reside in states that are conscious but non-phenomenal.

❀ In some ways the mind-body problem is actually a mind-*anything* problem. Consciousness is perplexing and paradoxical, no matter what sort of thing it turns out to be.

❀ To become "relentlessly modest" about introspection-based judgments, we must be willing to focus upon some experience and sincerely consider the possibility that a compelling belief about this experience is erroneous.

❀ Qualia are ontologically opaque. When we reflect upon our own qualia, we discover little or nothing of their essential nature. Thus we should be skeptical of ontological judgments based upon introspection, especially when competent theorists disagree.

❀ If introspection detects brain events, it detects highly specific neural activities rather than chunks of nerve tissue.

❀ One reason sensations and perceptions seem "real" is that the brain establishes what we take to *be* reality. Our reflections about our own sensory experiences start with them as real, as substantial, as thus-there-now. We can't peer through these experiences to see "the real reality" that's behind them. When we contemplate our own qualia, we are attending to a basic building block of what reality is for us.

❀ And for emphasis I'll repeat – ***beware of depressing poetry disguised as philosophy.***

We have made a long journey through our mental hall of mirrors, but there is much more work to be done. Here are a few items for future agendas.

As far as I know, few philosophers of mind have spelled out a well-developed theory of selfhood. No doubt some of them could sketch such theories and relate them to their own accounts of consciousness. I would find such an exploration quite helpful.

We could also reflect more deeply about the nature of pleasure and pain. I have suggested ways of synthesizing these states in a machine, but others will offer additional insights.

We obviously need to think more about diminished consciousness. As medical technology advances, we will keep more people "alive" whose awareness is minimal or nonexistent. What aspects of consciousness matter most, and how can we preserve these best during aging and disability?[380]

The psychology of religion is a well-established discipline, but the psychology of philosophy lags behind. Researchers have begun to open this can of writhing psyches, and the results are fascinating.[381] More, please!

And what about SOFAR itself? How can single-order fallibilist realism be refined and expanded? I see two issues as especially important, two points at which my view of consciousness collides with powerful intuitions.

Collision One: It seems as if qualia such as experienced redness and pains are "special" – inexplicable phenomena that are radically different from anything else we know.

Collision Two: It seems as if phenomenal presence is impossible to explain in physical terms, or in any terms whatsoever except, "that's just how it is."

---

[380]"Ethical issues that arise at the beginning and the end of life are often held to turn, in part at any rate, on whether the organism is conscious" (Levy 2014, p. 127).

[381]In a paper on the influence of personality on philosophical beliefs, Holtzman suggests that "the persistence of philosophical disagreement suggests that something very personal drives philosophical intuition" (2013, p. 28).

Since I have addressed both of these issues, I'm sure that all readers will enthusiastically agree, thank me kindly, and move on. (And that's the best joke in the whole book.) These are ferociously difficult conundrums. I will continue to reflect upon them, both consciously and unconsciously, and I encourage others to do the same. I look forward to your emails, and to reading what I'll scrawl in the night on the note pad beside my bed.

As we conclude

This book is about the mystery of consciousness *and* why it matters to you. At this point, how has considering these topics made a difference to you personally? Have you re-examined your opinions about consciousness and selfhood? Do some things that once seemed simple and obvious now seem mysterious? Are you more keenly aware of the need for careful analysis of complex issues and the difficulty of talking about deep subjects using ordinary English? Have you challenged some of your own assumptions? Have you seen how these have been shaped by biases and emotional reactions?

Speaking for myself, studying consciousness has helped me revise my sense of who I really am. Studying the mind helps me realize that the familiarity of our personal experiences should not breed complacency. We are mysteries to ourselves, inner universes to be explored. We – I – you – are so much more than we know or think.

My goal in writing this book has been both modest and grandiose. I do not claim to have proven that consciousness is deployed within the brain. We are not remotely close to accomplishing this feat. Instead I have tried to show how consciousness *could* be a complex system of brain events. But merely demonstrating this theoretical possibility is a maddeningly magnificent challenge.

I have argued that we do access our own mental states through introspection, and I have denied that we can fully understand them in this way. This combination of affirmation and negation helps us grasp the thorniest branches of the Hard Problem of consciousness.

It seems as if I have made progress, but I know I may be mistaken. As a dedicated fallibilist, I strive to maintain a ruthless modesty about my ability to understand the mind from within. I cannot rule out the possibility that I have been tripped up by my own cognitive limitations, with conceptually disastrous consequences. And perhaps some of my fallibilistic missiles have overshot their targets.

Speaking personally now, *I hope this book has helped you recognize what a miracle you are,* and that you will hold on to this realization. Watch your mind as it effortlessly conjures everyday magic. Without even trying, you are aware of yourself as a creature that endures through time. You can chuckle at jokes and feel your spine tingle while hearing Beethoven. You have a multidimensional inner life, with pain and pleasure, a capacity for love, and a sense of justice. And to top it all off you can *know* about all of these things. You can even reflect upon your place in the vastness of space and time. We are obviously not gods in any literal sense, but I can see why an ancient Hebrew wrote in the Book of Genesis that we are made in God's image.

I've been thinking lately that there are two very different sources of wonder – half-deliberate self-confusion, and hard-earned clarity. If we have been keeping ourselves pleasantly confused so as to feel that the world is magical, we may have become attached to our puzzlements. Losing them, we may feel, would leave us disenchanted. But whenever we see through illusory mysteries, we can find new mysteries to make our jaws go slack. Discovery opens doors to wider wonder. I began the book with Einstein's proclamation that mystery is the source of all art and science. He understood so much that others found incomprehensible, but these insights heightened his sense of awe instead of diminishing it.

Even after working on this book for three years and studying consciousness for a quarter-century, I still find myself thinking, "aren't we just astonishing?" This familiar stranger, our own inner experience, is to be cared for and cherished, however we conceive of its nature.

In some ways the great stream of consciousness is probably just as we imagine it, and in other ways it is probably quite different. Although I'll never answer Nagel's question about what it's like to be a bat, I can learn much more about what it's like to be me – and by reasonable extension, what it's like to be you. If we can tremulously venture through intimidating doorways, we will keep pressing forward, toward ever-deeper truths about the living human mind that is our home.

Definitions

These definitions have three purposes:

1. To briefly explain technical terms to non-philosophers
2. When a term is used in a variety of ways by philosophers, to clarify the way I use it
3. To define idiosyncratic terms such as SOFAR

Consciousness, conscious experience. This book is mostly concerned with what we are conscious *of*, especially sensations and perceptions. Like many others who write about consciousness, I do not define this word precisely, but in Chapter One I list five hallmarks of adult-human conscious experiences. Typical conscious experiences are *available for use by the parts of the mind that control behavior, are experienced by a conscious self, are remembered at least briefly, are at least partially reportable, and seem manifestly present.* All of these characteristics apply to phenomenally conscious states, and all but *seeming present* apply to non-phenomenally conscious states.

Direct realism. This is the claim that our perceptions put us directly in touch with the world. When we perceive an object, we experience the object itself, rather than experiencing it indirectly by being aware of one of our own mental states.

Dualism. According to dualists, all or part of the mind is non-physical. The mind is thus separate from the body, in at least some important respect.

Duality. This is the idea that consciousness involves both what we experience and the act of experiencing it. An experience of a green afterimage, for example, would include:

1. The mental state that constitutes the afterimage
2. The mental state that constitutes our being aware of the afterimage

Many believe that if no one is aware of an afterimage, that afterimage is not conscious – and if the afterimage does not exist, it isn't conscious either. This dual requirement generates the problem of duality.

Eliminativism. This is an attempt to solve problems by saying that certain things don't exist. Eliminativism about qualia says there are no qualia.

Epistemic. Having to do with knowledge and the way we know things. One of the epistemic aspects of the mind-body relationship is the problem of *how we could know* that the mind is in the brain. This is not a problem about whether the mind *actually is* a bodily state. That is an ontological problem.

Explanatory gap. This is the worry that no matter how much of the brain's activity we explain, we could never explain why a particular brain event is linked to a particular experience. Why should a certain pattern of neuronal activity cause or constitute an experience of redness rather than one of blueness?

Another sort of explanatory gap involves the challenge of explaining why some neural activity pattern would cause or constitute a conscious experience rather than an unconscious mental state. This puzzle is addressed in Chapter Thirteen as the problem of *presence*, which is defined below.

Externalism. The idea that a mental state is at least partly constituted by things outside of the mind. For example, if "orange" is defined as the assortment of entities which typically cause us to experience the color orange, the orangeness of a carrot is at least partly constituted by certain features of the carrot's molecular structure.

Fallibilism. I use this term to stand for the claim that we sometimes make important mistakes in thinking about and describing our own conscious experiences.

Higher-order theory; HOT theory. HOT theory holds that in order for a mental state to be conscious, there must be a certain sort of thought about that state. Thus to be conscious of seeing a tree, we must have a thought which could be roughly expressed as, "I am seeing a tree." The HOT itself is typically unconscious, but when we engage in introspection it may become so: *"I am aware that* I'm seeing a tree." See Chapter Six.

Indirect realism. In contrast to direct realism, this is the view that when we perceive the world we don't have direct access to real objects. Instead we experience an internal simulation of the world, unique to our minds, which we treat as if it were the world.

Intentional; intentionality. Intentionality means "aboutness." Intentional thoughts are those that are about something or other, that refer to or represent something. The intentional object of a thought about Adam would be a man who was directly created by God, regardless of whether one believes that Adam actually existed.

Internalism. The idea that a mental state is wholly situated within the mind. For example, if "orange" is defined in this way, this color would be a mental state and not a property of things that we see as orange. Strictly speaking, there would be no orange objects.

Introspection. Introspection means paying attention to our own mental processes. Introspection is often brief, casual, and automatic. For instance, if we become angry, we don't need to focus intently on this state to be introspectively aware that we are angry.

Manifest. See *presence.*

Materialism. Most commonly used synonymously with *physicalism* (see below), though this term predates physicalism.

Metaphysical. In this book this is a synonym for *ontological.*

Mindweaving. I use this word to refer to the notion that conscious states typically interweave sensory/phenomenal experiences, non-sensory/non-phenomenal experiences, and unconscious mental processes.

Ontological agnosticism. By this I mean the idea that introspection does not give us reliable access to the ontology of qualia.

Ontology, metaphysics. Ontology is the study of what exists, and the nature and properties of whatever does exist.

Pan-psychism. This theory holds that everything is in some sense mental. Every material object has some sort of consciousness or mentality.

Phenomena, sensory phenomena, phenomenal consciousness, introspectable phenomena. There are several philosophical definitions of phenomena. I typically use this term to refer to aspects of conscious experience that seem to be "there," present in our awareness in a way that we can mentally point to and describe. By contrast, non-phenomenally conscious states do not seem present in this way. Sensations and perceptions are the most obvious examples of phenomenal experiences, whereas thoughts are typically non-phenomenal. (But thoughts often occur with phenomenal accompaniments such as images that are related to the thought.)

Physicalism. This is the thesis that everything is physical, that there are no non-physical entities. This would mean that the mind is wholly physical.

Presence, manifest presence. Philosophers have expressed this idea in many ways, often using the term "phenomena" as a label for what they have in mind. When I speak of presence (or *manifest presence),* I am referring to mental states that seem to be "there," introspectable in a way that we can mentally point to and describe, such as sensations and perceptions.

Qualia. These are the qualities of sensory experiences. When you see a red rose, you will experience the quale of a certain shade of red. (Quale is pronounced *qua*-lay, not *quail.)*

Representationalism, strong representationalism, strong intentionalism. This is the view that all conscious experiences are intentional; that is, they are about something or other. This book mostly considers externalist versions of strong representationalism, which define qualia solely in terms of what they represent about the external world (including one's own body). See Chapter Seven.

Self, experiencing self, subject, subject of experience. These terms have many meanings. For our purposes, the *experiencing self* is the part of us that undergoes, enjoys, and suffers our experiences. The *self* or *subject* is the experiencing self plus additional components that provide a greater context for consciousness.[382]

Self-representationalism. This is the view that experiences are self-representing. An experience of seeing a tree both represents the tree and represents itself as an experience.

---

[382]These context-creating components might include our memories, our anticipations, our beliefs about what is or is not the case, our desires and priorities, and our action plans.

Sensory experiences, sensuous experiences. These are the sensations and perceptions that make up our day-to-day experiences – the taste of chocolate, or the sight of a sunset.

SOFAR. My account of consciousness: a single-order fallibilist approach that affirms the reality of introspectable experiences – **S**ingle-**O**rder **FA**llibilist **R**ealism. A single-order theory contrasts with higher-order theories. For example, HOT theory says that to be conscious of seeing a tree requires having a certain kind of thought that could be expressed as something like, "I'm seeing a tree." So we need the tree-seeing state *and* we need to be aware of that state. SOFAR suggests that a tree-seeing state *just is* being in a subjective state of seeing the tree.[383]

Zombie. In philosophy of mind, a hypothetical creature whose brain has precisely the same physical structures as ours and operates in the same ways that our brains do, but without consciousness. The creature *would* be conscious in the sense of being awake and able to report the contents of its mental states. A psychologist studying you and your zombie twin would discern no difference in behavior. But even though it would be conscious in a certain sense, it would be utterly devoid of sensory phenomena.

---

[383]Unconscious visual states would contribute to the occurrence of subjectively seeing the tree, and after we have that tree-seeing state we may think about and speak about this experience. But having the experience of seeing the tree consists of one state, not one state + another state that is aware of it. See Chapter Twelve for appallingly complex but important details.

For Further Reading

Chalmers, D. J. (1996) *The Conscious Mind: In Search of a Fundamental Theory* (Oxford: Oxford University Press). A scholarly presentation of the Hard Problem and related issues.

Churchland, P. M. *(1989) Neurophilosophy: Toward a Unified Science of the Mind/Brain* (Cambridge, MA: The MIT Press). Patricia Churchland explains neuroscience to philosophers and philosophy to neuroscientists, in a book that's accessible to any educated reader.

Dennett, D. C. (1991) *Consciousness Explained* (Boston: Little, Brown and Company). One of the few in-depth explorations of consciousness written for non-specialists. Although Dennett has moderated some of his views in response to criticisms, this book is still worth reading and re-reading.

Dretske, F. (1995) *Naturalizing the Mind* (Cambridge, MA: The MIT Press). A relatively clear presentation of externalist representationalism.

Flanagan, O. (1992) *Consciousness Reconsidered* (Cambridge, MA: The MIT Press). A thoughtful book about problems of consciousness.

Gennaro, R. J. (2012) *The Consciousness Paradox* (Cambridge, MA: The MIT Press). Includes excellent information about scientific investigations of infant consciousness and animal consciousness.

Hardin, C. L. (1988) *Color for Philosophers: Unweaving the Rainbow* (Indianapolis: Hackett Publishing Company). A lucid discussion of the philosophical implications of research into color perception.

Hofstadter, D. R. and Dennett, D. C. (1981) *The Mind's I: Fantasies and Reflections on Self and Soul* (New York: Bantam Books). A remarkable collection of essays on mind, brain, and consciousness, with incisive comments by the eminent co-authors.

Hooper, J. and Teresi, D. (1987) *The Three-Pound Universe* (Los Angeles: Jeremy P. Tarcher, Inc.). A fascinating account of neuroscience written for the general public.

Humphrey, N. (2011) *Soul Dust: The Magic of Consciousness* (Princeton and Oxford: Princeton University Press). A readable presentation of Humphrey's unique theory of consciousness.

Journal of Consciousness Studies, http://ingentaconnect.com/journals/bro wse/imp/jcs. A fascinating array of neuroscientific, philosophical, psychological, and parapsychological investigations.

Koch, C. (2012) *Consciousness: Confessions of a Romantic Reductionist* (Cambridge, MA: The MIT Press). Engaging reflections by a renowned scientist who isn't afraid to speak quite personally.

Kriegel, U. and Williford, K. (2006) *Self-Representational Approaches to Consciousness* (Cambridge, MA: The MIT Press). Scholarly papers by Gennaro, Hofstadter, Kriegel, Levine, Van Gulick, Williford, Woodruff-Smith and others, for those who want to delve into this topic.

Kriegel, U. (2009) *Subjective Consciousness: A Self-Representational Theory* (New York: Oxford University Press). A creative and resourceful effort to make self-representationalism work.

Levine, J. (2001) *Purple Haze: The Puzzle of Consciousness* (New York: Oxford University Press). An insightful exploration of core issues.

Robinson, W. S. (2010) *Your Brain and You: What Neuroscience Means for Us* (New York: Goshawk Books). Clear and concise explanations of brain science, along with philosophical analyses. Robinson is especially helpful and lucid in discussing free will.

Sacks, O. (1987) *The Man Who Mistook His Wife For a Hat and Other Clinical Tales* (New York: Harper & Row). Rightly regarded as a classic. Sacks discusses amazing brain syndromes, in a way that highlights the humanity of his patients rather than treating them as "cases."

Seager, W. (1999) *Theories of Consciousness: an Introduction and Assessment* (New York: Routledge). An informative overview of the debate.

Stanford Encyclopedia of Philosophy, http://plato.stanford.edu. A wonderful resource that explains technical terms in detail and explores major theoretical options. Although it can be hard going for non-philosophers, it's worth the effort.

References

Some internet URLs are listed in footnotes rather than in References.

Aleksander, I. and Morton, H. (2007) "Why Axiomatic Models of Being Conscious?" *Journal of Consciousness Studies*, July, 2007, Vol. 14, No. 7, pp. 15-27.

Allen, W. (1991) *The Complete Prose of Woody Allen*. (New York: Wings Books).

Alston, W. (2005) "Perception and Representation." *Philosophy and Phenomenological Research,* March, 2005, Vol. 70, No. 2, pp. 253-89.

Armstrong, D. M. (1980) "The Nature of Mind." In *Readings in Philosophy of Psychology, Volume One,* ed. N. Block (Cambridge, MA: Harvard University Press).

Baars, B. J. (1988) *A Cognitive Theory of Consciousness*. (Cambridge: Cambridge University Press).

Baars, B. J. (2004) "A Stew of Confusion." *Journal of Consciousness Studies*, January, 2004, Vol. 11, No. 1, pp. 29-31.

Baergen, R. (1992) "Perceptual Consciousness and Perceptual Evidence." *Philosophical Papers,* January, 1992, Vol. 21, No. 2, pp. 107-19.

Baggini, J. (2012) "Patricia Churchland, The Really Nice Guy Materialist." *The Philosopher's Magazine*, Issue 57, pp. 61-70.

Baggini, J. (2013) "Harry Frankfurt, Bullshit Detector." *The Philosophers' Magazine*, Issue 63, pp. 54-62.

Bain, D. (2011) "The Imperative View of Pain." *Journal of Consciousness Studies*, September/October, 2011, Vol. 18, No. 9-10, pp. 164-85.

Beaton, M. (2005) "What RoboDennett Still Doesn't Know." *Journal of Consciousness Studies*, December, 2005, Vol. 12, No. 12, pp. 3-25.

Beekmans, J. (2007) "Can Higher-Order Representation Theories Pass Scientific Muster?" *Journal of Consciousness Studies,* September/October, 2007, Vol. 14, No. 9-10, pp. 90-111.

Berger, J. (2013) Comment during discussion of "The Phenomenology of HOT, or What Is It Like to Think That You Think That p?" American Philosophical Association Conference, San Francisco, March 29, 2013.

Bermudez, J. (2007) "The Object Properties Model of Object Perception: Between the Binding Model and the Theoretical Model." *Journal of Consciousness Studies,* September/October, 2007, Vol. 14, No. 9-10, pp. 43-65.

Berryman, S. (2010) "Democritus." The Stanford Encyclopedia of Philosophy (Fall 2010 Edition), Edward N. Zalta (ed.), URL = <http://plato.stanford.edu/archives/fall2010/entries/democritus/>.

Birnbacher, D. (1995) "Artificial Consciousness." In *Conscious Experience,* ed. T. Metzinger (Thorverton, UK: Imprint Academic).

Block, N. (1980) "Troubles with Functionalism." In *Readings in Philosophy of Psychology, Volume One,* ed. N. Block (Cambridge, MA: Harvard University Press).

Block, N. (1981) "Introduction: What Is Philosophy of Psychology?" In *Readings in Philosophy of Psychology, Volume Two,* ed. N. Block (Cambridge, MA: Harvard University Press).

Block, N. (1995) "On a Confusion about a Function of Consciousness." *Behavioral and Brain Sciences,* June, 1995, Vol. 18, No. 2, pp. 227-47.

Block, N. (2007) "Consciousness, Accessibility, and the Mesh Between Psychology and Neuroscience." *Behavioral and Brain Science,* December, 2007, Vol. 30, No. 5-6, pp. 481-548.

Block, N. (2011a) "The Higher Order Approach to Consciousness is Defunct." *Analysis,* July, 2011, Vol. 71, No. 3. pp. 419-31.

Block, N. (2011b) "Response to Rosenthal and Weisberg." *Analysis,* July, 2011, Vol. 71, No. 3, pp. 443-48.

Block, N. (2012) "How Facts About Attention Constrain Theories of Perception." Oral presentation, December 5, 2012, Kant Lectures, Stanford University.

Bortolotti, L. (2009) "Review: *Neurophilosophy at Work,* by Paul Churchland." *Analysis,* January, 2009, Vol. 69, No. 1, pp. 176-78.

Botterell, A. (2001) "Conceiving What Is Not There." *Journal of Consciousness Studies*, August, 2001, Vol. 8, No. 8, pp. 21-42.

Bourget, D. (2013) "A General Reply to the Arguments from Blur, Double Vision, Perspective, and Other Kinds of Perceptual Distortion Against Representationalism." American Philosophical Association Conference, San Francisco, March 28, 2013.

Brogaard, B. and Marlow, K. (2013) "Hearing Colours." *The Philosopher's Magazine*, Issue 63, pp. 28-35.

Brown, H. I. (2008) "The Case for Indirect Realism." In *The Case for Qualia,* ed. E. Wright (Cambridge, MA: The MIT Press).

Brown, R. (2013) "Review: *Constructing the World*, by David Chalmers." *The Philosopher's Magazine*, Issue 61, pp. 115-18.

Campbell, A. (1995) "Review: *Journey to the Centers of the Mind: Towards A Science of Consciousness*, by Susan Greenfield." *Journal of Consciousness Studies*, Vol. 2, No. 2, pp. 191-92.

Carruthers, P. and Schechter, E. (2006) "Can Panpsychism Bridge the Explanatory Gap?" *Journal of Consciousness Studies*, October/November, 2006, Vol. 13, No. 10-11, pp. 32-39.

Carter, R. *et al.* (2009) *The Human Brain Book.* (London: D.K. Adult).

Cavanaugh, P. (2013) "Perceived Location: A New Measure of Attention." *Conference Handbook*, Association for the Scientific Study of Consciousness, July, 2013, p. 15.

Chalmers, D. J. (1995a) "Absent Qualia, Fading Qualia, Dancing Qualia." In *Conscious Experience*, ed. T. Metzinger (Thorverton, UK: Imprint Academic).

Chalmers, D. J. (1995b) "Facing up to the Problem of Consciousness." *Journal of Consciousness Studies,* Vol. 2, No. 3, pp. 200-19.

Chalmers, D. J. (1996) *The Conscious Mind.* (Oxford: Oxford University Press).

Chalmers, D. J. (1997) "Moving Forward on the Problem of Consciousness." *Journal of Consciousness Studies,* Vol. 4, No. 1, pp. 3-46.

Chalmers, D. J. (1999) "Materialism and the Metaphysics of Modality." *Philosophy and Phenomenological Research*, June, 1999, Vol. 59, No. 2, pp. 473-96.

Chalmers, D. J. (2013) "Panpsychism and Proto-Panpsychism." Oral presentation, February 5, 2013, Center for the Explanation of Consciousness, Stanford University.

Choisser, B. (2000) "A World without Faces: A Prosopagnosic's Perspective." Oral presentation, April 12, 2000, Toward a Science of Consciousness, Tucson, Arizona.

Churchland, P. M. (1984) *Matter and Consciousness.* (Cambridge, MA: The MIT Press).

Churchland, P. M. (1998) "Précis of The Engine of Reason, The Seat of the Soul: A Philosophical Journey into the Brain." *Philosophy and Phenomenological Research*, December, 1998, Vol. 58, No. 4, pp. 859-904.

Churchland, P. S. (1986) *Neurophilosophy.* (Cambridge, MA: The MIT Press).

Clark, A. (1993*) Sensory Qualities.* (Oxford: Clarendon Press).

Clark, A. (1997) *Being There: Putting Brain, Body, and World Together Again.* (Cambridge, MA: The MIT Press).

Clark, A. (2002) "Is Seeing All It Seems? Action, Reason and the Grand Illusion." *Journal of Consciousness Studies,* Vol. 9, No. 5-6, pp. 181-202.

Cole, D. (2011) "Review: *Consciousness Revisited: Materialism Without Phenomenal Concepts,* by Michael Tye." Springer Link, February 04, 2011, URL = <http://link.springer.com/article/10.1007/s11023-011-9225-3#page-1>.

Colter, L. W. (2009) "Review: *Consciousness Revisited,* by Michael Tye." *Metapsychology*, September 8, 2009, URL = <http://metapsychology.mental help.net/poc/view_doc.php?type=book&id=5121&cn=396>.

Cotterill, R. M. J. (1995) "On the Unity of Conscious Experience." *Journal of Consciousness Studies*, Vol. 2, No. 4, pp. 290-311.

Cottrell, A. (1999) "Sniffing The Camembert: On The Conceivability of Zombies." *Journal of Consciousness Studies*, January, 1999, Vol. 6, No. 1, pp. 4-12.

Cytowic, R. E. (1993) *The Man Who Tasted Shapes*. (New York: G. P. Putnam's Sons).

Davies, T. N. *et al.* (2002) "Visual Worlds: Construction or Reconstruction?" *Journal of Consciousness Studies*, Vol. 9, No. 5-6, pp. 72-87.

Dennett, D.C. (1978) *Brainstorms: Philosophical Essays on Mind and Psychology.* (Cambridge, MA: The MIT Press).

Dennett, D. C. (1981) "The Nature of Images and the Introspective Trap." In *Readings in Philosophy of Psychology, Volume Two*, ed. N. Block (Cambridge: Harvard University Press).

Dennett, D. C. (1984) *Elbow Room: The Varieties of Free Will Worth Wanting.* (Cambridge, MA: The MIT Press).

Dennett, D. C. (1988) "Quining Qualia." In *Consciousness in Contemporary Science*, ed. A. J. Marcel and E. Bisiach (Oxford: Clarendon Press).

Dennett, D. C. (1991) *Consciousness Explained.* (Boston: Little, Brown and Company).

Dennett, D. C. (1993) "Living on the Edge." *Inquiry,* March, 1993, Vol. 36, No. 1-2, pp. 135-59.

Dennett, D. C. (1993) "The Message is: There is no *M*edium." *Philosophy and Phenomenological Research,* December, 1993, Vol. 53, No. 4, pp. 919-31.

Dennett, D. C. (2002) "How Could I Be Wrong? How Wrong Could I Be?" *Journal of Consciousness Studies,* Vol. 9, No. 5-6, pp. 13-16.

Dennett, D. C. (2003) "Who's on First? Heterophenomenology Explained." *Journal of Consciousness Studies*, September/October, 2003, Vol. 10, No. 9-10, pp. 19-30.

Dennett, D. C. (2005) *Sweet Dreams: Philosophical Obstacles to a Science of Consciousness.* (Cambridge, MA: The MIT Press).

Dennett, D. C. (2007) "Review: *Seeing Red: A Study In Consciousness,* by Nicholas Humphrey." *Brain,* Vol. 130, No. 2, pp. 592-95.

Dennett, D. C. (2012) "The Mystery of David Chalmers." *Journal of Consciousness Studies,* January/February, 2012, Vol. 19, No. 1-2, pp. 86-95.

Derbyshire, S. and Raja, A. (2011) "On the Development of Painful Experience." *Journal of Consciousness Studies,* September/October, 2011, Vol. 18, No. 9-10, pp. 233-56.

Doyle, B. (2014) "Libet Experiments." *The Information Philosopher,* URL =<http://www.informationphilosopher.com/freedom/libet_experiments.html>.

Dretske, F. (1995) *Naturalizing the Mind.* (Cambridge, MA: The MIT Press).

Duncan, D. E. (2009) "Looking at Stress – and God – in the Human Brain." *Discover,* May, 2009, URL = <http://discovermagazine.com/2009/may/24-looking-at-stress-and-god-in-mans-brain>.

Dyson, F. (2012) "What Can You Really Know?" *New York Review of Books,* November 8, 2012, URL = <http://www.nybooks.com/articles/archives/2012/nov/08/what-can-you-really-know/?pagination=false>.

Eccles, Sir J. (1987) "Brain and Mind, Two or One?" In *Mindwaves,* ed. C. Blakemore and S. Greenfield (Oxford: Basil Blackwell).

Edwards, J. (2014) "Review: *Millikan and Her Critics,* by Dan Ryder, Justine Kingsbury and Kenneth Williford." *Journal of Consciousness Studies,* January/February, 2014, Vol. 21, No. 1-2, pp. 221-27.

Ellis, R. D. and Newton, N. (1998) "Three Paradoxes of Phenomenal Consciousness: Bridging the Explanatory Gap." *Journal of Consciousness Studies,* Vol. 5, No. 4, pp. 419-42.

Feser, E. (2001) "Qualia: Irreducibly Subjective But Not Intrinsic." *Journal of Consciousness Studies,* August, 2001, Vol. 8, No. 8, pp. 3-20.

Fink, S. B. (2011) "Independence and Connections of Pain and Suffering." *Journal of Consciousness Studies*, September/October, 2011, Vol. 18, No. 9-10, pp. 45-66.

Flanagan, O. (1992) *Consciousness Reconsidered.* (Cambridge, MA: The MIT Press).

Fodor, J. A. (1980) "Special Sciences, or The Disunity of Science as a Working Hypothesis." In *Readings in Philosophy of Psychology, Volume One,* ed. N. Block (Cambridge, MA: Harvard University Press).

Ford, J. and Smith, D. W. (2006) "Consciousness, Self, and Attention." In *Self-Representational Approaches to Consciousness*, ed. U. Kriegel and K. Williford (Cambridge, MA: The MIT Press).

Fox, C. A. (2012) "Freethinkers Undermine Libet." *The Philosophers' Magazine*, Issue 59, p. 8.

Freeman, A. (2006) "A Daniel Come To Judgement?" *Journal of Consciousness Studies*, March, 2006, Vol. 13, No. 3, pp. 95-109.

Gadenne, V. (2006) "In Defence of Qualia-epiphenomenalism." *Journal of Consciousness Studies*, January/February, 2006, Vol. 13, No. 1-2, pp. 101-14.

Gallagher, S. (1997) "Mutual Enlightenment: Recent Phenomenology in Cognitive Science." *Journal of Consciousness Studies*, Vol. 4, No. 3, pp. 195-214.

Garrett, B. J. (1999) "Review: On the Contrary; Critical Essays, 1987-97, by Paul and Patricia Churchland." *Journal of Consciousness Studies*, April, 1999, Vol. 6, No. 4, pp. 136-37.

Garvey, J. (2012) "Frank Jackson Interview." *The Philosophers' Magazine*, Issue 59, pp. 68-75.

Garvey, J. (2013) "From The Editor." *The Philosopher's Magazine*, Issue 60, p. 4.

Gazzaniga, M. (1985) *The Social Brain.* (New York: Basic Books, Inc).

Geach, P. (1981) "Selections from *Mental Acts.*" In *Readings in Philosophy of Psychology, Volume Two,* ed. N. Block (Cambridge, MA: Harvard University Press).

Gennaro, R. J. (2005) "The HOT Theory of Consciousness: Between A Rock And A Hard Place?" *Journal of Consciousness Studies,* December, 2005, Vol. 12, No. 12, pp. 3-21.

Gennaro, R. J. (2006) "Between Pure Self-Referentialism and the Extrinsic HOT Theory of Consciousness." In *Self-Representational Approaches to Consciousness,* ed. U. Kriegel and K. Williford (Cambridge, MA: The MIT Press).

Gennaro, R. J. (2007) "Consciousness and Concepts: An Introductory Essay." *Journal of Consciousness Studies,* September/October, 2007, Vol. 14, No. 9-10, pp. 1-19.

Gennaro, R. J. (2012a) *The Consciousness Paradox.* (Cambridge, MA: The MIT Press).

Gennaro, R. J. (2012b) "HOT Theory and the Prefrontal Cortex." Oral presentation, April 10, 2012, Toward a Science of Consciousness, Tucson, Arizona.

Gennaro, R. J. (2013a) "Defending HOT Theory & the Wide Intrinsicality View: A Reply to Weisberg, Van Gulick, & Seager." *Journal of Consciousness Studies,* November/December, 2013, Vol. 20, No. 11-12, pp. 82-100.

Gennaro, R. J. (2013b) "Precis of *The Consciousness Paradox: Consciousness, Concepts, & Higher-Order Thoughts.*" *Journal of Consciousness Studies,* November/December, 2013, Vol. 20, No. 11-12, pp. 6-30.

Goff, P. (2011) "A Posteriori Physicalists Get Our Phenomenal Concepts Wrong." *Australasian Journal of Philosophy,* January, 2011, Vol. 89, No. 2, pp. 191-209.

Goff, P. (2013) "The Zombie Threat to a Science of Mind." *Philosophy Now,* May/June, 2013, URL =<http://philosophynow.org/issues/96/The_Zombie_Threat_to_a_Science_of_Mind>.

Goldstein, I. (1994) "Identifying Mental States: A Celebrated Hypothesis Refuted." *Australasian Journal of Philosophy,* March, 1994, Vol. 72, No. 1, pp. 46-61.

Gopnik, A. (2011) "Review: *Soul Dust: The Magic of Consciousness,* by Nicholas Humphrey." *The New York Times,* May 20, 2011, URL = <http://www.nytimes.com/2011/05/22/books/review/book-review-soul-dust-the-magic-of-consciousness-by-nicholas-humphrey.html?_r=0>.

Gottlieb, A. (2011) "A Lion in the Undergrowth." *The New York Times Book Review,* January 30, 2011, p. BR12.

Gottlieb, A. (2014) "Let's Have a Dialogue." *The New York Times Book Review,* April 20, 2014, p. 14.

Graham, G. and Horgan, T. (2008) "Qualia Realism: Its Phenomenal Contents and Discontents." In *The Case for Qualia,* ed. E. Wright (Cambridge, MA: The MIT Press).

Gray, J. A. *et al.* (2002) "Implications of Synaesthesia for Functionalism: Theory and Experiments." *Journal of Consciousness Studies,* Vol. 9, No. 12, pp. 5-31.

Güzeldere, G. (1995a) "Is Consciousness the Perception of What Passes in One's Own Mind?" In *Conscious Experience,* ed. T. Metzinger (Thorverton, UK: Imprint Academic).

Güzeldere, G. (1995b) "Consciousness: What It Is, How To Study It, What To Learn From Its History." *Journal of Consciousness Studies,* Vol. 2, No. 1 pp. 30-51.

Hannay, A. (1990) *Human Consciousness.* (London: Routledge, Chapman and Hall, Inc.).

Hardin, C. L. (1988) *Color for Philosophers: Unweaving the Rainbow.* (Indianapolis: Hackett Publishing Company).

Hardin, C. L. (2008) "Color Qualities and the Physical World." In *The Case for Qualia,* ed. E. Wright (Cambridge, MA: The MIT Press).

Harman, G. (1990) "The Intrinsic Quality of Experience." *Philosophical Perspectives,* Vol. 4, pp. 31-52.

Heeger, D. (2006) "Perception Lecture Notes: Secondary Cortical Visual Areas and the What/Where Pathways." New York University, URL = <http://www.cns.nyu.edu/~david/courses/perception/lecture-notes.html>.

Hill, C. S. (2005) "Remarks on David Papineau's *Thinking about Consciousness*." *Philosophy and Phenomenological Research*, July, 2005, Vol. 71, No. 1, pp. 147-54.

Hill, C. S. (2006) "Perceptual Consciousness: How It Opens Directly Onto the World, Preferring the World to the Mind." In *Self-Representational Approaches to Consciousness*, ed. U. Kriegel and K. Williford (Cambridge, MA: The MIT Press).

Hofstadter, D. R. (1981a) "Introduction." In *The Mind's I*, ed. D. Hofstadter and D. Dennett (New York: Bantam Books).

Hofstadter, D. R. (1981b) "Reflections." In *The Mind's I*, ed. D. Hofstadter and D. Dennett (New York: Bantam Books).

Hofstadter, D. R. (1981c) "The Turing Test: A Coffeehouse Conversation." In *The Mind's I*, ed. D. Hofstadter and D. Dennett (New York: Bantam Books).

Holt, J. (2003) *Blindsight and the Nature of Consciousness*. (Peterborough, Canada: Broadview Press).

Holtzman, G. (2013) "Do Personality Effects Mean Philosophy is Intrinsically Subjective?" *Journal of Consciousness Studies*, May/June, 2013, Vol. 20, No. 5-6, pp. 27-32.

Honderich, T. ed. (1995) *The Oxford Companion to Philosophy*. (Oxford: Oxford University Press).

Hooper, J. and Teresi, D. (1987) *The Three-Pound Universe*. (Los Angeles: Jeremy P. Tarcher).

Horowitz, A. (1999) "Is There a Problem in Physicalist Epiphenomenalism?" *Philosophy and Phenomenological Research*, June, 1999, Vol. 59, No. 2, pp. 421-34.

Howell, R. J. (2008) "Subjective Physicalism." In *The Case for Qualia*, ed. E. Wright (Cambridge, MA: The MIT Press).

Humphrey, N. (2011) *Soul Dust: The Magic of Consciousness.* (Princeton and Oxford: Princeton University Press).

Jack, A. I. and Prinz, J. J. (2004) "Searching for a Scientific Experience." *Journal of Consciousness Studies*, January, 2004, Vol. 11, No. 1, pp. 51-56.

Jackson, F. (1982) "Epiphenomenal Qualia." *Philosophical Quarterly*, April, 1982, Vol. 32, No. 127, pp. 127-36.

Jackson, F. (1986) "What Mary Didn't Know." *Journal of Philosophy*, May, 1986, Vol. 83, pp. 291-95.

Jackson, F. (2004a) "Foreword: Looking Back on the Knowledge Argument." In *There's Something About Mary*, ed. P. Ludlow *et al.* (Cambridge, MA: The MIT Press).

Jackson, F. (2004b) "Mind and Illusion." In *There's Something About Mary*, ed. P. Ludlow *et al.* (Cambridge, MA: The MIT Press).

Jackson, F. (2004c) "Postscript." In *There's Something About Mary*, ed. P. Ludlow *et al.* (Cambridge, MA: The MIT Press).

Jackson, F. (2004d) "Postscript on Qualia." In *There's Something About Mary*, ed. P. Ludlow *et al.* (Cambridge, MA: The MIT Press).

Jackson, F. (2012) "Michael Tye on Perceptual Content." *Philosophy and Phenomenological Research*, January, 2012, Vol. 84, No. 1, pp. 199-205.

Jackson, F. (2013) Oral presentation, May 17, 2013, Center for the Explanation of Consciousness, Stanford University.

Johnson, G. (1991) *In the Palaces of Memory.* (New York: Vintage Books).

Jonkisz, J. (2012) "Consciousness: A Four-fold Taxonomy." *Journal of Consciousness Studies*, November/December, 2012, Vol. 19, No. 11-12, pp. 55-82.

Kant, I. (1788) *Critique of Practical Reason.* URL = <http://praxeology.net/kant4.htm>.

Kauffmann, O. (2011) "Brain Plasticity and Phenomenal Consciousness." *Journal of Consciousness Studies*, July/August, 2011, Vol. 18, No. 7-8, pp. 46-70.

Kim, J. (1993) *Supervenience and Mind: Selected Philosophical Essays.* (Cambridge, MA: Cambridge University Press).

Kind, A. (2008) "How to Believe in Qualia." In *The Case for Qualia,* ed. E. Wright (Cambridge, MA: The MIT Press).

Kirk, R. (1995) "How Is Consciousness Possible?" In *Conscious Experience,* ed. T. Metzinger (Thorverton, UK: Imprint Academic).

Kirk, R. (2012) "Zombies." The Stanford Encyclopedia of Philosophy (Summer 2012 Edition), Edward N. Zalta (ed.), URL = <http://plato.stanford.edu /archives/sum2012/entries/zombies/>.

Koch, C. (2012) *Consciousness: Confessions of a Romantic Reductionist.* (Cambridge MA: The MIT Press).

Kriegel, U. (2005) "Naturalizing Subjective Character." *Philosophy and Phenomenological Research,* July, 2005, Vol. 71, No. 1, pp. 23-57.

Kriegel, U. (2006) "Introduction: Consciousness and Self-Representation." *Psyche,* May, 2006, Vol. 12, No. 2, pp. 1-3.

Kriegel, U. (2009) *Subjective Consciousness: A Self-Representational Theory.* (New York: Oxford University Press).

Kriegel, U. (2011) "Self-Representationalism and the Explanatory Gap." *Consciousness and the Self: New Essays,* ed. J. Liu and J. Perry (New York: Cambridge University Press). URL = <http://uriahkriegel.com/ downloads/ gap.pdf>.

Kriegel, U. (2012) "In Defense of Self-Representationalism: Reply to Critics." *Philosophical Studies*, January, 2012, Vol. 159, No. 3, pp. 475-84.

Kriegel, U. and Williford, K. (2006) *Self-Representational Approaches to Consciousness.* (Cambridge, MA: The MIT Press).

Kurthen, M. (1995) "On the Prospects of a Naturalistic Theory of Phenomenal Consciousness." In *Conscious Experience*, ed. T. Metzinger (Thorverton, UK: Imprint Academic).

Lakoff, G. (1996) *Moral Politics.* (Chicago: The University of Chicago Press).

Levin, D. (2002) "Change Blindness Blindness As Visual Metacognition." *Journal of Consciousness Studies,* Vol. 9, No. 5-6, pp. 111-30.

Levin, J. (2002) "Is Conceptual Analysis Needed for the Reduction of Qualitative States?" *Philosophy and Phenomenological Research*, May, 2002, Vol. 64, No. 3, pp. 571-91.

Levine, J. (1983) "Materialism and Qualia: The Explanatory Gap." *Pacific Philosophical Quarterly*, October, 1983, Vol. 64, pp. 354-61.

Levine, J. (1995) "Qualia: Intrinsic, Relational or What?" In *Conscious Experience*, ed. T. Metzinger (Thorverton, UK: Imprint Academic).

Levine, J. (2001) *Purple Haze: The Puzzle of Consciousness*. (New York: Oxford University Press).

Levine, J. (2006) "Conscious Awareness and (Self-)Representation." In *Self-Representational Approaches to Consciousness*, ed. U. Kriegel and K. Williford (Cambridge, MA: The MIT Press).

Levine, J. (2013) "Three Problems for Higher-Order Thought Theories." Oral presentation, Association for the Scientific Study of Consciousness, July 13, 2013.

Levy, N. (2005) "Libet's Impossible Demand." *Journal of Consciousness Studies*, December, 2005, Vol. 12, No. 12, pp. 67-76.

Levy, N. (2014) "The Value of Consciousness." *Journal of Consciousness Studies*, January/February, 2014, Vol. 21, No. 1-2, pp. 127-38.

Lopes, D. M. M. (2000) "What is it Like to See with Your Ears? The Representational Theory of Mind." *Philosophy and Phenomenological Research*, March, 2000, Vol. 60, No. 2, pp. 439-53.

Lowe, E. J. (2008) "Illusions and Hallucinations as Evidence for Sense Data." In *The Case for Qualia,* ed. E. Wright (Cambridge, MA: The MIT Press).

Ludlow, P. *et al.* eds. (2004) *There's Something About Mary*. (Cambridge, MA: The MIT Press).

Lycan, W. G. (1987) *Consciousness*. (Cambridge, MA: The MIT Press).

Lycan, W. G. (1995) "A Limited Defence of Phenomenal Information." In *Conscious Experience*, ed. T. Metzinger (Thorverton, UK: Imprint Academic).

Lycan, W. G. (2009) "Giving Dualism its Due." *Australasian Journal of Philosophy*, Vol. 87, No. 4, URL = <http://www.unc.edu/~ujanel/Du.htm>.

Mack, A. (2002) "Is the Visual World a Grand Illusion? A Response." *Journal of Consciousness Studies*, Vol. 9, No. 5-6, pp. 102-10.

Mack, A. and Rock, I. (1998) *Inattentional Blindness*. (Cambridge, MA: The MIT Press).

Macpherson, F. (2005) "Colour Inversion Problems for Representationalism." *Philosophy and Phenomenological Research,* January, 2005, Vol. 70, No. 1, pp. 127-50.

Malpas, J. (2012) "Donald Davidson." The Stanford Encyclopedia of Philosophy (Summer 2014 Edition), Edward N. Zalta (ed.), URL = <http://plato.stanford.edu/archives/sum2014/entries/davidson/>.

Marcel, A. J. and Bisiach, E. eds. (1998) *Consciousness in Contemporary Science.* (Oxford: Clarendon Press).

Markman, A. *et al.* (2007) "Using Regulatory Focus to Explore Implicit and Explicit Processing in Concept Learning." *Journal of Consciousness Studies,* September/October, 2007, Vol. 14, No. 9-10, pp. 132-55.

Maund, B. (2008) "A Defense of Qualia in the Strong Sense." In *The Case for Qualia*, ed. E. Wright (Cambridge, MA: The MIT Press).

McClelland, T. (2013a) "The Neo-Russellian Ignorance Hypothesis." *Journal of Consciousness Studies*, March/April, 2013, Vol. 20, No. 3-4, pp. 125-51.

McClelland, T. (2013b) "Review: *Consciousness and the Prospects of Physicalism,* by Derk Pereboom." *Journal of Consciousness Studies*, September/October, 2013, Vol. 20, No. 9-10, pp. 193-200.

McGinn, C. (1991) *The Problem of Consciousness*. (Oxford: Blackwell).

McGinn, C. (2012) "All Machine and No Ghost?" *New Statesman,* February 20, 2012, URL = <http://www.newstatesman.com/ideas/2012/02/consciousness-mind-brain>.

McLaughlin, B. and Bartlett, G. (2004) "Have Noë and Thompson Cast Doubt on the Neural Correlates of Consciousness Programme?" *Journal of Consciousness Studies,* January, 2004, Vol. 11, No. 1, pp. 56-67.

Meeks, R. (2005) "Review: *Consciousness and Persons: Unity and Identity,* by Michael Tye." *Journal of Consciousness Studies,* April/May, 2005, Vol. 12, No. 4-5, pp. 150-51.

Metzinger, T. ed. (1995a) *Conscious Experience.* (Thorverton, UK: Imprint Academic).

Metzinger, T. (1995b) "Faster than Thought." In *Conscious Experience*, ed. T. Metzinger (Thorverton, UK: Imprint Academic).

Metzinger, T. (1995c) "The Problem of Consciousness." In *Conscious Experience*, ed. T. Metzinger (Thorverton, UK: Imprint Academic).

Minsky, M. (1985) *The Society of Mind.* (New York: Simon & Schuster).

Moody, T. (2014) "Consciousness and the Mind-Body Problem." *Journal of Consciousness Studies,* March/April, 2014, Vol. 21, No. 3-4, pp. 177-90.

Morgan, B. (2012) "Review: *Conceiving God,* by David Lewis-Williams." *Journal of Consciousness Studies,* March/April, 2012, Vol. 19, No. 3-4, pp. 251-57.

Morowitz, H. J. (1981) "Rediscovering the Mind." In *The Mind's I*, ed. D. Hofstadter and D. Dennett (New York: Bantam Books).

Nagel, T. (1974) "What Is It Like to Be a Bat?" *Philosophical Review*, October, 1984, Vol. 83, No. 4, pp. 435-50.

Nagel, T. (1995) *Other Minds: Critical Essays 1969-1994.* (New York: Oxford University Press).

Newton, N. (1991) "Consciousness, Qualia, and Reentrant Signalling." *Behavior and Philosophy*, Spring/Summer, 1991, Vol. 19, No. 1, pp. 21-42.

Nikolinakos, D. (1994) "General Anesthesia, Consciousness, and the Skeptical Challenge." *The Journal of Philosophy,* February, 1994, Vol. 91, No. 2, pp. 88-104.

Noë, A. and Thompson, E. (2004a) "Are There Neural Correlates of Consciousness?" *Journal of Consciousness Studies*, January, 2004, Vol. 11, No. 1, pp. 3-28.

Noë, A and Thompson, E. (2004b) "Sorting Out the Neural Basis of Consciousness." *Journal of Consciousness Studies*, January, 2004, Vol. 11, No. 1, pp. 87-98.

O'Dea, J. (2008) "Transparency and the Unity of Experience." In *The Case for Qualia*, ed. E. Wright (Cambridge, MA: The MIT Press).

O'Regan, J. K. (2000) "Change Blindness and the Visual World as an Outside Memory." Oral presentation, April 11, 2000, Toward a Science of Consciousness, Tucson, Arizona.

O'Regan, J. K. and Noë, A. (2001) "A Sensorimotor Account of Vision and Visual Consciousness." *Behavioral and Brain Sciences,* Vol. 24, No. 5, pp. 939-73.

Ornstein, R. (1986a) *The Amazing Brain,* Cassette tape. (Los Altos, California: Institute for the Study of Human Knowledge).

Ornstein, R. (1986b) *Multimind.* (Boston: Houghton Mifflin).

Ornstein, R. (1991) *The Evolution of Consciousness.* (New York: Prentice-Hall).

Papineau, D. (1995) "The Antipathetic Fallacy and the Boundaries of Consciousness." In *Conscious Experience*, ed. T. Metzinger (Thorverton, UK: Imprint Academic).

Papineau, D. (2005a) "Precis of *Thinking about Consciousness*." *Philosophy and Phenomenological Research*, July, 2005, Vol. 71, No. 1, pp. 143-46.

Papineau, D. (2005b) "Replies to Commentators." *Philosophy and Phenomenological Research*, July, 2005, Vol. 71, No. 7, pp. 171-86.

Papineau, D. (2006) "Comments on Galen Strawson: 'Realistic Monism: Why Physicalism Entails Panpsychism.'" *Journal of Consciousness Studies*, October/November, 2006, Vol. 13, No. 10-11, pp. 100-09.

Papineau, D. (2007) "Review: *Ignorance and Imagination: The Epistemic Origin of the Problem of Consciousness*, by Daniel Stoljar." *Notre Dame Philosophical Reviews: An Electronic Journal,* April 15, 2007, URL = <https://ndpr.nd.edu/news/25270-ignorance-and-imagination-the-epistemi c-origin-of-the-problem-of-consciousness/>.

Pauen, M. *et al.* (2006) "Epiphenomenalism: Dead End or Way Out?" *Journal of Consciousness Studies*, January/February, 2006, Vol. 13, No. 1-2, pp. 7-19.

Pauen, M. (2011) "Materialism, Metaphysics, and the Intuition of Distinctness." *Journal of Consciousness Studies*, July/August, 2011, Vol. 18, No. 7-8, pp. 71-98.

Pereboom, D. (2011) *Consciousness and the Prospects of Physicalism.* (Oxford: Oxford University Press).

Pitt, D. (2004) "The Phenomenology of Cognition Or What Is It Like to Think That P?" *Philosophy and Phenomenological Research*, July, 2004, Vol. 69, No. 1, pp. 1-32.

Pitt, D. (2013) "Mental Representation." The Stanford Encyclopedia of Philosophy (Fall 2013 Edition), Edward N. Zalta (ed.), URL = <http://plato. stanford.edu/archives/fall2013/entries/mental-representation/>.

Pockett, S. (2004) "Does Consciousness Cause Behavior?" *Journal of Consciousness Studies*, February, 2004, Vol. 11, No. 2, pp. 23-40.

Pollock, J. L. (1989) *How to Build a Person.* (Cambridge, MA: The MIT Press).

Prinz, J. (2007) "Mental Pointing: Phenomenal Knowledge Without Concepts." *Journal of Consciousness Studies*, September/October, 2007, Vol. 14, No. 9-10, pp. 184-211.

Putnam, H. (1980) "The Nature of Mental States." In *Readings in Philosophy of Psychology, Volume One,* ed. N. Block (Cambridge, MA: Harvard University Press).

Raggett, S. (2014) "Review: *The Conscious Brain: How Attention Engenders Experience*, by Jesse Prinz." *Journal of Consciousness Studies*, January/February, 2014, Vol. 21, No. 1-2, pp. 215-21.

Ramachandran, V.S. and Hubbard, E.M. (2001) "Synaesthasia – A Window Into Perception, Thought and Language." *Journal of Consciousness Studies*, December, 2001, Vol. 8, No. 12, pp. 3-34.

Rey, G. (1981) "Introduction: What Are Mental Images?" In *Readings in Philosophy of Psychology, Volume Two,* ed. N. Block (Cambridge, MA: Harvard University Press).

Rey, G. (1992) "Sensational Sentences Switched." *Philosophical Studies*, December, 1992, Vol. 68, No. 3, pp. 289-319.

Rey, G. (1995) "Towards a Projectivist Account of Conscious Experience." In *Conscious Experience*, ed. T. Metzinger (Thorverton, UK: Imprint Academic).

Rey, G. (2007) "Phenomenal Content and the Richness and Determinacy of Colour Experience." *Journal of Consciousness Studies,* September/October, 2007, Vol. 14, No. 9-10, pp. 112-31.

Robinson, H. (2008) "Why Frank Should Not Have Jilted Mary." In *The Case for Qualia,* ed. E. Wright (Cambridge, MA: The MIT Press).

Robinson, W. S. (1996a) "The Hardness of the Hard Problem." *Journal of Consciousness Studies*, Vol. 3, No. 1, pp. 14-25.

Robinson, W. S. (1996b) "Qualia Realms and Neural Activation Patterns." *Journal of Consciousness Studies*, October, 1996, Vol. 6, No. 10, pp. 65-80.

Robinson, W. S. (2005) "Thoughts Without Distinctive Non-Imagistic Phenomenology." *Philosophy and Phenomenological Research*, May, 2005, Vol. 70, No. 3, pp. 534-61.

Robinson, W. S. (2006) "Knowing Epiphenomena." *Journal of Consciousness Studies,* January/February, 2006, Vol. 13, No. 1-2, pp. 85-100.

Robinson, W. S. (2008) "Experience and Representation." In *The Case for Qualia*, ed. E. Wright (Cambridge, MA: The MIT Press).

Robinson, W. S. (2010) *Your Brain and You: What Neuroscience Means for Us*. (Astoria, New York: Goshawk Books).

Robinson, W. S. (2014) "Developing Dualism." *Journal of Consciousness Studies*, January/February, 2014, Vol. 21, No. 1-2, pp. 156-82.

Rogers, P. (1997) "Review: *Other Minds: Critical Essays 1969-1994.* by Thomas Nagel." *Journal of Consciousness Studies*, Vol. 4, No. 2, pp. 186-88.

Rosenthal, D. M. (1995) "Multiple Drafts and the Facts of the Matter." In *Conscious Experience*, ed. T. Metzinger (Thorverton, UK: Imprint Academic).

Rosenthal, D. M. (1997) "A Theory of Consciousness." In *The Nature of Consciousness*, ed. N. Block, O. Flanagan, and G. Güzeldere (Cambridge, MA: The MIT Press).

Rosenthal, D. M. (2011) "Exaggerated Reports: Reply to Block." *Analysis*, July, 2011, Vol. 71, No. 3, pp. 431-37.

Rosenthal, D. M. (2012) "Conscious Awareness, Unconscious Perceiving, and Overflow." Oral presentation, April 12, 2012, Toward a Science of Consciousness, Tucson, Arizona.

Roskies, A. L. and Wood, C. C. (1992) "A Parliament of the Mind." *The Sciences,* May/June, 1992, Vol. 32, No. 3, pp. 44-50.

Rudd, A. J. (1999) "Review: *The Significance of Consciousness,* by Charles P. Siewert." *Journal of Consciousness Studies*, April, 1999, Vol. 6, No. 4, pp. 150-51.

Ryle, G. (1949) *The Concept of Mind*. (Chicago: The University of Chicago Press).

Sacks, O. (1970) *The Man who Mistook His Wife for a Hat.* (New York: Harper & Row).

Salomon, R. (2013) "Body-Building Awareness: Bodily Factors Shaping Our Consciousness." *Conference Handbook*, Association for the Scientific Study of Consciousness, July, 2013, p. 17.

Schriner, R. C. (1992a) "Dr. Dennett and the Mis-Appearance of Consciousness." Oral presentation, February 16, 1992, Laguna Beach, California.

Schriner, R. C. (1992b) "You Don't Really See this Title: The Plausible Denial of Conscious Experience." Oral presentation, March 1, 1992, Laguna Beach, California.

Schriner, R. C. (2002) "The Plausibility of Fallibilist Experiential Realism." Poster presentation, April 11, 2002, Toward a Science of Consciousness, Tucson, Arizona.

Schriner, R. C. (2006a) "Joseph Levine's Problem of Duality." Poster presentation, April 7, 2006, Toward a Science of Consciousness, Tucson, Arizona.

Schriner, R. C. (2006b) "Ontological Agnosticism and the Hard Problem of Consciousness." Unpublished manuscript, September 30, 2006.

Schriner, R. C. (2008) "Strong Representationalism and Selective Attention." Poster presentation, April 9, 2008, Toward a Science of Consciousness, Tucson, Arizona.

Schriner, R. C. (2009) *Do Think Twice: Provocative Reflections on Age-Old Questions.* (Fremont, California: Living Arts Publications).

Schriner, R. C. (2014) "Having Experiences That Don't Exist: The Odd Possibility of Targetless HOTs." Oral presentation, April 22, 2014, Toward a Science of Consciousness, Tucson, Arizona.

Schwitzgebel, E. (2011) *Perplexities of Consciousness.* (Cambridge, MA: The MIT Press).

Schwitzgebel, E. (2014) "Introspection." The Stanford Encyclopedia of Philosophy (Summer 2014 Edition), Edward N. Zalta (ed.), URL = <http://plato.stanford.edu/archives/sum2014/entries/introspection/>.

Seager, W. (1993a) "The Elimination of Experience." *Philosophy and Phenomenological Research,* June, 1993, Vol. 53, No. 2, pp. 345-65.

Seager, W. (1993b) "Verificationism, Scepticism, and Consciousness." *Inquiry*, January, 1993, Vol. 36, No. 1-2, pp. 113-33.

Seager, W. (1996) "Review: *Supervenience and Mind: Selected Philosophical Essays,* by Jaegwon Kim." *Philosophy and Phenomenological Research,* September, 1996, Vol. 56, No. 3, pp. 730-33.

Seager, W. (1999) *Theories of Consciousness: an Introduction and Assessment.* (New York: Routledge).

Seager, W. (2013) "Transitivity, Introspection, and Conceptuality." *Journal of Consciousness Studies,* November/December, 2013, Vol. 20, No. 11-12, pp. 31-50.

Searle, J. R. and Freeman, W. J. (1998) "Do We Understand Consciousness?" *Journal of Consciousness Studies*, Vol. 5, No. 5-6, pp. 718-33.

Sheets-Johnstone, M. (2011) "The Corporeal Turn: Reflections on Awareness and Gnostic Tactility and Kinaesthesia." *Journal of Consciousness Studies,* July/August, 2011, Vol. 18, No. 7-8, pp. 145-68.

Shoemaker, S. (1994a): "Self-Knowledge and 'Inner Sense.'" *Philosophy and Phenomenological Research,* September, 1994, Vol. 54, No. 3, pp. 254-55.

Shoemaker, S. (1994b) "The First-Person Perspective." *Proceedings and Addresses of The American Philosophical Association,* November, 1994, Vol. 68, No. 2, pp. 7-22.

Siegel, S. (2010) *The Contents of Visual Experience.* (Oxford: Oxford University Press).

Siewert, C. (1993) "What Dennett Can't Imagine and Why." *Inquiry,* January, 1993, Vol. 36, No. 1-2, pp. 93-112.

Sloman, A. and Chrisley, R. (2003) "Virtual Machines and Consciousness." *Journal of Consciousness Studies*, April/May, 2003, Vol. 10, No. 4-5, pp. 133-72.

Stoljar, D. (2006) *Ignorance and Imagination: The Epistemic Origins of the Problem of Consciousness.* (Oxford: Oxford University Press).

Strawson, G. (2006) "Realistic Monism: Why Physicalism Entails Panpsychism." *Journal of Consciousness Studies*, October/November, 2006, Vol. 13, No. 10-11, pp. 3-31.

Strawson, G. (2011) "Review: *Soul Dust,* by Nicholas Humphrey." *The Observer*, Jan 8, 2011, URL = <http://www.theguardian.com/books/2011/jan/09/soul-dust-nicholas-humphrey-review>.

Taylor, J. G. (2012) "The Problem of 'I': A New Approach." *Journal of Consciousness Studies*, November/December, 2012, Vol. 19, No. 11-12, pp. 233-64.

Taylor, K. A. (2007) "Without the Net of Providence: Atheism and the Human Adventure." In *Philosophers without Gods,* ed. L. Antony (New York: Oxford University Press).

Tooley, M. (2011) "The Skeptical Challenges of Hume and Berkeley: Can They Be Answered?" *Proceedings and Addresses of The American Philosophical Association*, Vol. 85, No. 2, pp. 27-46.

Turausky, K. E. (2014) "'The Most Interesting Problem in the Universe': Twenty Years of TSC: Report on the Toward a Science of Consciousness Conference 2014." *Journal of Consciousness Studies*, July/August, 2014, Vol. 21, No. 7-8, pp. 220-40.

Tye, M. (1991) *The Imagery Debate.* (Cambridge, MA: The MIT Press).

Tye, M. (1994) "Qualia, Content, and the Inverted Spectrum." *NOUS,* June, 1994, Vol. 28, No. 2, pp. 159-83.

Tye, M. (1995) *Ten Problems of Consciousness, A Representational Theory of the Phenomenal Mind.* (Cambridge, MA: The MIT Press).

Tye, M. (1997) "Review: *Raw Feeling: A Philosophical Account of the Essence of Consciousness,* by Robert Kirk." *Philosophy and Phenomenological Research,* December, 1997, Vol. 57, No. 4, pp. 968-71.

Tye, M. (2000) *Consciousness, Color, and Content.* (Cambridge, MA: The MIT Press).

Tye, M. (2009) *Consciousness Revisited: Materialism without Phenomenal Concepts.* (Cambridge, MA: The MIT Press).

Tye, M. (2013) "Response, Author Meets Critics: *Seven Puzzles of Thought (and How to Solve Them): An Originalist Theory of Concepts.*" American Philosophical Association Conference, San Francisco, March 28, 2013.

Van Gulick, R. (1998) "Reduction, Supervenience and Phenomenal Consciousness." Oral presentation, April 28, 1998, Toward a Science of Consciousness, Tucson, Arizona.

Van Gulick, R. (2000) "Inward and Upward - Reflection, Introspection and Self-Awareness." New York University, URL = <http://www.nyu.edu/gsas /dept/philo/courses/gradmind01/Papers/vanGulick.html>.

Van Gulick, R. (2002) "Nonreduction, Consciousness and Physical Causation." *Journal of Consciousness Studies*, Vol. 9, No. 11, pp. 41-49.

Van Gulick, R. (2006) "Mirror Mirror – Is That All?" In *Self-Representational Approaches to Consciousness*, ed. U. Kriegel and K. Williford (Cambridge, MA: The MIT Press).

Van Gulick, R. (2011) "Life, Holism, and Emergence." *Journal of Consciousness Studies,* May/June, 2011, Vol. 18, No. 5-6, pp. 139-47.

Van Gulick, R. (2013) "Rival Views of Consciousness and Self-Awareness." *Journal of Consciousness Studies,* November/December, 2013, Vol. 20, No. 11-12, pp. 51-68.

Van Gulick, R. (2014) "Consciousness." The Stanford Encyclopedia of Philosophy (Spring 2014 Edition), Edward N. Zalta (ed.), URL = <http://plato.stanford.edu/archives/spr2014/entries/consciousness/>.

Varela, F. J. and Shear, J. (1999) "First-person Methodologies: What, Why, How?" *Journal of Consciousness Studies*, February/March, 1999, Vol. 6, No. 2-3, pp. 1-14.

Vargas, M. (2014) "Can Neuroscience Show That Free Will Does Not Exist?" *The Philosopher's Magazine*, Issue 64, pp. 46-53.

Velmans, M. (2011) "Review: *Soul Dust: The Magic of Consciousness*, by Nicholas Humphrey." *Journal of Consciousness Studies*, November/December, 2011, Vol. 18, No.11-12, pp. 252-53.

Vermersch, P. (1999) "Introspection as Practice." *Journal of Consciousness Studies*, February/March, 1999, Vol. 6, No. 2-3, pp. 17-42.

Voorhees, B. (2000) "Dennett and the Deep Blue Sea." *Journal of Consciousness Studies*, March, 2000, Vol. 7, No. 3, pp. 53-69.

Warfield, T. A. (1999) "Against Representational Theories of Consciousness." *Journal of Consciousness Studies*, January, 1999, Vol. 6, No. 1, pp. 66-69.

Watt, D. F. (2000) "Emotion and Consciousness: Part II." *Journal of Consciousness Studies*, March, 2000, Vol. 7, No. 3, pp. 72-84.

Watts, A. (1972) *The Book: On the Taboo Against Knowing Who You Are.* (New York: Vintage Books).

Weisberg, J. (1999) "Review: *Consciousness and Qualia*, by Leopold Stubenberg." *Journal of Consciousness Studies*, April, 1999, Vol. 6, No. 4, pp. 154-55.

Weisberg, J. (2003) "Being All That We Can Be: A Critical Review of Thomas Metzinger's *Being No One: The Self-Model Theory of Subjectivity.*" *Journal of Consciousness Studies*, November, 2003, Vol. 10, No. 11, pp. 89-96.

Weisberg, J. (2008) "Same Old, Same Old: the Same-order Representation Theory of Consciousness and the Division of Phenomenal Labor." *Synthese*, January, 2008, Vol. 160, No. 2, pp. 161-81.

Weisberg, J. (2011) "Abusing the Notion of What-it's-like-ness: a Response to Block." *Analysis*, July, 2011, Vol. 71, No. 3, pp. 438-42.

Weisberg, J. (2013) "A Problem of Intimacy." *Journal of Consciousness Studies,* November/December, 2013, Vol. 20, No. 11-12, pp. 69-81.

Weiskrantz, L. (1988) "Some contributions of neuropsychology of vision and memory to the problem of consciousness." In *Consciousness in Contemporary Science,* ed. A. J. Marcel and E. Bisiach, (Oxford: Clarendon Press).

Westphal, J. (1984) "The Complexity of Quality." *Philosophy*, October, 1984, Vol. 59, No. 230, pp. 457-71.

Williams III, G. (1992) "How To Become Immortal: Give Your Mind To A Robot." *Longevity*, May, 1992, pp. 22-24.

Williford, K. (2006) "The Self-Representational Structure of Consciousness." In *Self-Representational Approaches to Consciousness*, ed. U. Kriegel and K. Williford (Cambridge, MA: The MIT Press).

Wright, E. (2008) *The Case for Qualia.* (Cambridge, MA: The MIT Press).

Wright, E. (2008) "Introduction." In *The Case for Qualia,* ed. E. Wright (Cambridge, MA: The MIT Press).

Wright, R. (1996) "Can Machines Think?" *Time Magazine,* March 25, 1996, Vol. 147, No. 13, pp. 50-56.

Zeki, S. (1992) "The Visual Image in Mind and Brain." *Scientific American,* September, 1992, Vol. 267, No. 3, pp. 69-76.

About the Author

Roger Christan Schriner, AKA Chris, is Minister Emeritus of Mission Peak Unitarian Universalist Congregation in Fremont, California. He graduated from the University of Redlands *summa cum laude* in religion, philosophy, and psychology. He received a Doctorate in Religion from Claremont School of Theology and an M.S. in Marriage, Family, and Child Counseling from the University of LaVerne.

In addition to his ministry, Dr. Schriner worked for 25 years as a psychotherapist, and he has conducted personal growth workshops throughout his career. *Your Living Mind* is his sixth book. His previous publications include *Feel Better Now*; *Do Think Twice: Provocative Reflections on Age-Old Questions;* and *Bridging the God Gap: Finding Common Ground Among Believers, Atheists and Agnostics.*

Dr. Schriner has studied neuroscience and philosophy of mind for over 20 years. He regularly attends philosophy conferences and academic colloquia, and has presented papers several times at the biennial Toward a Science of Consciousness conferences in Tucson, Arizona, which he has attended every two years from 1996 through 2014.

Chris lives in Fremont, California with his wife Jo Ann. He enjoys sharing ideas as a speaker, workshop leader, and panelist at conferences, classes, and colloquia. His workshop and lecture topics include "Your Mysterious Mind: New Insights into Baffling Enigmas," "The Loom of Experience: How the Mind is Woven from Darkness and Light," and "Bridging the God Gap: Communication, Cooperation, and Common Ground Among Believers, Atheists and Agnostics." Contact Chris at rcschriner@aol.com, or search the Internet for his web site and blogs.

Web site: **http://www.schrinerbooksandblogs.com.** Current blogs:

Theists & Atheists: Communication & Common Ground
http://theistsandatheists.wordpress.com
The Mystery of Consciousness, and Why It Matters
http://mysteryofconsciousness.wordpress.com

Printing Notes

This book was first printed in September of 2014. In October, Chapter Thirteen was modified for clarity, and material was added to the first footnote of Chapter Twelve. At that point the text was finalized, and will not be substantively altered unless factual errors are discovered. However from time to time, typographical errors will be corrected, illustrations and textual formatting may be improved, and material preceding and following the text may be modified.

In April, 2015, certain software considerations required the book to be reformatted. In some cases page breaks were changed slightly, but page numbers in the index were unaffected by these alterations. In August, 2015, a new citation was inserted in footnote 122, p. 88.

INDEX OF NAMES

INDEX OF TOPICS